a Generous Or+hodoxy

BRIAN D. McLAREN

a Generous Or+hodoxy

WHY I AM A missional + evangelical +
post/protestant + liberal/conservative +
mystical/poetic + biblical +
charismatic/contemplative +
fundamentalist/calvinist + anabaptist/anglican +
methodist + catholic + green + incarnational +
depressed-yet-hopeful + emergent +
unfinished CHRISTIAN

ZONDERVAN

A Generous Orthodoxy
Copyright © 2004 by Brian D. McLaren

Youth Specialties Books, 300 South Pierce Street, El Cajon, CA 92020, are published by
Zondervan, 5300 Patterson Avenue SE, Grand Rapids, MI 49530

Library of Congress Cataloging-in-Publication Data

McLaren, Brian D., 1956-
A generous orthodoxy : why I am a missional, evangelical,
post/Protestant, liberal/conservative, mystical/poetic, biblical,
charismatic/contemplative, Fundamentalist/Calvinist,
Anabaptist/Anglican, Methodist, Catholic, Green, incarnational,
depressed-yet-hopeful, emergent, unfinished Christian / by Brian
McLaren.
   p. cm.
Includes bibliographical references.
ISBN-10: 0-310-25747-6 (hardcover)
ISBN-13: 978-0-310-25747-9 (hardcover)
1. Christianity--Essence, genius, nature. I. Title.
BT60.M37 2004
270.8'3--dc22

           2004008614

Editorial direction by Dave Urbanski
Art direction by Jay Howver
Editing by David Sanford
Proofreading by Kristi Robison & Janie Wilkerson
Cover design by Mark Arnold
Cover photography by Blair Anderson
Jacket photography by Jennifer Hughes
Interior design by Holly Sharp
Interior photography by Ryan Sharp
Printed in the United States of America

05 06 07 08 09 10 · 16 15 14 13 12 11

To all the people who have given, lent, or recommended good books to me—books that have enriched my life.

To all who wrote those books.

To Mark Oestreicher and the whole YS family, thank you for supporting the emergent community and making needed books available.

To God, who is the source of every good idea (old or new), which writers accidentally discover or unintentionally steal or by grace glimpse and then wrestle into fresh words for strangers, who in turn pass them on to others—in a wonderful process of receiving and giving that's a lot like Christmas.

CONTENTS

Generous Orthodoxy and a Changing World

Foreword to *A Generous Orthodoxy*

John R. Franke, DPhil

Associate Professor of Theology

Biblical Theological Seminary, Hatfield, PA

"The world is changed. I feel it in the water. I feel it in the earth. I smell it in the air. Much that once was, is lost, for none now live who remember it." So speaks Galadriel of Middle Earth at the opening of the cinematic version of J. R. R. Tolkien's mythic tale *The Lord of the Rings*. Like the inhabitants of Middle Earth, followers of Jesus Christ from across the diverse ecclesiastical and theological spectrum of North American Christianity have a growing sense that the world they have known is changing. Strange things are happening in unexpected places, long-familiar assumptions are being called into question, and new conversations are taking place between longtime adversaries, sometimes resulting in surprising alliances. Residents of the liberal and conservative precincts of the church are engaging in respectful and constructive dialogue across the metaphorical divide that has separated them for nearly two centuries; Protestants are growing in their appreciation for ancient Christian tradition; Lutherans and Catholics have issued a joint declaration on justification; evangelicals and Catholics are working together and expressing mutual appreciation for each other. The maps of North American Christianity that not so long ago provided reliable orientation and guidance are being redrawn.

Many of these developments can be traced to the failure of modernity's categories and paradigms to recognize the social and cultural diversity of the human experience. This failure has prompted the emergence of postmodern theory with its critique of certain, objective, universal knowledge and its quest to construct new forms of thought in the aftermath of modernity. These new forms of thought have significantly reshaped our common cultural and intellectual life in a variety of ways, including the standard assumptions that have guided Western culture and expressions of Christian faith since the Enlightenment. Of course, not everyone believes these developments are positive, and this has triggered considerable discussion and controversy in many ecclesiastical and theological circles. In the context of this debate, it is important to remember that postmodern theory does not support the rejection of rationality but rather supports rethinking rationality in the wake of modernity. This rethinking has resulted not in irrationality, as is often claimed by less informed critics of postmodern thought, but rather in numerous redescriptions and proposals concerning the understanding of rationality and knowledge. These postmodern ideas produced a more inherently self-critical view of knowledge than modernity.

In this setting, Yale theologian Hans Frei sought to move beyond the liberal/conservative impasse of modernity and coined the term *generous orthodoxy* to describe an understanding of Christianity that contained elements of both liberal and conservative thought. However, he also envisioned an approach to Christian faith that moved beyond the views of knowledge and certainty that liberals and conservatives held in common. This entailed the rejection of philosophical foundationalism characteristic in both liberal and conservative theology. Foundationalism refers to a conception of knowledge that emerged during the Enlightenment and sought to address the lack of certainty generated by the human tendency toward error and to overcome the inevitable, often destructive disagreements and controversies that followed. This quest for certainty involved reconstructing knowledge by rejecting "premodern" notions of authority and replacing them with uncontestable beliefs accessible to all individuals. The assumptions of foundationalism, with its goal of establishing certain and universal knowledge, came to dominate intellectual pursuit in the modern era.

This conception of knowledge also significantly influenced the church as Christian leaders and thinkers reshaped their understandings of the faith in accordance with its dictates. In the nineteenth and twentieth centuries, the foundationalist impulse produced a theological division between the "left" and the "right" among Anglo-Americans—liberals constructed theology upon the foundation of an unassailable religious experience while conservatives looked to an error-free Bible as the incontrovertible foundation of their theology. But in spite of all their differences, we can see that while liberal and conservative Christians appeared to be going their separate ways throughout the twentieth century, both were responding in different ways to the same modern, foundationalist agenda.

In response to this situation, "post-liberals" and "post-conservatives" have sought to move in the direction suggested by generous orthodoxy through a nonfoundationalist conception of the Christian faith. They can be identified by some common characteristics and commitments, such as strong ecumenical interests, a desire to move beyond the liberal/conservative divide, and a willingness to think through old questions in new ways that foster the pursuit of truth, the unity of the church, and the gracious character of the gospel. These common commitments have provided a fruitful context for conversation between postliberal and postconservative thinkers who together are seeking an understanding of Christian faith that is both orthodox and generous.

While this conversation continues to proceed and develop in the academy, its real significance lies in its implications for the church. If generous orthodoxy is to make a difference in the church and the world, it must move beyond lecture halls, textbooks, and conference agendas and come to be embodied in the lives and fabric of Christian communities as a genuine alternative to the fragmented and fractured witness of the contemporary church in our post-Christian society. Many resources will be required in order for the vision of generous orthodoxy to become a reality, and indeed many have already started to become available. I believe this book to be such a resource, and a potentially significant one at that. Brian D. McLaren offers a provocative, stimulating, and challenging account of a committed Christian orthodoxy that is truly inviting. In so doing he has provided a model for those who are seeking to develop, nurture, and practice a postmodern, ecumenical, and missional Christian faith.

Several virtues of the book are particularly significant in the quest for generous orthodoxy. First, it maintains a focus on Jesus Christ as the center of the Christian faith. In Brian's survey of the different ways Jesus has been perceived in the various traditions of the church, he implicitly identifies both the diversity that characterizes the Christian tradition and its unity through the living presence of Christ. And while the presence of Christ has been manifested and experienced by the power of the Spirit in richly diverse ways throughout the history of the church, he identifies the centrality of Christ as the single unifying force in a multifaceted tradition.

Second, the centrality of Christ is combined with openness appropriate for generous orthodoxy. For instance, the biblical witness to Jesus Christ as the unique Savior and hope of the world does not demand a restrictive posture concerning salvation for those who have never heard the gospel or those in other religious traditions. Brian addresses the questions in this area that many Christians wrestle with and suggests that these need not be finally closed, but may remain open to hopeful engagement without undermining or compromising the importance of Christian witness and responsibility. His discussion follows in the spirit of the influential missionary theologian Lesslie Newbigin who articulated his own position concerning Christ and salvation along the following lines: exclusive in the sense of affirming the unique truth of the revelation in Jesus Christ, but not in the sense of denying the possibility of salvation to those outside the Christian faith; inclusive in the sense of refusing to limit the saving grace of God to Christians, but not in the sense of viewing other religions as salvific; pluralist in the sense of acknowledging the gracious work of God in the lives of all human beings, but not in the sense of denying the unique and decisive nature of what God has done in Jesus Christ (Newbigin, *The Gospel in a Pluralist Society*, Eerdmans, 1989, 182-3).

Third, the tone of the book is honest, authentic, and self-critical. Brian does not present himself as one with "all the answers," but rather as a pilgrim thinker seeking after truth in the midst of missional Christian work. The questions and challenges he addresses emerge not from the confines of a secluded study, but from the perspective of a thoughtful and reflective working pastor grappling with the issues and problems that people are struggling with, both inside the church and out. He is honest about his doubts and struggles, self-critical with respect to his own tradition, and willing to listen and learn from others without sacrificing his own convictions. In this way Brian models the contextual and interpretive character of theology that informs generous orthodoxy.

Finally, because generous orthodoxy is aware of the need to keep listening and learning in openness to the Spirit and the world for the sake of the gospel, it seeks to keep conversations going and not to end them. Generous orthodoxy does not so much specify a particular point or position as it establishes a spacious territory defined by certain distinct boundaries in which there is space to live, move, and breathe while exploring the wonders and mysteries of the faith. In this context ongoing conversation is nothing less than the gracious gift of God through the work of the Spirit in fulfillment of the promise to guide the church into the fullness of truth. In this book Brian models the art of conversation admirably. He does not covet the last word, he is honest about his presuppositions and potential blind spots, he is forthright in his convictions, and he is willing to engage with the many voices found in the church and in our culture. The last thing he wants to do is end conversation—his desire is to keep it going for the sake of the Way, the Truth, and the Life. Some readers will undoubtedly be disturbed at points and wish that this were otherwise, especially in some of the more controversial parts of the book. It is worth remembering that Brian makes clear at the outset his intention to be "provocative, mischievous, and unclear" for the purpose of encouraging readers to think and enter into the conversation themselves.

In conclusion, readers are encouraged to keep in mind the words of Hans Frei, who once commented on the term he had coined: "Generosity without orthodoxy is nothing, but orthodoxy without generosity is worse than nothing."

INTRODUCTION

You may not be a Christian and wondering why anyone would want to be. The religion that inspired the Crusades, launched witch trials, perpetuates religious broadcasting, presents too-often boring and irrelevant church services with schmaltzy music—or else presents manic and overly aggressive church services with a different kind of schmaltzy music—baptizes wars and other questionable political programs, promotes judgmentalism, and ordains preachers with puffy haircuts (and others who are so superficial as to complain about puffy haircuts or whose baldness makes the complaint seem suspiciously tinged with envy)...it doesn't make sense to you why anyone would want "in" on that.[1]

   You may not yet be a Christian, and you're thinking of becoming one, but you're worried that if you do you'll become a worse person—judgmental, arrogant, narrow-minded, bigoted, and brainwashed. You feel attracted to something good on the path of Jesus, but you wish you could get that "something good" without a lot of extra religious, social, and maybe political baggage (Do I have to like organ music? Do I have to say "Praise the Lord!" all

---

[1] Me either. See chapter 15.

the time? Do I have to vote Republican? Do I have to oppose civil rights for homosexuals?). You wonder if there's any way to follow Jesus without becoming a Christian.[2]

You may already be a Christian, struggling, questioning, and looking for reasons to stay in. Or you may have officially left the Christian community, but part of your heart is still there, and you wonder if you might someday return. So many of us have come close to withdrawing from the Christian community. It's not because of Jesus or his Good News, but because of frustrations with religious politics, dubious theological propositions, difficulties in interpreting passages of the Bible that feel barbaric (especially to people sensitized by Jesus to the importance of compassion), and/or embarrassments from recent and not-so-recent church history.[3] Or perhaps it's simply boredom—dreary music, blasé sermons, sappy answers to tough questions, and other adventures in missing the point. Or perhaps it's fatigue—a treadmill of meetings and books and programs and squabbles that yield more duties, obligations, guilt trips, and stress.

You may be a Christian leader who has heard terms like _postmodern_ and _missional_.[4] You keep hearing about post-evangelicals, post-liberals, and postmoderns, about missional churches and missional faith communities. You may hope to get

---

[2] If you need permission, _YES, you can follow Jesus without identifying yourself as a Christian._ See chapter 17. Of course, as a follower of Jesus, you will learn to love and draw near to everyone, whatever their religion or lack thereof, including Christians. In so doing, you will exemplify what a Christian should be.

[3] _Question:_ Why have we stayed in? _Answer:_ Where else would we go? Would divesting ourselves of our faith in Jesus be an improvement? Would becoming just another uncommitted, secular American (or any nationality) consumer, dreaming of a bigger car or mortgage or savings account, be a step in the right direction? And if we decided to disassociate from the checkered career of the Christian community, are we so arrogant or naïve as to think we and our descendants would do better? Wouldn't the very act of disassociation itself be a kind of arrogant and elitist move, and therefore spiritually dangerous? Doesn't the checkered career, once fully acknowledged, help to make recurrences less likely, by humbling us, sensitizing us to the abuses of religion? See Chapter 19.

[4] Several of my books deal directly with the issue of postmodernity, and although the term is used about 20 times in these pages (including its use in this sentence), it is not dealt with directly or extensively here. See www.emergentvillage.com and www.anewkindofchristian.com for more on postmodernity.

some constructive insight about this post-familiar vantage point here. You may have read some other books (by me or my friends) using this strange language, and they made you want to hear more from whatever this strange post-perspective is. One of the great honors of my life is to serve my colleagues in Christian leadership by sharing whatever insights I have gained in our common journey and mission, trying to find words for insights that thousands of us seem to reach nearly simultaneously. I'm not all that original; I just seem to be able to get the tune out of my head and onto my lips a little before others do. When I hum it, others often say, "That tune was in my mind already, but I just couldn't quite access it."

You may be looking for dirt so you can write a hostile review. Chances are you'll find exactly what you're looking for, whether it's here or not. You'll quickly discern that I'm no G. K. Chesterton, who wrote the original book on orthodoxy.[5] Though I'm just shy of two-thirds his weight (he was a 300-pounder), I'm not half the writer or a quarter the Christian he was. I can only hope to offer the faintest, quietest, perhaps most pathetic echo of his brilliance in these pages. His orthodoxy was truly generous, as this quote regarding his critics makes clear: "I offer this book with the heartiest sentiments to all the jolly people who hate what I write, and regard it (very justly, for all I know), as a piece of poor clowning or a single tiresome joke" (*Orthodoxy*, 6).

You may be new to the Christian way, and you're trying to learn the lay of the land. I'm especially glad to have you on the journey, and I'll try to keep you in mind on every page. In a way I wish every reader could pretend to be you, exploring the Christian story and family for the first time. It would be my honor to introduce you to what I've found. I would also be glad to help you avoid the mistaken beliefs, the attractive shortcuts that turn out to be dead

---

[5] All further references to Chesterton's masterpiece, *Orthodoxy* (originally published in 1908 and now available from Shaw [1994]), will be noted in the text.

ends, and the other needless sidetracks that I wish I would have avoided along the way. I often think my most valuable credential is my vast repertoire of stupid mistakes through the years, mistakes that can't help but teach their perpetrator something the hard way. A warning—there will be some terminology here that's unfamiliar to you, no doubt. I'll do my best to define terms in the text or in footnotes, but if a term comes along that you don't know, just let it slide. My grandmother had good advice for reading the Bible that would apply here, too: *Reading the Bible is like eating fish. Enjoy the meat that's easy to eat first; come back and work on the bones later if you're still hungry.*

Whatever your reasons for beginning this book, I hope by its end you'll find even more than you're looking for now. The approach you'll find here, which might be called *postcritical*, seeks to find a way to embrace the good in many traditions and historic streams of Christian faith, and to integrate them, yielding a new, generous, emergent approach that is greater than the sum of its parts.[6] This approach is both ancient/historical and avant-garde/innovative. My friend Leonard Sweet uses the image of a swing to capture this simultaneous kicking-back/leaning-forward, kicking-forward/leaning-back. He also uses the image of a pole vaulter, who, in order to move forward and fly upward, begins by going backward to get a running start. He calls this an *ancient-future* approach, as does Robert Webber, another wise Christian thinker looking for ways ahead for the Christian faith by reaching back at the same time.[7]

The Christian family through the centuries and across cultures provides rich resources for your journey through life.

---

[6] *Postcritical* does not mean "uncritical," as you will see in Chapter 19. Bishop N. T. Wright calls this approach the "hermeneutic of love" as opposed to the "hermeneutic of suspicion." *Hermeneutic* here means an approach to reading and interpreting. We best understand something, Wright says, not merely by critiquing, dissecting, and doubting it, but also by trusting, loving, and respecting it. In fact, when critique and questioning come in the context of love, they yield even more insight than otherwise.

[7] See Leonard Sweet's *Postmodern Pilgrims* (Broadman & Holman, 2000) and Robert Webber's *Ancient-Future Faith* (Baker, 1999).

There are heroes and saints whose lives inspire. As well, many rich resources come via the embarrassments and tragedies we Christians have experienced and perpetrated through the years. You can learn a lot from others' mistakes if you don't distance yourself from them too quickly. Whether through heroes or catastrophes, you'll find much you need.

And you'll find that you are needed, too. Because the story isn't over, and the family isn't complete. I hope that in these pages you'll get a feeling for the important contributions we need you to make.

The subtitle of this book creates a term so awkward and confusing that it's certain not to catch on. Which is a good thing, because what we need is not new sectarian terminology or new jargon or a new elitist clique, but rather a humble rediscovery of the simple, mysterious way of Jesus that can be embraced across the whole Christian horizon (and beyond). What we need is something lived, not just talked or written about. The last thing we need is a new group of proud, super protestant, hyper puritan, ultra restorationist reformers who say, "Only we've got it right!" and thereby damn everybody else to the bin of five minutes ago and the bucket of below-average mediocrity.

The word *orthodoxy* means "straight thinking" or "right opinion." The last thing I want is to get into nauseating arguments about why this or that form of theology (dispensational, covenant, charismatic, whatever) or methodology (cell church, megachurch, liturgical church, seeker church, blah, blah, blah) is right (meaning approaching or achieving timeless technical perfection). Hence the important adjective *generous* in the title of this book.

If I seem to show too little respect for your opinions or thought, be assured I have equal doubts about my own, and I don't mind if you think I'm wrong. I'm sure I am wrong about many things, although I'm not sure exactly which things I'm wrong about. I'm even sure I'm wrong about what I think I'm right about in at least some cases. So wherever you think I'm wrong, you could be right. If, in the process of determining that I'm wrong, you are stimulated to think more deeply and broadly, I hope that I will have somehow served you anyway. See Chapter 0 for additional disclaimers.

I write as a lifelong participant in the Christian religion. As a little boy I was sometimes unfathomably bored and uncomfortable in church. Bored because I didn't understand what the grown-ups were saying; and uncomfortable because I had to wear a white shirt, clip-on tie, jacket, slippery socks, and stiff, tight shoes with slippery soles. (Most churches don't torture children that way anymore.) As a teenager I was indignant about the hypocrisy I saw in others, though sadly, not yet in myself. Perhaps I just hadn't lived long enough to develop my own personal style of hypocrisy. I have lived long enough now. Then I had a series of experiences with Jesus Christ that ruined my life—ruined it for good—in a good way, I mean.[8]

To my surprise I felt this love growing in me for the church, for the little suburban church I attended, and for the Church as a whole in all its forms and denominations. I actually ended up planting two churches over the years (one that still survives, one that had a short but glorious lifespan before its tragic and ugly demise), and I've helped several other churches get started, too. I never planned on being a pastor, but it turned out that I became one (after several years in my planned profession—teaching college English).

---

[8] I share some of my own spiritual journey in a book called *Finding Faith* (Zondervan, 2000). As well, I share some of my ministry experience in a chapter called "Ruining Your Ministry for Good" in *Seeing Beyond Church Walls: Action Plans for Touching Your Community*, edited by Steve Sjogren (Group, 2002), pp. 49-63.

Years later I started writing books that some pastors and other Christian leaders found helpful (and others didn't), which then put me in front of thousands of them, many of whom needed some encouragement and appreciation. I've had countless discussions with sincere Christians from nearly every major North American denomination, and I've learned much from nearly every one. So I'm deep into this thing we call Christianity. I also hope in the process that I've grown deeper into the simple way of Jesus, knowing that the two (Christianity and the way of Jesus) may or may not go together.

Meanwhile I have realized that my deepest passion isn't for church people: it has always been for those outside the church. I want to welcome them in, to help them become part of our life and mission. But often I have felt like an ambulance driver bringing injured people to a hospital where there's an epidemic spreading among the patients and doctors and nurses. You know the feeling? What do you do? You try to help the hospital get the epidemic under control again, so they can get back to helping people heal.

I'm naïve in many ways, with an uncorrected leaning toward optimism and hope. But then again, I'm not as naïve as I may seem. I've been around long enough and involved deeply enough to see the dark downsides, the dirty closets, and the ugly realities of the Christian community in its many forms. The hospital can be a pretty sick place sometimes. A friend of mine once said that every new Christian should be equipped at baptism with a manure detector (not his exact words) because there's plenty of it around in the church world, and I agree. I've seen it and smelled it (and too often tracked it through the house). Sometimes, honestly, I've felt like giving up and walking away in search of fresher, healthier air. But there's something here that I love and can't stop loving, and that something is actually Someone.

The real purpose of this book, and much of my writing

and preaching, is to try to help us realign our religion and our lives at least a little bit more with that Someone. Doing so, I believe, will be good for us and good for our world. Christianity is the biggest and richest religion in the world, and if it goes anemic or compromised, backward or confused, aggressive or passive— everyone loses, Christian and non-Christian. If its heart is right and its vision clear, everyone wins. In my own feeble and flawed way, I hope I can contribute to the church's health and vision... with your help, and of course, God's.

For some reason my name is often associated with a book I wrote, *A New Kind of Christian*. That title might suggest a claim to understand and even exemplify a *New! and ***IMPROVED!!! kind of Christianity. In this book I hope people will understand how a new kind of Christian is also an old kind of Christian, a person who knows and embraces our shared Christian history (the sweet, the spicy, the sour, and the smelly), and who seeks to move forward into the future resourced by the church in all its many current and past forms.

For those who have accused me of being excessively original, this book should affirm my basic unoriginality.[9] I'm saying little or nothing new, but rather I'm listening to a wider variety of older and newer voices than most people do. I'm trying to take them all seriously, which itself is, perhaps, my chief novelty. Chesterton described his own relationship with novelty and orthodoxy like this: "I am the man who with utmost daring discovered what had been discovered before...I did try to found a heresy of my own; and when I had put the last touches to it, I discovered it was orthodoxy" (*Orthodoxy* 6–7).

A warning: as in most of my other books, there are

---

[9] To read what some of my critics have said about my work to date, do a search of my name at www.christianitytoday.com.

places here where I have gone out of my way to be provocative, mischievous, and unclear, reflecting my belief that clarity is sometimes overrated, and that shock, obscurity, playfulness, and intrigue (carefully articulated) often stimulate more thought than clarity.

A friend of mine tells me it is a mistake to challenge readers to think because most readers simply want to hear what they already know and agree with, expressed with minimum personality and maximum blandness. I would probably do this if I could because those books seem to sell best, and I have kids in colleges with high tuitions. But another friend told me that learning is not the consequence of teaching or writing, but rather of thinking. So a playful, provocative, unclear, but stimulating book could actually be more worth your money than a serious, clear book that tells you what to think but doesn't make you think.

Besides, writing for me has always been a way of discovery and questioning: I write not to stop my mind from thinking, but because I can't stop it. Writing (whether in a journal, in an e-mail, on a Web site, or through an article, book, or sermon) at least produces some fruit from the labor of compulsive thinking.[10]

As for the term *generous orthodoxy,* I first came across it in the work of my respected friend and mentor-from-a-distance Dr. Stanley Grenz of Carey Theological Seminary. In *Renewing the Center,* Dr. Grenz quotes Hans Frei (a key figure in the emergence of what is known as post-liberal theology): "My own vision of what might be propitious for our day, split as we are, not so much into denominations as into [liberal/mainline and conservative/ evangelical] schools of thought, is that we need a kind of generous

---

[10] My favorite lyric from my favorite songwriter (Bruce Cockburn, also a compulsive thinker) goes—"All these years of thinking ended up like this: in front of all this beauty, understanding nothing" ("Understanding Nothing," *Big Circumstance,* Sony, 1989).

orthodoxy which would have in it an element of liberalism...and an element of evangelicalism."[11]

This generous orthodoxy does not mean a simple merging, mixing, conflating, or reconciling of the two schools of thought, though. Rather it disagrees with both regarding the "view of certainty and knowledge which liberals and evangelicals hold in common," a view Grenz describes as "produced... by modernist assumptions." Grenz adds that this generous orthodoxy must "take seriously the postmodern problematic" and suggests "the way forward is for evangelicals to take the lead in renewing a theological 'center' that can meet the challenges of the postmodern...situation in which the church now finds itself."

Sharing Stanley's sense of the reality and importance of the "postmodern transition" (and acknowledging both problems with defining the term and the outrageous things that are said by its enemies and friends alike), here I find myself trying in my own amateurish ways to explore some of the possibilities "a generous orthodoxy" might present.

So this book is offered with all due apology and retraction for my errors, with sincere gratitude for the good friends who read drafts of this book in manuscript form, along with a ready acknowledgement that this is neither the first nor the last word on anything. It is simply one attempt at offering something helpful in a needed and ongoing conversation, along with a sincere request for your prayers wherever you think I've said something ridiculous.

---

[11] (Baker, 2000), pp. 325, 331. Also, see the important and helpful work of Richard Foster and Renovare (www.renovare.org).

So here's my take on *a generous orthodoxy*,[12] and here's **Why I am a** *missional, evangelical, post/protestant, liberal/conservative, mystical/poetic, biblical, charismatic/contemplative, fundamentalist/calvinist, anabaptist/anglican, methodist, catholic, green, incarnational, depressed-yet-hopeful, emergent, unfinished* **Christian.**

As in many areas of life, the last should be first; I must begin by explaining why I am a Christian in Part One.

First, though, a warning.

Brian D. McLaren

www.anewkindofchristian.com

www.emergentvillage.com

www.crcc.org

---

[12] I hope it is clear what the term "generous orthodoxy" implies: that both generosity and orthodoxy are needed, neither at the expense of the other. One might slip in Paul's term *charity* from 1 Corinthians 13 for *generosity* in the previous sentence if one would prefer a more biblical adjective that makes the point even more strongly. I understand the term is used by a reform group within a major U.S. denomination. My use of it here should imply no association with that or any other group and should bring no blame on Hans Frei, Stanley Grenz, or anyone else who has used the term.

A GENEROUS REFUND

You are about to begin an absurd and ridiculous book. Those who like it and those who hate it, those who get it and those who don't, equally stand in some peril. So some words of warning are required. It is not too late to turn back, as you have not yet reached Chapter 1.

The book is absurd because it advocates an orthodoxy that next to no one actually holds, at least not so far. Most people aren't interested in an orthodoxy anyway—generous or otherwise; they want *THE* orthodoxy. From the look of things, this book will do little to change the situation, although hope dies hard.

The word *generous* in the title is already a bad sign, since many if not most orthodoxies of the past have not displayed much generosity toward others outside their tribe. You have every reason to believe, based on a cursory understanding of church history, that a *generous orthodoxy* is oxymoronic (like a heavy lightness, a dark flash, or dry rain), and that generosity leads to unorthodoxy, and vice versa, as *orthodoxy* and *generosity* are typically defined. This book plays with those typical definitions (sin enough to some) and expresses the naïve hope that generosity and orthodoxy actually have gone and actually can and should go together.

Many will agree: the choice of the word *orthodoxy* in the title is a terrible mistake. For most people, *orthodoxy* means right thinking or right opinions, or in other words, "what *we* think," as opposed to "what *they* think." In contrast, orthodoxy in this book may mean something more like "what God knows, some of which we believe a little, some of which they believe a little, and about which we all have a whole lot to learn." Or it may mean "how we search for a kind of truth you can never fully get into your head, so instead you seek to get your head (and heart) into it." Most people are too serious, knowledgeable, and busy for such an unorthodox definition of orthodoxy.

Many hold a minimalist concept of orthodoxy, seeking "the least common denominator," which limits the list of requirements for orthodoxy to a few core essentials. The generous orthodoxy of this book never seeks to dispute with those lists, but rather, it consistently, unequivocally, and unapologetically upholds and affirms the Apostles' and Nicene Creeds. It also acknowledges (rather perversely) that a number of items many hold as vital for orthodoxy are found nowhere in those seminal creeds and adds (somewhat sheepishly) that the creeds should never be used as a club to batter into submission people with honest questions and doubts. It also affirms (this is so Protestant) that Scripture itself remains above creeds and that the Holy Spirit may use Scripture to tweak our creedal understandings and emphases from time to time, so that new creeds are needed to give voice to the cry of faith today.

In contrast, for others, orthodoxy is not the least common denominator at all but rather the historical accumulation of precedents, like an annotated legal code that grows every legislative season. (After all, what are we paying legislators for, if not to write new laws for us every year? Imagine how happy we'll be in a thousand years when we have a hundred times as many laws to improve our lives.)

The approach found in this book may make you feel nervous about the accumulating-opinion style of orthodoxy, since accumulating orthodoxy makes it harder year by year to be a Christian than it was in Jesus' day. To be orthodox one has to have right opinions about far more things than one needed to have back then, when having a right attitude toward Jesus (i.e., confidence or trust in him) was about all it took. If Christian orthodoxy is defined as the hard mental work of holding in one's mind an increasing bank of complex opinions about a lot of things before breakfast, one might ask, hasn't something important been lost? But this is itself an opinion, which may be right or not, and may have little to do with orthodoxy.

My quarrel with accumulating orthodoxy does not mean I advocate a "know-nothing" approach to church history. The very opposite is the case. The orthodoxy explored in this book invites us as never before to study not only the history of the church, but also the history of writing the church's history. Bearing in mind the old saying, "Those who win the battles write the history," it's easy to see the danger of describing orthodoxy by looking in the rearview mirror. Where there has been diversity of opinion in the past, the winners label previous divergences as heretical and unorthodox and unchristian, leaving the impression for their descendants that everyone everywhere under the banner of orthodoxy has always agreed with them. In that light orthodoxy might seem to follow those who fight the hardest and perhaps the dirtiest. Not a pleasant thought.

Some defend this time-honored approach, saying that the Holy Spirit always protects the true church from making mistakes, so all those whom the true church (i.e., theirs) judges unorthodox truly are. This book doesn't assume that, although it does agree that where the Holy Spirit is shown the door by the church, an unlocked window is found through which the Spirit will sneakily enter. Thus the Holy Spirit stubbornly refuses to abandon the church even when the church quenches the Spirit—all in spite of the fact that the church has little idea how unorthodox it is at any given moment. While this view is humbling for the church, it also holds out the hope that if a church can't yet be perfectly orthodox, it can—with the Holy Spirit's help and by the grace of God—at least be perpetually re-formable.

Scandalously, the generous orthodoxy you will explore (if you proceed) goes too far, many will say, in the direction of identifying orthodoxy with a consistent practice of *humility, charity, courage,* and *diligence: humility* that allows us to admit that our past and current formulations may have been limited or distorted. *Charity* toward those of other traditions who may understand some things better than our group—even though we are more conscious of what we think we understand better. *Courage* to be faithful to the true path of our faith as we understand it even when it is unpopular, dangerous, and difficult to do so. *Diligence* to seek again and again the true path of our faith whenever we feel we have lost our way, which seems to be pretty often. While I see this practice as a way of seeking and cherishing truth, some will interpret this approach as an abandonment of truth, doctrine, theology, etc. You are free to be among them.

To link orthodoxy with a *practice*, as the previous paragraph does, further makes this book seem ridiculous because many orthodoxies have always and everywhere assumed that ortho*doxy* (right thinking and opinion about the gospel) and ortho*praxy* (right practice of the gospel) could and should be separated, so that one could at least be proud of getting an A in orthodoxy even when one earned a D in orthopraxy, which is only an elective class anyway. In fact, one could even get into a good graduate school based on high orthodoxy grades alone. In that traditional setting, orthodoxy could be articulated and debated by scholars or officials who had little responsibility to actually live by or live out the orthodoxy they defended. Defenders of orthodoxy were seen more like referees than basketball players; nobody cared if they could pass, dribble, or shoot, as long as they could blow a whistle and name an infraction in their black-and-white striped shirts.

In contrast, this book assumes that we're all on the court, so to speak. Since we're all players, this book can rightly be accused of blurring that distinction between the orthodoxy of the referees and the orthopraxy of the players. Absurdly (to some at least) this book seems to approach orthodoxy as a tool or means to achieve orthopraxy. You want to know the rules, not so you can blow whistles as a referee, but so you can have a lot of glorious good clean fun as a player, throwing passes and making assists and sinking three-pointers and layups without fouling out. In sum, this book sees orthopraxy as the point of orthodoxy—again, a concept so unorthodox as to encourage a good many good readers to abandon this book right now.

The generous orthodoxy explored in the pages ahead assumes, for example, that the value of understanding the Trinity is to love and honor and serve the Trinity, and that allegedly right Trinitarian opinions that do not lead to divine adoration are worth little. More, this view would assert that so-called orthodox understandings of the Trinity that don't lead so-called orthodox Christians to love their neighbors in the name of the Trinity (including those neighbors who don't properly understand the Trinity) are more or less worthless, which trivializes their orthodoxy.

By the way, even though I could have parenthetically referenced 1 Corinthians 8:1-3 or 13:1-4 to validate the previous points, I did not. I assume that thoughtful and noble readers will want to test what I say in reference to the Scriptures rather than me trying to save them the time and effort of doing so through the time-honored practice of proof-texting (Acts 17:11).

This isn't to say that doctrine doesn't matter—not at all! Let me go on record as saying that I believe sound doctrine is very, very, *very* important (Titus 2:1–3:11), and that bad doctrine, while not the root of all evil, is a despicable accomplice to a good bit of the evil in the world. In fact, this book is an attempt to correct what I perceive to be some bad doctrine, including bad doctrine *about* doctrine. Having wholeheartedly affirmed the importance of orthodox doctrine, I would quickly add that it is of little use to correctly say, "Lord, Lord" if one doesn't do what the Lord says.

While this approach affirms the importance of orthodox doctrine (as contained, again, in the Apostles' and Nicene Creeds), it severely doubts the long-term value of highly emphasizing doctrinal *distinctives*, distinctives being those secondary doctrines beyond the core beliefs contained in the ancient creeds that are unique to this or that denomination. This book comes to celebrate orthodox doctrine-in-practice, and it comes not to bury doctrinal distinctives but rather to put them in their marginal place. These distinctives have real value, I believe, however overrated that value generally is. And much of the value may lie in accidental side effects of holding the distinctives. For those who are certain and proud of their doctrinal distinctives, this will sound like unorthodox rubbish, and so again it's not too late to return the book.

True, one might point to Michael Polanyi's distinction between tacit and conscious knowledge as a defense of this book's strange approach. Consider, Polanyi might say, the experience of pounding a nail or playing jazz on the clarinet. When one pounds a nail, she is not conscious of the hammer at all; the hammer becomes an unconscious extension of her hand, a tool which she indwells and takes into herself. With each blow she is not aware of the pressure of the hammer handle against her palm, but rather she is aware of the bang of the hammerhead on the nail head. She focuses through the hammer to the nail.

When one plays the clarinet, one is not thinking about the pressure of the lower teeth against the lower lip, nor of the tightness of the lower lip against the reed, nor of the touch of the upper teeth to the mouthpiece, nor of the pressure of the fingers on the holes and keys, nor of the contraction of the hand and finger muscles, nor of the weight of the instrument borne by the right thumb and right elbow and right shoulder, nor of the tapping of the left foot to keep time, nor of the air pressure produced by the diaphragm on the lungs and in turn on the windpipe and in turn on the inner mouth and reed. Rather, through the unconscious absorption of the instrument into the body, through indwelling the instrument through one's fingers and breath, one attends through it to the notes, to the tone filling the air and room outside one's body, to the feeling of the musical phrase, to the passionate exuberance of the melody, to the free play of improvisation, to the rhythm and movement of the band, to the almost intangible but real response of the audience as it sways and smiles and maybe even dances. One focuses through the instrument to the music, and through the music to the audience. If one were to think consciously of all the intricate movements of muscles, tendons, bones...one would go nuts and be completely unable to play.

In this vein, orthodoxy in this book is seen as a kind of internalized belief, tacit and personal, that becomes part of you to such a degree that once assimilated, you hardly need to think of it. We enter it, indwell it, live and love through it. We concentrate on hitting the nail on the head, on the music touching, delighting, moving the audience. Orthodoxy in this book is similarly caught up in the practice (orthopraxy) of love for God and all God's creations. Such an outlandish idea, in the name of orthodoxy, is so unorthodox that it is hardly worth your continued consideration.

More damning: I myself will be considered by many to be completely unqualified to write such a book of theology, being neither a trained theologian nor even a legitimate pastor if legitimacy is defined by ordination qualifications in a bona fide denomination. Rather I am only a lowly English major who snuck into pastoral ministry accidentally through the back doors of the English department and church planting, and whose graduate education consisted of learning how to read—a skill most people feel they have mastered by about the third grade. In other words, I am a confessed amateur. You may define amateur as "one who works for love, not money," as I might prefer, or you may define it as "unskilled, a rude beginner, unprofessional" if you wish. Either way, I can't blame you for deciding to read a book by a certified professional instead of this one.

Even as an English major I'm a failure. My sentences are too long. As you've already seen. I overuse parentheses, which many readers find highly obnoxious (and having been told this, I still yield to almost every parenthetical temptation that presents itself). And the book is laced with overstatement, hyperbole, and generalizations...which, as the self-refuting saying goes, always must be wrong. At least I could have footnoted reputable scholars who make the same generalizations I do, to add some aura of credibility. All good English majors know how to do this. But I seldom do so, leaving you to wonder whether I am even aware of the scholarship, or whether I am just too lazy or ornery to give sufficient documentation, or whatever.

On top of all this absurdity, if the generous orthodoxy described in this book is valid, it implies a necessary critique of ungenerous tendencies in other orthodoxies, which could, ironically, result in this orthodoxy becoming no more generous than the others. In other words, this orthodoxy could present itself as tolerant and generous, but really, beneath the surface, it could be just as disgusted with rival approaches to orthodoxy as any other self-proclaimed orthodoxy has been. While this is not necessarily the case, and I sincerely hope it will not be, I must acknowledge that it could be. So this generous orthodoxy is dangerous. It can as easily be abused by its friends as its foes—yet another reason to go for a refund while you still can.

To add insult to injury, nearly all orthodoxies of Christian history have shown a pervasive disdain for other religions of the world: Buddhism, Hinduism, Judaism, atheism, etc. A generous orthodoxy of the kind explored in this book, while never pitching its tent in the valley of relativism, nevertheless seeks to see members of other religions and non-religions not as enemies but as beloved neighbors, and whenever possible, as dialogue partners and even collaborators. It seeks to remove splinters from the eyes of other religions only after removing its own planks, a process that will take a lot of time and energy, postponing intense critical examination of other eyes perhaps beyond this week or even next.

No wonder some will call this book a generous unorthodoxy, or an ungenerous unorthodoxy, or a dangerous unorthodoxy, or worse. At least, for all these reasons and more, it will be easy to ignore by those bound to disagree with it.

Beyond all these warnings, you should know that I am horribly unfair in this book, lacking all scholarly objectivity and evenhandedness. My own upbringing was way out on the end of one of the most conservative twigs of one of the most conservative branches of one of the most conservative limbs of Christianity, and I am far harder on conservative Protestant Christians who share that heritage than I am on anyone else. I'm sorry. I am consistently oversympathetic to Roman Catholics, Eastern Orthodox, even dreaded liberals, while I keep elbowing my conservative brethren in the ribs in a most annoying—some would say *ungenerous*—way. I cannot even pretend to be objective or fair. This is simply an inexcusable shortcoming of the book that serves no good purpose, unless by some chance it could generously be included under the proverb, "Faithful are the wounds of a friend" (Proverbs 27:6 NASB). Even so, will I be grateful and gracious when this friendly wounding is generously reciprocated?

In this regard, in addition to concluding that I have issues and reminding me that one shouldn't bite the hand that fed it, thoughtful readers may also conclude any or all of the following about me:

1. That I need professional counseling to resolve my neuroses about my religious heritage.

2. That I'm naïve about the other sectors of the Christian church; if I knew them better, I'd be just as hard on them, but since I don't, I let them slide. In other words, my generosity is born of ignorance, not virtue.

3. That I actually believe the problems of my conservative religious heritage pose a greater threat to or throw greater obstacles at a generous orthodoxy than the problems of other heritages.

4. That I am reticent to critique other religious families, just as I would feel presumptuous to correct my neighbors' children, so I feel it is best to let others in other religious families deal with the problems in their respective houses, while I do the same in my own, even though doing so may get me kicked out of it.

5. That I believe people who claim higher status on the scale of orthodoxy should be held to a higher standard.

6. That I am actually writing these conservative critiques for the benefit of non-conservatives, validating the concerns

they have, letting them know that I see what they see, which is important for me to do since my name (in the past anyway, though maybe less so after the publication of this book) has been associated with the term *evangelical*, which has a conservative reputation (although there are many who break this stereotype).

Further, since the kind of generous orthodoxy described in this book has never had much of a following—so much so that many who consider themselves orthodox watchdogs will consider the message of this book an intruder on their turf—you risk guilt by association just by being seen in public with this book. If you must proceed, trade dust jackets with another more respectable book so no one will know what you're reading. Just so you know, I plan to change my name and apply to either *Extreme Makeover* or a witness protection program as soon as the book comes out to save my fragile skin, so I urge you to protect yourself, too.

If all this weren't bad enough, I often indulge in a sense of humor that few find as funny as I do. This lack of seriousness is laughable in a writer who takes himself seriously.

Speaking of serious: people who try to label me an exclusivist, inclusivist, or universalist on the issue of hell will find here only more reason for frustration. To them this categorization is essential for determining whether I'm orthodox (by their definition); but in my definition of orthodoxy, these terms and the question they seek to answer easily become "weapons of mass distraction."[13] To say that I seek to believe whatever Jesus taught about hell, and for whatever purpose, will not satisfy them, even though it's true. They'll say I'm being evasive, cowardly, afraid to take a stand, and write smoke. No one can blame them.

---

[13] Thanks to Muslim journalist Irshad Manji for this turn of phrase, found in *The Trouble with Islam: A Muslim's Call for Reform in Her Faith* (St. Martin's, 2003). Ms. Manji's sparklingly written, courageous, and insightful book has much to teach Christians on many levels.

Speaking of smoke, this book suggests that relativists are right in their denunciation of absolutism. It also affirms that absolutists are right in their denunciation of relativism. And then it suggests that they are both wrong because the answer lies beyond both absolutism and relativism. I'll bet that sounds like nonsense to nine of 10 readers, which should bring the words *store credit* to mind.

Finally, in addition to all these egregious shortcomings, this book is woefully incomplete. It lacks chapters on Franciscan, Benedictine/monastic, patristic/Eastern, Celtic, feminist, immigrant, and third world Christianity, for example, subjects of great interest to me that I have not covered, without any explanation as to why not. One might almost think I'm keeping the option open for *A Generous Orthodoxy II* or *The Revenge of a Generous Orthodoxy* or some similar sequel, which would be truly pathetic if it were true.

No wonder, in light of these shortcomings, that later in the book I identify its genre as "confession." One imagines a couple of cops at police headquarters, pacing a dingy, undecorated room with a single light bulb hanging from the ceiling, under which I sit in a metal folding chair, head in hands. They barrage me with tough questions about orthodoxy, and finally I break down in sobs: "I confess, I confess!" Then the cops soften, get me a cup of bitter black coffee in a white paper cup, pull out a tape recorder, and push the red record button as I pour out with remorseful tears the pathetic contents of this book.

Speaking of confession, I confess I just reread this Chapter 0, and it strikes me as so weird—arrogant? defensive? tortured? complex? anxious?—that I can't imagine why anyone would push through it to Chapter 1.

If you ignore all of these sound warnings and read chapters with numbers beyond zero, I hope you will agree not to use any ideas found here in a dangerous or divisive way. The unity of the Spirit in the bond of peace is a precious thing that we must be diligent to preserve. If you try to create an elite "generous orthodoxy club," holding meetings at which you look down your long, crooked noses on everybody else who is so obviously less generous or less orthodox than you, please do not invite me to be your guest speaker. In fact, please disband the club immediately and throw a party to celebrate its demise. Far more than an adults-only Web site or a film with really scary scenes in it, this book is for mature audiences only. You have been forewarned.

If this were a Web site, there would now be a message like this:

By clicking the button below, you acknowledge that you have read the previous warnings and agree to the unreasonable terms and strange conditions they describe.

☐ I agree

Only then would you be given access to the pages that follow.

Now that the crowd has thinned out a bit, let me explain something.

The people I'm primarily writing for are the Christians (or former Christians)—evangelical, liberal, Catholic, whatever—who are about to leave (or have just left) the whole business because of the kinds of issues I raise in this book. And equally, I'm writing for the spiritual seekers who are attracted to Jesus, but they don't feel there's room for them in what is commonly called Christianity unless they swallow a lot of additional stuff. *Not* essential orthodoxy, but rather doctrinal distinctives—the fine print added to the contract of orthodoxy—that are fine to explore and discuss but threaten to become far more important than the gospel warrants.

Perhaps I'm trying to tell them, "Don't leave! Don't give up! There's room for you!" But maybe I'm just wrong, overly idealistic, and naive. Maybe it's not right to tell these people there is room for them in most Christian circles—because there's not.

If that thought breaks your heart, you should read this book.

Many—no, most—are happy with their orthodoxy and unbothered about the people who are about to leave or the outsiders who feel unwelcome. I have no wish to disturb them in any way, just as one doesn't want to disturb a hornet's nest (unless, say, it's hanging right in front of your front door, and its inhabitants keep stinging your kids and scaring away your guests). Enough. On to part one, and why I am a Christian.

PART ONE: WHY I AM A CHRISTIAN

CHAPTER 1

THE SEVEN JESUSES I HAVE KNOWN

I am a Christian because I have a sustained and sustaining confidence in Jesus Christ. I've lost and rediscovered that confidence a few times, which is a long and messy story worth simplifying and boiling down to manageable length in these first chapters.

I know my original attraction to Jesus came as a young child. In my home and at Sunday school, I heard stories about Jesus. I remember a children's picture Bible that had a simple but beautiful picture of Jesus, seated, in a blue and white robe, with children of all races gathered around his knees. Some were leaning on him. Some were seated at his feet. Some had their arms around him. His arms were opened in an embrace that took them all in, and his bearded face carried a gentle smile a boy could trust.

Looking back, I realize the illustration wasn't historically accurate. It was influenced more by a popular Sunday school song that I also loved ("red and yellow, black and white, they are precious in his sight. Jesus loves the little children of the world") than by ancient Middle Eastern realities. But in a way the picture was even truer than a historically accurate picture would have been; it probably would have had no red, yellow, black, or white children at all, but only brown Middle Eastern ones.

The picture Bible was augmented in my imagination by flannel graph stories about Jesus. Flannel graph was a kind of 1950s high-tech precursor of overhead projectors, laptop video projectors, videos, and DVDs. The teachers were always kind women, sometimes even my own mother. Each would tell stories with an easel behind her. On the easel would be a piece of flannel cloth with a scene drawn on it with markers—a countryside, a storm at sea, a courtyard with marble columns, a home, a roadside with big boulders beside it. As the story unfolded, cut-out figures backed with felt would be stuck on the flannel background (felt and flannel being a gentle precursor of Velcro®)—blind Bartimaeus, Zacchaeus, a woman near a well, a nameless leper and his nine friends, a Roman centurion, or a Syrophonecian woman with a sick child. Through these stories, Jesus won my heart.

When I reached my teenage years, though, I lost that Jesus as one loses a friend in a crushing, noisy, rushing crowd. The crowd included arguments about evolution (which seemed elegant, patient, logical, and actually quite wonderful to me, more wonderful even than a literal six-day creation blitz), arguments about the Vietnam War (which made no sense to me—even if communism was as bad as everyone said, were people better off bombed and napalmed to death?), arguments about ethical issues like civil rights and desegregation and a hundred other things. I wondered if women were really supposed to be submissive to men and if rock 'n' roll was really of the devil. Were Catholics really going to burn in hell forever unless they revised their beliefs and practices to be *biblical* like us?

After a short foray into doubt and a rather mild (all things considered) youthful rebellion, my faith in Jesus was revitalized, largely through the Jesus Movement. For those who were part of it, especially in its early days, the Jesus Movement was a truly wonderful thing. There was a simplicity, a childlikeness, a naïveté, and a corresponding purity of motive that I have seldom seen since. In fact, this book may simply be an attempt to articulate what many of us felt and "knew" during those years.

But all too soon the Jesus Movement was co-opted. It was to a different Jesus that I was gradually converted.[14]

The first new Jesus I met had a different face, a different tone, a different function. "Jesus was born to die," I was told again and again, which meant his entire life—including the red, yellow, black, and white children around his knees...Zacchaeus in the sycamore tree (which gave me a lifelong love for sycamores)... Bartimaeus by the road...the one grateful leper returning...the woman by the well...the caring parents who begged him to heal their children—was quite marginalized. Everything between his birth and death was icing at most, assuredly not cake. This marginalization was unintentional, but in my experience it was very real.[15] I was losing something but gaining something, too: the conservative Protestant (or Evangelical) Jesus.

The Conservative Protestant Jesus

For conservative Protestants, the Good News centers on the crucifixion of Jesus. Jesus saves us by dying on the cross. "Jesus was born to die," I heard again and again. By dying, Jesus mysteriously absorbs the penalty of all human wrongdoing through all of history. The cross becomes the focal point where human injustice—past, present, and future—meets the unconquerable compassion and forgiveness of God. Jesus, hanging in agony, says, "Father, forgive

---

[14] Several forces, I think, cooperated in the co-opting of the Jesus Movement, including Classic Pentecostalism, the Religious Right, parachurch Christianity, the contemporary Christian music industry, and the religious marketing machine.

[15] Have you noticed that our great creeds tend to do this, too—to affirm Jesus' birth and then skip to his death? What does that say about us? What unintended consequences come from this focus on the beginning and end of Jesus' life and neglect or avoidance of the middle?

them, for they do not know what they are doing." We are given confidence that at our worst moment, the moment at which we humans behave as badly as is possible in this universe by torturing and killing God's ultimate messenger and representative to us, his prayer is answered. His innocent self-sacrifice somehow cancels out human guilt.

At the cross, the powerful horror of human evil and the more powerful glory of God's mercy meet, and human evil is exhausted, but not God's mercy. Exactly how this happens is understood through various metaphors, with the following four perhaps being most popular.[16]

A legal metaphor: God is judge and humanity is guilty, deserving the death penalty. Jesus, a perfect representative of humanity, willingly takes the death penalty deserved by all humanity. Justice is satisfied, and evildoers can be forgiven. In this metaphor the forensic language of law, guilt, punishment, penalty, and justification is all-important. Sometimes the cool, impersonal guilt pronounced by the law is replaced by the hot wrath erupting from the Judge, but both styles reflect the same legal metaphor.

An economic metaphor: God is the good master, and we are God's servants, but we run away (or are lured away, perhaps kidnapped) by the Evil One, who makes us his slaves. Jesus offers himself to Satan as the representative of the human race: "Take me and let them go," Jesus says, offering himself as a kind of ransom payment. Satan takes Jesus, and as a result, we are potentially set free. (And Satan gets double-crossed in the end because after killing Jesus and thinking he has triumphed, Jesus triumphs by rising from the dead.) In this metaphor the business language of selling, buying, price, and payment is paramount.

---

[16] Too few Christians realize how metaphorical our language about God is. See Chapter 9 for more on this subject.

A governmental metaphor: The human race has rebelled against the King. To be forgiven and restored as citizens in good standing, humanity must repent and resubmit itself to God's will. But humans are so distorted by evil that they are unable to sincerely repent and resubmit to God. Jesus, through his obedient life and voluntary death, acts as a representative for all humanity and enacts repentance and submission to God's will for all humanity. As the representative of the human race, his perfect obedience and submission extend to all who will trust Jesus. In this metaphor, political terms like *representation*, *reconciliation*, and *citizenship* are essential.

A military metaphor: The human race has been conquered by an alien power or powers (Sin, the Devil, and Death are the most common antagonists, although Paul's more ambiguous "principalities and powers" could also be included). Jesus goes to battle with the alien power(s), and appears to be defeated in death, but his death turns out to be the undoing of the antagonist. In this metaphor, military terms such as *battle*, *defeat*, and *conquering* are predominant.

Many conservative Protestants develop little analogies to explain, on a more popular and less technical level, how the death of Jesus "works" to bring us forgiveness within these metaphorical contexts. There are well-circulated stories, for example, about an impending train wreck averted by a man whose son is killed in the process, a bad boy in school whose punishment is taken by a good boy, etc. There's a diagram about a chasm and a bridge. I used to share these diagrams and stories enthusiastically, although over time each analogy presented logical and ethical problems that dulled my enthusiasm.[17]

---

[17] For a helpful overview of problems with the most popular conservative Protestant understanding of Jesus' death, see *Recovering the Scandal of the Cross* by Joel Green and Mark Baker (Baker, 2000) and its sequel, as yet unpublished.

Ultimately, most thoughtful conservative evangelical Protestants will agree that none of these explanations, metaphors, or theories perfectly or completely explains how the death of Jesus brings good news to the world: the full answer includes and yet eludes all these metaphors, analogies, and diagrams.[18] However it happens, conservative Protestants agree that by dying, Jesus opens the door, not just to heaven beyond this life, but to true communion and relationship with God in this life—whoever you are, whatever you've done. This Good News captured my heart in my late teenage years and recaptured my allegiance to Jesus.

In particular, it meant (and means) a lot to me because I don't think I've ever gone very long without sinning in some more or less obvious way: pride, lust, greed, untruthfulness (exaggeration, excuses), ungratefulness—not to mention the subtler ways. This understanding of Jesus focuses directly, and nearly exclusively, on the problem of individual moral guilt.

But as precious and indispensable as this perspective is for me, over the years a feeling grew within me, usually vague but sometimes acute, that I was missing something, perhaps something important. Jesus' cross in the past saved me from hell in the future, but it was hard to be clear on what it meant for me in the struggle of the present. And more importantly, did the gospel have anything to say about justice for the many, not just the justification of the individual? Was the gospel intended to give hope for human cultures and the created order in history, or was history a lost cause, so that the gospel only could give hope to individual souls beyond death, beyond history—like a small lifeboat in which a few lucky souls escape a huge sinking cruise ship?

And did the conservative Protestant emphasis on the death

---

[18] Sadly, some conservative Protestants unwittingly reduce the gospel to a theory of atonement. Dallas Willard calls this "the gospel of sin management" and says it produces "vampire Christians" who want Jesus for his blood and little else. See *The Divine Conspiracy* (Harper, 1998).

of Jesus necessarily marginalize Jesus' life—his wise teachings and his kind deeds, which had captured my childhood imagination? Over time I began to feel as though, from my perspective, the gospel became simply an individualistic theory, an abstraction with personal but not global import. It became about the solution to a cosmic legal/business/political problem, real and serious, but a bit dry, a bit removed from real life. In my heart grew a deep, subtle, unspoken sense that something was missing, which gradually opened my heart to search for other ways of seeing Jesus.

I should add that this dissatisfaction with the conservative Protestant Jesus intensified just last Christmas when one of my children was home for the holidays from college. I asked him how he was doing spiritually.

"I'm struggling, Dad," he said.

"Tell me about that," I said.

He replied, "Well, Dad, if Christianity is true, then nearly everyone I love is going to be tortured in the fires of hell forever. And if it's not true, then life has no meaning." He was silent for a moment and then added, "I just wish there were a better option."

My heart was broken. I asked, "Is that the understanding of Christianity you got from me?"

He replied, "No, but that's the way most Christians think. They just kind of bottom-line everything to heaven or hell, and that makes life feel kind of cheap."

My son's insight doesn't apply to the best expressions of conservative Protestants, but it does, I fear, apply too often to the most popular ones. He put into blunt and powerful terms exactly what I felt vaguely and inarticulately when I was his age.

The Pentecostal/Charismatic Jesus

The second Jesus I met in my spiritual journey as a young adult—back when I was about my son's age—was the Pentecostal or Charismatic Jesus.[19] If the conservative Protestant Jesus can tend to become something of an abstraction, necessary for the solution to my legal problem with God the Judge, but somewhat removed from daily experience apart from guilt removal, the Pentecostal Jesus was up close, present, and dramatically involved in daily life. If the conservative Protestant Jesus saves from a future hell by his death in the past, the Pentecostal Jesus also saves by his powerful presence in this present moment.

Sadly, much of my early exposure to the Pentecostal Jesus was clouded by a technical argument with relational implications. The argument had to do with whether all those who were truly following Jesus and therefore "Spirit-filled" had to "speak in tongues," which was an experience of the earliest Christians on a Jewish holiday called Pentecost (hence the name of the group or movement) involving speaking in unknown (some would say ecstatic) languages. The argument, happily beyond the scope of our discussion here, doubly forced one to think in terms of "who's in/who's out." Not only must one monitor who's a Christian or "saved" or "born again" (a distinction practiced by nearly all conservative Protestants including Pentecostals), but also one must be aware of who's "Spirit-filled" or not. I found this constant judging of in/out, us/them to be fatiguing and distracting from loving everyone I met as a neighbor, which I was pretty sure should be primary for Christians.

My Pentecostal friends wanted me to be "in" and share

---

[19] I'm using these terms interchangeably here, knowing that there are reasons to distinguish them. If these terms are unfamiliar to you, all you really need to know is that there are groups of Christians called charismatic or Pentecostal, and they celebrate the view of Jesus I am about to explain.

"the gift." But in spite of my sincere prayers and even tears, for many years I never received "the gift of tongues" and was made to feel like a second-class citizen in Pentecostal circles. Even after I did "receive the gift" (which turned out to be quite anticlimactic after all the fuss), I never bought into the belief that there were two easy-to-distinguish classes of Christians: Spirit-filled tongues speakers and everyone else. I resisted this Pentecostal teaching for three reasons (not including the fact that I didn't find the biblical arguments convincing).

First, by that time I had met too many certified tongues-speaking Christians who were consistently dishonest, weird, unhealthy, and mean-spirited. Any understanding of being "Spirit-filled" that didn't include helping people to become healthy, Christlike, and kind didn't seem to be worth much. Second, I had met too many non-tongues speakers who were sincere and Christ-like, radiant and fragrant with the Spirit of Christ. Third, I didn't want to do to others as had been done to me by creating a two-tier, in-group/out-group status.[20]

In spite of this rocky start, from the Pentecostals I became convinced that Jesus is here and now present, active, alive and well, and that the stories of Jesus that had so won my heart as a child were not marginalized at all—and even better, they were not over, either. I began to understand and expect that Jesus would continue to intervene in powerful, wonderful ways. I realized that, although invisible, the Holy Spirit was no less than the real presence of Jesus, and that my experiences and those of my friends with the Spirit of Jesus were no less real than those flannel graph and picture-Bible stories from my childhood. Jesus is alive and active! Signs and wonders still occur! I wasn't surprised that Pentecostals often used

---

[20] Many Pentecostals and/or Charismatics have let go of this two-class distinction and have come to see being filled with the Spirit as an ongoing way of life that may or may not have a dramatic beginning and that may or may not be accompanied by speaking in tongues. Others see this as a dangerous, liberalizing tendency.

the term *full gospel* to explain their understanding of Jesus, because it was fuller than the understanding I previously had.

But over time I realized that this "full gospel" terminology could have two dangerous side effects: pride (*our gospel is fuller than yours!*) and un-teachability (*we have it all—what more is there to learn?*). And not only that, but also I faced a problem of expectations. Jesus was present via the Holy Spirit to heal, for example—but could I expect every disease to be healed? Did God promise miracles on demand? What happens when someone prays for healing and Jesus doesn't do it? I refused to "blame the victim," to say he or she didn't have enough faith or any nonsense like that. The person was already sick, for crying out loud! The Jesus I knew came to help them, not blame them or make them feel worse.

As well, the Pentecostal Jesus didn't have much to say about God's concern for the whole world, for history, and for creation. It was focused on "the sweet here and now" as well as "the sweet by and by." But only for individuals who believed—really believed. Was that all there was? What about justice for non-Christians? Could the Good News of Jesus be even fuller than "the full gospel"? Were there social and historical dimensions to the gospel that went beyond personal health, prosperity, and happiness for believers now and in "eternity"? So, for all I gained from meeting the Pentecostal Jesus, I was still unsettled. About that time, quite by accident, I met a third Jesus.

The Roman Catholic Jesus

In graduate school I ended up writing a master's thesis on novelist Walker Percy. Raised in an intellectual and agnostic home, Percy became a theist, a Christian, and a Roman Catholic as a young adult, which is a short, bland summary of a long, fascinating story.[21] I loved his novels and essays, and his story and literary work reduced my ignorance and prejudice about Roman Catholicism.

Through him I discovered other Roman Catholic writers—twentieth-century writers such as Flannery O'Connor, Thomas Merton, Henri Nouwen, Romano Guardini, and Gabriel Marcel, as well as the medieval mystics and others.

If conservative Protestants focus on the way Jesus initially saves individuals by dying on the cross, and Pentecostals focus on the way Jesus continues to save individuals by giving the Holy Spirit, Roman Catholics focus on the way Jesus saves the church by rising from the dead. Through the resurrection, God has defeated death and all that comes with it—fear (when will death come?), hurry (how much time do I have in this short, terminal life?), greed (you only go around once in life, so you have to grab for all the gusto you can get), envy (why does her short life go better than mine?), injustice (the evil often prosper and live long while the good often suffer and die young), materialism (the one who dies with the most toys wins), despair (life is full of pain and then you die), and selfishness (in the end all you have is you). By entering life's worst—suffering and death —and breaking through it, Jesus opens the way to heaven, to life with God beyond this life. Through the resurrection, Jesus changes forever the whole equation of existence.[22]

Generosity, courage, gratitude, hope, and love fit as perfectly in this new equation of resurrection as desperation, greed, anxiety, and cynicism did in the old equation of death. Now, since death never has the last word, it makes sense to do right even if your just cause is, humanly speaking, hopeless. Jesus' resurrection guarantees that in the end God will win. You can spend your

---

[21] My favorite biography of Percy is by Jay Tolson: *Pilgrim in the Ruins* (Simon & Schuster, 1992).

[22] I realize that this is a very sympathetic interpretation of the Catholic Jesus. Less sympathetic interpretations should also be heard—for example, that Jesus is important because he establishes the institutional church hierarchy, which then marginalizes Jesus and takes the spotlight itself, assuming a powerful position in the world as dispenser of salvation. Similarly unsympathetic interpretations are possible for each group discussed in this chapter, and, no doubt, unsympathetic interpretations could be given of my interpretations here as well! For a constructively critical survey of church history to complement this one, read my friend Dave Andrews' important book *Christi-anarchy: Discovering a Radical Spirituality of Compassion* (Oxford: Lion, 1999).

life caring, giving, serving, and sacrificing, unconcerned about whether you've "succeeded" or received as much as you've given or sacrificed, convinced that you will have "treasures in heaven" beyond this life that are greater by far than any "treasure on earth" in this life. And even if you live and die as a nobody here, you hold your head high, because beyond this life your true value, wisdom, and identity will shine through.

This new equation confronts as well as encourages: you can fight to the top to be first in this life, only to find out that you're at the end of the line beyond this life; you can "store up treasures on earth" and fail to be "rich toward God." The resurrection of Jesus, then, puts human life in a new eternal context, and the new context calls for a whole new way of living.

This view, called the "Christus Victor" theory of atonement by theologians, is not exclusively Catholic. It celebrates that Jesus is risen and alive, intersecting with our lives on earth, and waiting for us beyond this life. In this view, Christians are especially aware of how the risen Jesus continues to encounter his followers through public worship, and especially through the Eucharist, which is one reason (among many) why the Eucharist is so important to Roman Catholic Christians and their close cousins, Anglican Christians.[23] The Eucharist is a constant celebration of good news, a continual rendezvous with the risen Christ, and through him, with God. That such a rendezvous is possible is amazingly good news for everyone in the church.

The Roman Catholic Church is so broad that it includes many "little churches" (*ecclesiolae*) in the "big church" (*ecclesia*). Many

---

[23] The Eucharist (or communion, or the Lord's Supper) is a ritual or practice in which bread and wine are used to celebrate Jesus' death, resurrection, abiding presence, and promised return. Different tribes in the Christian family focus on different aspects of its many-layered meaning. For a warmhearted devotional reflection on the Eucharist, see my friend Dan Schmidt's book *Taken by Communion: How the Lord's Supper Nourishes the Soul* (Baker, 2003).

of those little churches in the contemplative tradition emphasize how God may be mystically experienced through contemplation, through a quiet mindfulness. Other *ecclesiolae*, such as the Catholic Worker Movement, emphasize the social implications of Jesus' life and message. I didn't discover these *ecclesiolae* until later, though.

So by my mid-20s, I had met the conservative Protestant Jesus, the Pentecostal Jesus, and the Roman Catholic Jesus. And by the grace of God, I didn't think of them as different saviors, requiring a lateral conversion to a new denomination each time. Rather I believed that each was a new facet, a new dimension, of the Jesus I had met as a child and rediscovered as a teenager, and that each could enrich my ongoing conversion in my spiritual journey. But I was still unsatisfied, especially because I sensed that if Jesus were truly the Savior, he wasn't just my personal Savior, but was the Savior of the whole cosmos. The Eastern Orthodox Jesus would lead me into this new territory.

The Eastern Orthodox Jesus

I think I was first introduced to the Orthodox way through the writings of Dostoyevsky and Tolstoy in college. Years later I came across a book on prayer by Metropolitan Anthony Bloom (*Beginning to Pray*, Paulist, 1988). I had read a lot of Christian books by my early 30s, especially books on prayer; and with most, after reading a page or two, I could predict what they'd say, how they'd say it, etc. But this book surprised me on page after page. This Eastern tradition, of which I had known little beyond stereotypes, turned out to have rich resources that attracted me and sparked my curiosity.

In particular I became intrigued with the way the Eastern Orthodox family (which includes the Greek, Russian, Serbian, Antiochian, and several other communities) celebrated the Trinity—not as an abstract exercise in theological hairsplitting, but as an introduction to a powerful and dynamic view of God.

I learned that the early church leaders described the Trinity using the term *perichoresis* (*peri*—circle, *choresis*—dance): the Trinity was an eternal dance of Father, Son, and Spirit sharing mutual love, honor, happiness, joy, and respect. Against this backdrop, God's act of creation means that God is inviting more and more beings into the eternal dance of joy. Sin means that people are stepping out of the dance, corrupting its beauty and rhythm, crashing and tackling and stomping on feet instead of moving with grace, rhythm, and reverence. Then, in Jesus, God enters creation to restore the rhythm and beauty again.[24]

If the Evangelical Jesus saves by dying, the Pentecostal Jesus by sending his Spirit, and the Catholic Jesus by rising from death, the Eastern Orthodox Jesus saves simply by being born, by showing up, by coming among us.[25] In Jesus' birth, these Christians believe two wonderful things happen. First, God takes the human life of Jesus into God's own eternal life, and in so doing, Jesus' people (the Jews), species (the human race), and history (the history of our planet and our whole universe) enter into—are taken up into—God's own life. God's life, love, joy, and power are so great that all our death, hate, pain, and failures are eradicated, swallowed up, cancelled, extinguished, and overcome by being taken up into God. In this way Jesus will ultimately bring blessing to the whole world, to all of creation.

---

[24] For those who are tired of abstract arguments about the Trinity that seem to box God into a mathematical equation, listen to Chesterton: "For to us Trinitarians (if I may say it with reverence)—to us God Himself is a society. It is indeed a fathomless mystery of theology...This triple enigma is as comforting as wine and open as an English fireside; this thing that bewilders the intellect utterly quiets the heart" (*Orthodoxy*, 145-146). In the last few years, there has been a hopeful, heartwarming, and mind-expanding resurgence of interest in the Trinity—a wonderful contribution to a generous orthodoxy. See, for example, Colin Gunton's *The Triune Creator* (Eerdmans, 1998).

[25] If you're wondering where these different streams of Christian faith arose, here's a brief historical sketch. Eastern Orthodoxy and Roman Catholicism officially split about 1000 A.D.; this was roughly speaking an East-West split. Protestants in Northern Europe (including Anabaptists) split off from Roman Catholics in Southern Europe in about 1500 A.D. Liberal and Conservative Protestants began to diverge in the 1800s, and Pentecostals arose from within Conservative Protestants—also called Evangelicals—about 1900. These latter divergences were conceptual, without geographical correlates.

Second, as humanity (and all creation) enters into God through Jesus, God also enters Jesus' people, species, and history. And by entering all creation through Jesus, God's heart is forever bound to it in solidarity, faithfulness, loyalty, and commitment. God will never give up until all creation is healed of its diseases, cured of its addictions, retrained from its foolishness, reclaimed from its lost state. Jesus saves by coming, by being born. It's no wonder that, for the Eastern Orthodox, Christmas is celebrated with such profound joy and rich, sustained intensity. It's the celebration of God's saving (rescuing) of the world—that God has entered creation through Jesus (*incarnation* is the theological term for God's embodiment in Jesus) and creation has been taken up into God so that all will be well. This is surely Good News!

How does this happen? A powerful story was told in the fourth century by Athanasius, one of the most important theologians in Eastern Orthodoxy, to illustrate how, in Jesus, God came as a human to save all of creation. I'll adapt and expand his story here:

Once upon a time there was a good and kind king who had a great kingdom with many cities. In one distant city, some people took advantage of the freedom the king gave them and started doing evil. They profited by their evil and began to fear that the king would interfere and throw them in jail. Eventually these rebels seethed with hatred for the king. They convinced the city that everyone would be better off without the king, and the city declared its independence from the kingdom.

But soon, with everyone doing whatever they wanted, disorder reigned in the city. There was violence, hatred, lying, oppression, murder, rape, slavery, and fear. The king thought: *What should I do? If I take my army and conquer the city by force, the people will fight against me, and I'll have to kill so many of them, and the rest will only submit through fear or intimidation, which will make them hate me and all I stand for even more. How*

*does that help them—to be either dead or imprisoned or secretly seething with rage? But
if I leave them alone, they'll destroy each other, and it breaks my heart to think of the
pain they're causing and experiencing.*

So the king did something very surprising. He took off his
robes and dressed in the rags of a homeless wanderer. Incognito,
he entered the city and began living in a vacant lot near a garbage
dump. He took up a trade—fixing broken pottery and furniture.
Whenever people came to him, his kindness and goodness and
fairness and respect were so striking that they would linger just to
be in his presence. They would tell him their fears and questions,
and ask his advice. He told them that the rebels had fooled them,
and that the true king had a better way to live, which he exemplified
and taught. One by one, then two by two, and then by the hundreds,
people began to have confidence in him and live in his way.

Their influence spread to others, and the movement grew
and grew until the whole city regretted its rebellion and wanted
to return to the kingdom again. But, ashamed of their horrible
mistake, they were afraid to approach the king, believing he
would certainly destroy them for their rebellion. But the king-in-
disguise told them the good news: he was himself the king, and he
loved them. He held nothing against them, and he welcomed them
back into his kingdom, having accomplished by a gentle, subtle
presence what never could have been accomplished through brute
force.

For the first time, through the Eastern Jesus, I began to
have a glimpse of how Jesus could indeed be the Savior not just of
a few individual humans, but of the whole world.[26] I began to see
the wisdom, the necessity of the incarnation, and its expanding

---

[26] By "the whole world," I do not necessarily mean every individual in it, but rather, I mean the
cosmos, creation, the earth in history, not just beyond history. Also, I should add here that I
am unqualified to be a spokesperson for the Eastern tradition, and so my thoughts on Eastern
Orthodoxy should be considered the impressionistic observations of an outside admirer, not
technically precise pronouncements of an inside spokesperson.

impact not just beyond this life and this history, but within it. And somehow I began to see how my personal salvation was not *apart from* the salvation of the world but was *a part of* it. The more I learned from Jesus "the ways of the king," the more I could influence others in his ways, too, and the closer we came to the salvation of the whole world. This dynamic, transcendent, and cosmic Eastern Orthodox Jesus opened the door for three more.

The Liberal Protestant Jesus

For reasons I'll explain later, I was deeply prejudiced against liberal or mainline Protestants (see Chapter 8). But in my mid-20s, newly married, my wife and I began attending an Episcopal church. The church was not a typical Episcopal congregation: "Evangelical in the pulpit, Anglican at the altar, and charismatic in the pew," Rector Renny Scott, who became one of my early important mentors, would say to describe it.

While Scott himself was conservative or evangelical, he loved and respected his more liberal colleagues, and his attitude began to rub off on me. "Scratch the paint of a liberal," he once told me, "and you'll find an alienated fundamentalist underneath." Over years I found out how true that little saying was. As I began to realize how liberal Protestants were seeking to fill in the deficiencies they found in the conservative Protestant Jesus, I realized I could learn a lot from them; I was on a similar quest.

In my 30s, as I got to know a number of liberal Protestants as friends. I became willing to appreciate how for them, the gospel centers in the words and deeds of Jesus Christ—the story of his life, between his birth (of such importance to the Eastern Orthodox), and his death and resurrection (the focal points for conservative Protestants and Roman Catholics). His teachings and acts of love, healing, justice, and compassion offer a way of life that, if practiced, brings blessing to the whole world. Our mission, then, is to bring the teaching and example of Jesus to bear on our world—not only on our personal relationships, but also on the political structures and cultural systems of our world.

For some complex reasons that we can't go into here, some (not all) liberal Protestants will question whether some or all of the miraculous deeds recounted in the Gospels (and elsewhere in the Bible) actually happened. Instead they often read the miracle accounts as instructive fictions, parables, fables, myths not intended by the storytellers of the early church to be historically accurate or inaccurate, but intended instead to dramatically convey a deeper meaning, given by God. So, when Jesus multiplies a boy's loaves and fish to feed a multitude, we are being told in the language of poetry that if we will give whatever little we have, God will make it more effective than we could imagine. Or when Jesus heals a paralytic, we can see our spiritual paralysis more clearly and believe it can be healed. Or when Jesus heals blindness, we acknowledge our own blindness and need for enlightenment or new vision.

Beyond these personal applications, these stories inspire us to actually feed the hungry by sharing our bread and our hospitality, to build and staff hospitals to help the sick, to cure the blindness of ignorance through education and art, to cross racial and cultural boundaries in love, to face corrupt systems even at risk of our lives. Even for many liberal Protestants who question the literal validity of many of the stories of Jesus, the stories' meaning or message is true and God-given, and can have an impact on us, and through us, on our world.[27]

While I believe that actual miracles can and do happen (though I notice they sometimes create nearly as many problems

---

[27] Some liberal Protestants even go beyond what I'm describing here, denying the reality of a personal, relational God. While I understand in part what they're reacting *against*, I have never been clear about what is left to be *for*, or why.

as they solve, and so I see why they aren't given "on demand"), I am sympathetic with those who believe otherwise, and I applaud their desire to live out the meaning of the miracle stories even when they don't believe the stories really happened as written.[28] (I find it harder to be sympathetic with those who take pride in believing the miracles really happened but don't seek to live out their meaning.)

The Anabaptist Jesus

I think I first heard the term *Anabaptist* associated with "Christian pacifism" back in the days of the Vietnam War when I was a teenager. Nearly all the pacifists I met then were nonreligious, and nearly all the religious people I knew tended toward the "hawk" side when it came to the war. But even as a teenager, I resonated with the ideal of pacifism for Christians, and I remember hoping I'd meet some Anabaptists someday. It turns out I had already met some but didn't realize it.

In high school, our marching band (I played saxophone) did an exchange weekend with a band in rural Ohio, and I stayed with a warm, hospitable Mennonite family there. Amish families surrounded their farm. From that visit I got the idea that Mennonites were a slightly less conservative version of the Amish, but I had no idea that together they were prime examples of Anabaptists. In my 20s, I read John Howard Yoder's *The Politics of Jesus*, and although I wasn't immediately convinced of all his arguments, I was certainly convinced that Anabaptists had a lot to teach me.

Anabaptist Christians, not unlike liberal Protestants, find the heart of the gospel in the teachings of Jesus—and in particular, the ethical teachings of Jesus. Anabaptists have (for better and

---

[28] Accidental theologian Jim Carrey brilliantly illustrates some of the problems with miracles on demand in his delightful 2003 film *Bruce Almighty*.

for worse) traditionally been wary of too much speculation about theological abstractions such as atonement theories (which are so important to conservative Protestants), literal or figurative biblical interpretation (a.k.a., hermeneutics, which has been so important to both liberal and conservative Protestants), or rites and rituals like the Eucharist (of such importance to Roman Catholics and Eastern Orthodox). Instead they feel their calling is to focus on living out Jesus' teachings about how we are to conduct our daily lives, especially in relation to our neighbors. As more and more people take Jesus' teachings on neighborly nonviolence and peacemaking seriously, as more and more people live out the simple way of Jesus in their communities, our whole world comes closer to the day when God's will is done on earth—which includes the extinction of war.

For conservative Protestants and Roman Catholics, then, Jesus saves individuals through the cross and resurrection; for Eastern Orthodox followers, Jesus saves the world through the incarnation; for liberal Protestants and Anabaptists, Jesus saves through his teaching and example. But in addition, Anabaptists uniquely emphasize Jesus' role in convening and leading a community of disciples. For them the church is not at heart an institution (as it has tended to be for the other groups we have considered) with hierarchies and policies, headquarters, and bureaucracy. Above all, the church is a continuation and extension of the original band of disciples, a group of people learning the ways of Jesus as a voluntary community.

The Jesus of the Oppressed

Add one more key element to the Anabaptist vision, and you have the seventh and final Jesus that I have met...so far, at least. This is the Jesus of nonviolent liberation theology. In my readings and travels (especially in Latin America), I have been exposed to many committed Christians who believe that Marxism and Communism were filling in the gap that should have been filled by Christians—Christians who understood the revolutionary social and political implications of the teaching and example of Jesus, whose gospel was good news to the poor, along with a challenge toward generosity for the rich.

Because Christians failed to preach and practice this dimension of the gospel, secular movements arose to fill the gap. Sadly, because these secular movements had ideology without truly spiritual good news, the poor received from these secular movements yet another disappointment and yet another delay in experiencing true liberation. Sadly, because these secular movements often preached that violence could overcome violence, even if they had succeeded in liberating the poor from poverty, they never could have liberated the poor from violence. Nonviolent liberation theology sought to rediscover the Jesus who is the hero to the poor and oppressed, and the prophet who bravely confronts the establishments of power and privilege.

Like the Jesus of the liberal Protestants and Anabaptists, this Jesus leads a band of disciples, but the liberation mind-set gives special attention to the activism of this band of disciples in relation to systems of oppression. Through them, with them, Jesus works for liberation of all oppressed people. Jesus' death on the cross is seen in a unique way from this vantage point: in his dying, Jesus confronts the corrupt, compromised religious system and violent, unjust political and economic powers of his day through nonviolent resistance.[29] He does not inflict suffering but willingly suffers. In the process, the corrupt systems show themselves for what they are, sowing the seeds for their own destruction and making way for the peace and justice of God to replace them—not just beyond history in heaven but here in history on planet Earth.

---

[29] I am aware that some liberation theologians have promoted violence, but I have tended to discount them and only paid attention to those who were nonviolent.

The Jesus of liberation theology, firmly rooted in the struggles of the first century, inspires Christians to continue his work and mission in all centuries throughout history, believing that history is exactly the venue into which God's kingdom comes and in which God's will can increasingly be done.

Through the years I have found that there are many pictures of Jesus afoot in the Christian world. My sketches here in this chapter are just that—simple impressions drawn with a few lines; for detailed portraits you'll need to read elsewhere. Perhaps we could summarize using this table:

Type of Christian	Focus/Problem	Good News
Conservative Protestant	The human race is guilty of sin and wrongdoing.	Jesus' death pays the full penalty for human sin.
Pentecostal	The human race is held down by disease and poverty.	Jesus teaches us how to receive miracles and healings from God through faith in God's promises.
Roman Catholic	The human race is enslaved by the fear of death.	Jesus' resurrection defeats death and liberates humanity.
Eastern Orthodox	The human race is spiritually sick and needs healing; it has dropped out of the "dance" of creation.	Jesus' entry (or incarnation) into humanity and history brings God's healing to the human race and all of creation.

Liberal Protestant	The human race suffers from ignorance of the teachings and ways of Christ.	Jesus' example and teachings inspire us to work compassionately for social justice.
Anabaptist	The human race is divided and violent and needs to learn the ways of Christ in community.	Jesus convenes a learning community of disciples who seek to model lives of love and peace.
Liberation Theology (nonviolent)	Humanity is oppressed by corrupt powers, systems, and regimes.	Jesus commissions and leads bands of activists to confront unjust regimes and make room for the shalom of God.

This table is far from complete; I can think of at least one new Jesus that is arising from within the evangelical tradition in recent years. And there are many crossovers and hybrids among these visions of Jesus as well. For example, most Pentecostals share a close affinity with what I'm calling Conservative Protestants in their attention to human guilt and the forgiveness Jesus' death brings. Many Catholics share a concern for social justice with Liberal Protestants and Anabaptists and Liberationists. Furthermore, each of these groups has nuances, sub-streams, counter-streams, weaknesses, problems, and minority opinions that my simple table doesn't begin to show.

In the end, the purpose of this table and this whole chapter is not to further distinguish, delineate, or divide these various types of Christians by setting up competing independent portraits of Jesus, but rather, the reverse.

In short, I tell the story of my encounters with Jesus to say that now, after many years of following Jesus and learning from many different communities of his followers, I'm just beginning to arrive at a view of Jesus that approaches the simple, integrated richness I knew of him as a little boy—picture Bible on my father's lap, flannel graph characters on my mother's easel, and a pure, childlike love welling up within me. You could say I'm finding a new simplicity on the far side of complexity. I am a Christian because I believe the real Jesus is all that these sketches reveal and more. Saying that, a question comes to mind....

Why not celebrate them all? Already, many people are using terms like *post-Protestant, post-denominational, post-liberal,* and *post-conservative* to express a desire to move beyond the polarization and sectarianism that have too often characterized Christians of the past (as we'll discuss in Chapters 6 and 7). Up until recent decades, each tribe felt it had to uphold one image of Jesus and undermine some or all of the others. What if, instead, we saw these various emphases as partial projections that together can create a hologram: a richer, multidimensional vision of Jesus?

What if we enjoy them all, the way we enjoy foods from differing cultures? Aren't we glad we can enjoy Thai food this week, Chinese next, Italian the following week, Mexican next month, and Khmer after that? What do we gain by saying that Chinese food is permissible, but Mexican food is poison? Isn't there nourishment and joy (and pleasure) to be had from each tradition?

No, I am not recommending we throw each offering in a blender, press the "liquefy" button, and try to create a gray porridge of all cuisines. That doesn't sound appetizing at all. Neither would it be helpful. Rather I'm recommending that we acknowledge that

Christians of each tradition bring their distinctive and wonderful gifts to the table, so we can all enjoy the feast of generous orthodoxy—and spread that same feast for the whole world.

CHAPTER 2

JESUS AND GOD B

I am a Christian because I have confidence in Jesus Christ—in all his dimensions (those I know, and those I don't). I trust Jesus. I think Jesus is right because I believe God was in Jesus in an unprecedented way. Through Jesus I have entered into a real, experiential relationship with God as Father, and I have received God's Spirit into my life. I have experienced the love of God through Jesus, and as the old hymn says, "love so amazing, so divine, demands my heart, my life, my all." As I seek to follow Jesus as my leader, guide, and teacher, I believe I am experiencing life in its fullest dimensions—full of joy and love, and yes, full of struggle and challenge, too. For all these reasons and more, I love Jesus. I believe Jesus embraces me, and you, and the whole world in the love of God.

It pained me to write the name *Jesus* so many times in the previous paragraph because I'm worried I will sound like those people whose mouths seem to drool with Jesus-talk. As Catholic novelist Walker Percy suggested, you can say "Jesus" so much that it sounds like a cheap product or slogan, as if you're shouting "Exxon! Exxon!"[30] For some it's a kind of *shibboleth*, a code word that, when used often enough, proves to some that you're truly "one of us," orthodox, legit, an insider in the "Jesus Club." But I don't like playing those code-word games (because I don't think Jesus would, either).

As well, as many of my Jewish friends realize, *Jesus* can sound like a political slogan threatening repression (as in, "We're going to take this country for JEEZUSSSS!"). To my Jewish friends who listen to Christian radio just to keep an eye on us, that doesn't sound very good.[31] For too many people the name *Jesus* has become a symbol of exclusion, as if Jesus' statement "I am the way, and the truth, and the life; no one comes to the Father except through me" actually means, "I am in the way of people seeking truth and life. I won't let anyone get to God unless he comes through me." The name of Jesus, whose life and message resonated with acceptance, welcome, and inclusion, has too often become a symbol of elitism, exclusion, and aggression. This pains me, and I imagine it pains Jesus, too, who was himself Jewish and knew what it felt like to be treated with disdain.

I am sympathetic to my Jewish friends in this regard for another reason: Jewish people try to avoid overusing the name of God out of deep respect for the commandment (one of the Big 10) about not taking the name of the Lord in vain. Like them, out of reverence for any sacred name associated with God, I don't want to use it too often or in "vain" ways.

Meanwhile I fully sympathize with the people who use Jesus-talk a lot because once you've begun to understand and, even better, experience, and—even better still—follow Jesus, you are

---

[30] See *The Message in the Bottle* (Picador, 2000).

[31] I once saw a small, old synagogue in the shadow of a big, new church. A huge cross towered above the church entrance, which abutted the synagogue entrance. It pained me that the good Jewish people of that synagogue had to enter it under the sign of that huge cross every Sabbath, a symbol that has often carried horrible associations for Jewish people. "Jesus wouldn't have done that," I thought. Jesus, a Jew himself, would have understood how having to drive under that cross would have been humiliating and oppressive—humiliation and oppression being two things he experienced but never imposed on others.

tempted to gush about him like a junior-high school girl with a new hunk of a boyfriend. Her heart gushes because (a) *he is* just so *wonderful*, and (b) *she's* just so *proud* to be associated with him. I agree: Jesus really is so wonderful, and I really am amazed and grateful that I get to be associated with him! But the innocent and humble "proud to be associated with Jesus" can too easily become the elitist and annoying "proud to be superior to everyone who's not," and I sure hope to avoid that.

So it's good, at the start, to say that if you don't get the whole Jesus thing (again, I hate using his name that way), I am sympathetic. I have a friend who is Jewish (by birth and practice) and agnostic (by persuasion). One day we were talking about things spiritual. He said, "Brian, what's the deal with Jesus?" I think his question meant, "Why do Christians emphasize Jesus so much?" It's a fair question, and one I'm trying to answer on these pages, knowing that I will fail.

I will fail because (a) every Christian who reads these pages will feel that I haven't *begun* to do him justice, that they see him as being so much more wonderful than I can explain here, and (b) they're right. Jesus is more wonderful than I will ever be able to say.[32] So I must admit defeat even before I begin in the next few chapters to explain my attachment to Jesus in terms of three important confessions from the Bible, each deserving a book in itself. Why am I a Christian? Because I believe Jesus is Savior of the world, Lord, and Son of God. It is with the third of these confessions that I will begin.

To say Jesus is the Son of God is to say a lot, although

---

[32] I'm not alone in my feeling of frustration at not being able to do justice to Jesus: the Gospel of John says something very similar (John 20:30-31; 21:25). I've written about Jesus at length, equally unsuccessfully, in several of my other books, especially *A New Kind of Christian* (Jossey-Bass, 2001) and *The Story We Find Ourselves In* (Jossey-Bass, 2003). Ultimately, one shows regard for Jesus not just by what he or she says or writes, but by how he or she lives life. Here I fail as well, but perhaps in both arenas—living and writing—trying one's best (and failing) is all one can do.

many Christians use the phrase all their lives without ever really thinking about it. Perhaps you've heard the phrase currently used in the Middle East, "mother of." The "mother of all geniuses" means "the epitome of all geniuses" or "the ultimate genius." Similarly, "mother of all wars" means "the ultimate war" or "the quintessential war." The words *son of* works in a similar way.

In the Gospels (the four stories of Jesus included in the New Testament), we find that peaceful people are called "sons of peace," two rambunctious brothers are called "sons of thunder," dishonest, evil-hearted people are labeled "sons of the devil," and perhaps most importantly, Jesus is also referred to as "son of man" or "son of humanity." Clearly the meaning of this construction suggests "carrying the essence of" or "embodying the heart of." Some people carry the essence of peace or have the essential quality of thunder (loud? bombastic?) or embody evil. In this sense "son of man"—another of Jesus' favorite terms for himself—would mean "the essential human, the ultimate embodiment of humanity."

And in this sense "Son of God" would mean "embodying God" or "carrying the essence of God," just as in English a son who is the "spittin' image" of his father carries his father's genetic code or family likeness, or is a "chip off the old block," or is "his father's son." This likeness is what the earliest followers of Jesus were so struck with. When they were around Jesus, they felt—no, more than that, they somehow *knew*—they were experiencing God.[33]

This experience found its way into the language of the early church documents:

---

[33] It's instructive and beautiful to consider that the Gospels use the terms *son of man* and *Son of God* virtually interchangeably, suggesting, I think, that the true essence of humanity is to be in the true image of God. It's also instructive to contrast our use of the term *human* in statements such as "I'm only human" (where *human* means prone to do wrong) and "That was very human of him" (where *human* means prone to godlike kindness). True humanity, this "son of Man" language suggests, follows the latter use; distorted humanity, the former. It is equally instructive and beautiful to realize that the term *son of man* suggests that Jesus is the *son of all*—that he belongs to all humanity, not just one sect of it, whether Jewish or Christian.

He is the image of the invisible God, the firstborn over all creation. For by him all things were created: things in heaven and on earth, visible and invisible, whether thrones or powers or rulers or authorities; all things were created by him and for him. He is before all things, and in him all things hold together. And he is the head of the body, the church; he is the beginning and the firstborn from among the dead, so that in everything he might have the supremacy. *For God was pleased to have all his fullness dwell in him,* and through him to reconcile to himself all things, whether things on earth or things in heaven, by making peace through his blood, shed on the cross (Colossians 1:15-20, emphasis mine).

In the past God spoke to our forefathers through the prophets at many times and in various ways, but in these last days he has spoken to us by his Son, whom he appointed heir of all things, and through whom he made the universe. *The Son is the radiance of God's glory and the exact representation of his being,* sustaining all things by his powerful word (Hebrews 1:1-3, emphasis mine).

For God, who said, "Let light shine out of darkness," made his light shine in our hearts to give us the light of the knowledge of *the glory of God in the face of Christ* (2 Corinthians 4:6, emphasis mine).

This full, radiant, glorious experience of God in Jesus Christ eventually revolutionized the whole concept of God, so that the word *God* itself was reimagined through the experience of encountering Jesus, seeing him act, hearing him speak, watching him relate, and reflecting on his whole career.

First, the earliest Christians had to account for the fact that Jesus' relationship with God was less formally *religious* than it was intimately *relational* or *familial*: for him, God was Father, Abba (an Aramaic word that resonates, both in meaning and form, with "papa," "dada" or "daddy"). Second, they remembered that Jesus promised his own Spirit would be with and in them. *Spirit* in this sense means person, heart, soul, presence, so that he could say "My Spirit will be with you" and "I will be with you," and mean the same thing. They not only remembered Jesus saying this, but they also experienced his promise coming true. When they experienced the Spirit of Jesus in them and among them, they recognized "it" as a "he," and the "he" was both Jesus and God.

This is as good a place as any to apologize for my use of masculine pronouns for God in the previous sentence. You'll notice that wherever I can, I avoid the use of masculine pronouns for God because they can give the false impression to many people today that the Christian God is a male deity. *God is not a male.* Instead God is personal (we might say super-personal) in a way that human maleness and femaleness together image better than either can alone. Maleness and femaleness are biological categories, and God is Life beyond biological categories.

In English, there just isn't a personal pronoun to express this kind of Life/Personality that isn't either exclusively male or exclusively female. The only nongender pronoun in English is *im*personal (it). Since God is neither impersonal nor exclusively male nor exclusively female nor neuter (meaning less than male or female), none of these pronoun options satisfy.

There are many ways of trying to overcome this dilemma. Some of these solutions are using *she* for a while, in a kind of linguistic affirmative action (which disturbs some, satisfies others), or using *he* with the understanding that it means personal but not-exclusively-male when referring to *her* (which disturbs others and satisfies some and mirrors rather than solves the current problem, thus creating a second wrong, which, for many people, including myself, doesn't add up to a right solution). Others suggest using *s/he* (which creates the additional problems of requiring him/her, his/hers, etc., and which suggests "both/either male and female" but not necessarily "comprising and beyond male and female"). Another option is capitalizing *He* (which for some successfully moves the male masculine pronoun beyond human masculinity to divine Personality, but for others creates a kind of Super-Masculinity, which is even worse). These days I simply try to avoid pronouns altogether, but use them when I must for stylistic reasons, and hereby beg the reader's pardon, reaffirming my belief (shared by C. S. Lewis, et al.) that God is not a male or a female, whatever pronouns we use.

The masculine biblical imagery of "Father" and "Son" also contributes to the patriarchalism or chauvinism that has too often characterized Christianity, maybe even more significantly than the pronoun problem. Two deeper problems underlie this problem of masculine imagery. First is the problem of language itself, which will be dealt with in Chapter 9. Second is the problem of the Bible itself, which will be explored in Chapter 10.

Significantly, seeing Jesus as the "Son of God" can actually help remove the macho-power and patriarchal-dominance ideas often associated with God. Jesus comes not as a loud, bullying macho general but as a vulnerable baby. Jesus lives as a poor Jew without ecclesiastical or political power and models not a conquering arrogance but a filial submission, not rugged independence but courageous obedience, not angry dominance that threatens with suffering but loving faithfulness that suffers instead. If Jesus truly reveals and images God, this vision of God is vastly different from the tough, macho judge and angry male potentate that many people think of when they think of God.

There is so much more that could be said, but for now, let's conclude: "Son of God" is not intended to reduce or masculinize

God, but it is intended to express what the early Christian writers meant by such phrases as "radiance of God's glory," "the glory of God in the face of Jesus," "the fullness of God dwelling in bodily form," and the like.

Again, beyond these masculine/feminine issues, the experience of God in Jesus was so powerful that it forever transformed what followers of Jesus meant when they said the word *God*. What was God like? What was God about? When they thought about what they had learned, seen, and experienced in Jesus, their understanding was revolutionized. Eventually, after a few centuries of reflecting on God as revealed and experienced through Jesus (in the context of some major controversies with varied forms of Greek philosophy), the church began to describe God as Father-Son-Spirit in Tri-unity or the Trinity. For them, God could no longer be conceived of merely as "God A," a single, solitary, dominant Power, Mind, or Will, but as "God B," a unified, eternal, mysterious, relational community/family/society/entity of saving Love.

Think of the kind of universe you would expect if God A created it: a universe of dominance, control, limitation, submission, uniformity, coercion.[34] Think of the kind of universe you would expect if God B created it: a universe of interdependence, relationship, possibility, responsibility, becoming, novelty, mutuality, freedom. I'm not sure which comes first—the kind of universe you see or the kind of God you believe in, but as a Christian who believes in Jesus as the Son of God, I find myself in universe B, getting to know God B.

This is why, for starters, I am a Christian: the image of God conveyed by Jesus as the Son of God, and the image of the

---

[34] Most forms of Islam and certain forms of Christianity reflect belief in this kind of God—"God A"—and this kind of universe.

universe that resonates with this image of God best fit my deepest experience, best resonate with my deepest intuition, best inspire my deepest hope, and best challenge me to live with what my friend, the late Mike Yaconelli, called "dangerous wonder," which is the starting point for a generous orthodoxy.[35]

---

[35] Mike always minimized his own intelligence, but I consider *Messy Spirituality* (Zondervan, 2002) and *Dangerous Wonder* (NavPress, 1998) to display surprising theological savvy and sensitivity. His death, which occurred during the writing of this book in late 2003, leaves us all with pangs of sadness and memories of joy.

CHAPTER 3

WOULD JESUS BE A CHRISTIAN?

When you read Chapter 1, you may have thought, "Wow, Brian is a nice guy. He seems to see the good in everything. He's so accepting of all different Christian traditions." The perception may have been sustained through Chapter 2, but it's about to crash. I wish I were that nice. The fact is that I've always had a cynical and critical streak that borders on nasty. A famous pacifist often says, "If you knew what a mean son of a gun I am, you'd realize why I need to be a pacifist." I suppose that's why I work hard to be irenic and compassionate: I need to be.

But in this chapter, I'd like to indulge in some critical and maybe even cynical thinking expressed in statements like these:

1. The more I study the Bible and reflect on the life and teachings of Jesus, the more I think most of Christianity as practiced today has very little to do with the real Jesus found there.

2. Often I don't think Jesus would be caught dead as a Christian, were he physically here today.

3. Generally, I don't think Christians would like Jesus if he showed up today as he did 2,000 years ago. In fact, I think we'd call him a heretic and plot to kill him, too.[36]

These statements are surely exaggerations, dyspeptic and cranky ruminations. But they are more widespread than you may realize. I helped a dear friend get on the path of following Jesus a few years ago, and she began attending seminary. I asked her how her studies were going one day, and she said, "After studying church history, I can see why people believe in hell. I just can't figure out why all Christians don't go there." I think you can feel what she meant (if not, wait until Chapter 18): the more one respects Jesus, the more one must be brokenhearted, embarrassed, furious, or some combination thereof when one considers what we Christians have done with Jesus. That's certainly true when it comes to calling Jesus *Lord*, something we Christians do a lot, often without the foggiest idea of what we mean. Has he become (I shudder to ask this) less our Lord and more our Mascot?

Lord means "master" (the very opposite of mascot), and there are at least three senses of the word *master* that apply to Jesus. First, *Lord suggests authority and kingship.* Now whenever we use words like *king, kingdom, kingship,* or *reign,* we run into problems similar to those when using *son* and *father.* In addition to dominance and masculinity issues, we face the problem that for contemporary people these words all feel archaic—quaintly archaic or barbarously archaic. Associating monarchy with nondemocratic and corrupt regimes (because "absolute power corrupts absolutely," we've seen again and again) or with symbolic monarchies without much real power, it's so hard, perhaps impossible, for us to have a feel for the word *king* even remotely similar to what people would have felt in Bible times.

---

[36] Philip Yancey has addressed some of these issues more graciously and in more detail than I am doing here. See *The Jesus I Never Knew* (Zondervan, 1995) and *What's So Amazing About Grace?* (Zondervan, 2002).

Perhaps, though, we can at least imagine this: what would it be like to live in times of perpetual violence, horrific brutality, ever-present danger, and constant vulnerability to whichever warlord (another bad association with *lord*) threatened us? Perhaps under those circumstances, we can imagine what good news it would be that a good king had come into power.[37]

Ironically, though, when many modern Christians use the word *sovereignty* (another form of "kingship" or "lordship"), they make matters worse, much worse, because for them, sovereignty means absolute control, and control is a very tricky word. Again, if you're living in danger and chaos, to say "A good king will soon be in control" would be good news.

But it's not good news at all if you live, as we do, at the end of modernity, a period that told us in a hundred different ways how we're *already controlled*: by our genes (genetic determinism), by class struggle (Marxism), by primitive psychosexual aggressions (Freudianism), by operant conditioning (Skinnerism), by evolutionary competition (social Darwinism), by laws of physics and chemistry (naturalism, reductionism), by linguistic and social constructions (some forms of extreme postmodernism), by Euro-American military and economy (colonialism), by technique and machinery (industrialism), and by advertising (consumerism).

Against this backdrop, theistic determinism is just another determinism, and in that case, talking about God as the all-powerful, all-controlling Lord/King is just more bad news, reducing us to plastic chessmen on a board of colored squares, puppets on strings in a play we don't write, characters in a video game that we aren't even playing, cogs in a contraption whose levers and buttons God and God alone pulls and pushes.

---

[37] Reading or watching the film version of *The Lord of the Rings* can, in this regard, become an important theological exercise, furnishing our imagination with bad and good visions of what being a lord or king can mean.

Meanwhile, for me, in the U.S.—now the undisputed Superpower in the world—I feel surrounded by Christians who very much like the idea of an American God and a middle-class Republican Jesus, first and foremost concerned about Our National Security and Our Way of Life. "The Lord Is My Shepherd" becomes "The Lord Is Our President," elected by us for our national interest, or "The Lord Is Our Secretary of Defense," ready to sacrifice 10,000 lives of noncitizens elsewhere for the safety of U.S. citizens here. The language of lordship and authority in this context only seems to serve the "powers that be," to bolster the status quo, to legitimize and protect and baptize whatever regime is in power. This feels like a tired old story that history has seen rise and fall many times, and it sickens me.

Good news under these circumstances would be a leader who liberated us from all determinisms, who deconstructed oppressive authority and the self-interest of leaders and nations, who destabilized the status quo and made way for a better day, who delivered us not only from corrupt power, but also from the whole approach to power that is so corruptible...

...which is exactly (I say) what is meant by the phrase "Jesus is Lord." In Jesus' day, "Caesar is Lord" was the political pledge of allegiance, required in a way not unlike "Heil Hitler" was required in the 1930s and early 1940s in Nazi Germany. To call Jesus "Lord" meant that there is a power in Jesus more important than the power of the king of the greatest state in history. To say "Jesus is Lord" was then (and should be now!) a profoundly political statement— affirming the authority of a "powerless" Jewish rabbi with scarred feet over the power of Caesar himself with all his swords, spears, chariots, and crosses.

Similarly, today there are plenty of other authority figures around, Caesars in various realms: presidents national and corporate, experts scientific and social, celebrities and media moguls, priests and pastors and bishops and cult leaders, various people in various high places who exert whatever control they can. But Jesus comes as a liberating, revolutionary leader, freeing us from the dehumanization and oppression that come from all "the powers that be" in our world (including religious powers). His kingdom, then, is a kingdom not of oppressive control but of dreamed-of freedom, not of coercive dominance but of liberating love, not of top-down domination but of bottom-up service, not of a clenched iron fist but of open, wounded hands extended in a welcoming embrace of kindness, gentleness, forgiveness, and grace.[38]

Caesar's authority was symbolized in a cross on which rebels and revolutionaries suffered and failed. Jesus' authority is symbolized in a cross on which he suffered as a rebel and revolutionary and succeeded. But how many Christians in a thousand understand that? How many of us have used the cross in Caesar's way, to dominate, rather than in Jesus' way, to liberate?

Of course, all this talk of a revolutionary approach to power may seem to be completely undone when I say that a second meaning of *Lord* suggests *a master in relation to a servant or slave.* Here we are, using more language of oppression, domination, coercion. (You may be so used to the language that you can't even see what I'm talking about. Try.)

But again Jesus takes the image of master-slave relations and deconstructs it, turns it inside out, empties it of old meaning and refills it with new meaning, and thus redefines and revolutionizes it. "I no longer call you servants," Jesus says, "but friends." He sets a shocking example of revolutionary mastership by stripping down to his undergarment and washing the feet of his

---

[38] Miroslav Volf's *Exclusion and Embrace* (Abingdon, 1996) profoundly explores the meaning of the image of Christ's extended arms.

disciples, something only a slave would do (never a master!), and thus highlights that this is his absurd, unheard-of way of showing mastery—by serving. He commands his disciples to practice this inverted form of leadership by humble service ("not as the Gentiles," he says), so the last are first, and the first, last. No one can call Jesus "Lord" without letting Jesus define the word in this radical, revolutionary new way. Otherwise they're letting lords other than the Lord determine what the word means.

Of course, in the midst of his radical deconstruction and reconstruction of the idea of Lord as master, Jesus asserts that he is the leader who gives commands (not our wish-granting genie, taking commands from us). He has authority; we answer to him, not the reverse. His commands should be followed wholeheartedly (it's those who actually "walk the walk" by practicing his teachings who are blessed, Jesus says, not just those who "talk the talk" by mouthing, "Lord, Lord"). As the saying goes, there is one Lord, and you are not it.

Of course, the more you think about it, the more you realize that without wise and firm authorized guidelines (i.e., don't kill, treat others as you'd be treated, forgive rather than seeking revenge, etc.) from a good authority, a good household (master-slave metaphor) or kingdom (king-subject metaphor) wouldn't stay good for very long. Followers of Jesus believe that Jesus' teachings and example give us a way of life that leads to a "good household" or "good kingdom," and we learn, too often the hard way, that ignoring or disobeying the Lord's wisdom leads to the opposite result. Carrying out his commands, respecting him as master, and in this way identifying as his servants feel like liberation not subjugation, an honor not an insult, a promotion not a demotion, a joy not an obligation, a calling to the highest way of life possible.

Your identity as a servant of Jesus takes on even more significance when you consider the alternatives: as Bob Dylan sang, "You're gonna have to serve somebody." There's no neutral ground. The meaning of your life could be defined by serving your family (or not), serving your political party (or not), serving your corporation, serving an economy, serving an "—ism" (racism, chauvinism, feminism, Marxism, conservatism, liberalism, scientism, nationalism, etc.), even serving a church or other religious organization. And then there's the ever-popular option of serving yourself. Unwittingly, through these servitudes, one can actually be serving darkness, as Jesus and many biblical writers tell us.

In contrast, your life could be centered in serving Jesus Christ—which would not replace or eradicate, but rather transform and enrich the way you serve any other legitimate groups or causes. Jesus defined his own identity not as being served, but as giving his life in service, and in this way, *acknowledging Jesus as master means one voluntarily "takes his yoke" and learns from Jesus how to serve God, plus one's neighbor, plus one's enemy, and so the whole world. Confessing Jesus as Lord means joining his revolution of love and living in this revolutionary way.*

How many children in Sunday school learn that radical sense of Christian servant identity as opposed to *Christians are nice people who know the truth and do good. Non-Christians are bad people who don't. Therefore we need to avoid non-Christians or convert them as fast as possible or try to pass laws to keep them under control and protect ourselves from them—until we can escape them forever in heaven?*

The difference between these two views is no small thing.

The third meaning of *Lord* grows from the first two: *Lord also means a master-teacher or rabbi,* one who tells us what to do and how to live, and here we may go even further astray. If I were a conspiracy theorist, I would write a book about how Christianity has successfully dethroned Jesus as Lord to such a degree that the "Jesus" who is preached, pasted on bumper stickers, serenaded in gooey love songs on religious radio and TV, and prayed to is an impostor. Here's how I might make that argument:

1. We retained Jesus as Savior but promoted the apostle Paul (or someone else) to Lord and Teacher. (Even as Savior, though, we limited Jesus to saving us from hell, which explains why we have had comparatively little interest in his saving us from greed, gossip, prejudice, violence, isolation, carelessness about the poor or the planet, hurry, hatred, envy, anger, or pride.)

2. We did this in various ways: by assuming that the purpose of Jesus and his gospel was to get people's souls into heaven after death and therefore concluding that the only really important thing about Jesus was his death (or birth, or resurrection) to solve our guilt problem that kept us out of heaven. Or by deciding that Jesus' message was "spiritual" and therefore pertained to "eternity" and not "history," and/or by deciding that Jesus' life and teachings were completely interpreted by Paul (or a particular church hierarchy) so they deserved little attention on their own, apart from the uses to which Paul (or whoever) put them.[39]

3. We developed theological systems that taught us how to avoid many of Jesus' teachings and reinterpret those we couldn't avoid.

4. We made up for our demotion of Jesus from being our Lord and Teacher by saying or singing his name more often, and by saying "Lord, Lord" as much as possible, preferably

---

[39] I should add here that I am *not* one who pits Paul against Jesus. Not at all. Rather I think we have misunderstood and misused Paul in a way that pits *us* against Jesus. But that's another story far removed from generous orthodoxy. For more on this important subject, N.T. Wright's works have all been valuable to me in contributing to a better, more integrated understanding of Jesus and Paul.

with deep feeling and high volume. This allowed us to still feel like good Christians whether or not we did, or cared about doing, anything he said.

If we were to try to reinstate Jesus as Lord/Teacher, we would have to go outside the world of popular modern theology to find ways to think about the meaning of Lord/Teacher. We would go to the world of arts and trades and notice how a *master* violinist, a *master* carpenter, a *master* electrician, a *master* of martial arts passes on her mastery to students or apprentices. The only way to learn this mastery is through the disciple's voluntary submission to the discipline and tradition of the master.

In this sense, *tradition* doesn't just mean "traditions," such as a way of bowing before a karate lesson or after a violin performance, although "traditions" are included in tradition. Tradition means a whole way of practice or way of life that includes systems of apprenticeship, a body of knowledge (of terms, history, lore), a wide range of know-how (skills, technique, ability), and something else—a kind of "unknown knowledge" that philosopher Michael Polanyi calls *personal knowledge*: levels of knowledge that one has and knows but doesn't even know one has and knows.[40]

Imagine an adult human with a double Ph.D. in engineering and ornithology trying to use grass, feathers, scraps of paper, and mud to build a common robin's nest. His fingers and thumbs form a muddy blob that would crumble in the first rainstorm. Then imagine a robin building the same nest with nothing but her beak. The robin (as far as I can tell) doesn't know that she knows how to build a nest and doesn't know how she knows, but she *knows*; she *has a feel* for it, as we see every spring. She can do something the certified, lettered expert human can't. Her unknown

---

[40] Fortunately, Michael Polanyi's book *Personal Knowledge: Towards a Postcritical Philosophy* (University of Chicago, 1974) goes so deep into this subject that I can only touch the surface of here, as does Dallas Willard's *The Divine Conspiracy* (Harper, 1998).

knowledge illustrates the deepest level of human knowledge that is learned not just from a "teacher" but from a "master." If you ask, "How do you *do* that, how do you *know* that?"—the only answer can be, "I don't know; I just know!"

This is the kind of inwardly formed learning that Jesus, as master, teaches his apprentices; a knowledge about how to live that can't be reduced to information, words, rules, books, or instructions, but rather that must be seen in the words-plus-example of the Master.

Not only that, but the master's students continue and expand the master's tradition so that one learns the way of the master most fully by being in the community of other students, including those who can remember and tell the stories about members of the community long departed. These gone-but-not-forgotten members are re-membered (kept alive through memory as important, ongoing members of the community). In this way the master-apprentice relationship is not merely individual tutoring but membership in a learning community that lives around the globe and across generations, as well as around the corner or across the street.

But so little if any of this is necessary for Christianity today in nearly all of its forms. We're doing just fine (we think) with Jesus as Savior and not Lord in any meaningful sense. If the real Lord Jesus were to knock on our door as Revolutionary King/Master/Teacher, I think we'd look through the peephole and judge him an imposter, since our "Buddy Jesus" as Savior is already sitting on the couch inside, watching TV with us, thumbs up and grinning, "meeting our needs" very well, thank you very much. Our domesticated, romanticized, spiritualized Jesus has become for us the orthodox Jesus, so an alternative one looks unorthodox, unfamiliar, maybe even dangerous and deserving of...what?

The result is a religion that Jesus might consider about as useful as many non-Christians consider it today, just as the Lord said they would (Matthew 5:13-16, 7:21-23).

Now I've gone and depressed myself. I'm wondering what right we—and especially I—have to even *talk* about a generous orthodoxy. I feel completely lost and stupid and pathetic. Lord, have mercy.

CHAPTER 4

JESUS: SAVIOR OF WHAT?

If the previous chapter wasn't disturbing enough—claiming that we Christians have demoted Jesus from Lord while retaining him as Savior—it's about to get worse. I believe we've also misconstrued, reduced, twisted, and torqued the whole meaning of what words like *savior*, *save*, and *salvation* are supposed to mean for generously orthodox Christians.

Vincent Donovan was a Roman Catholic priest from the U.S. who served as a Spiritan missionary in Tanzania for 17 years in the 1960s and 1970s, evangelizing the Masai. *Christianity Rediscovered*, his memoir of ministry in Masailand is, I think, one of the most important mission-related books of the twentieth century, a treasure that too few have discovered.[41] His experience there propelled him into the kinds of disillusioning reflections in which we indulged in the previous chapter, but as his title suggests, the disillusionment led to rediscovery.

Donovan found himself caught between the "heathen Masai" and a very confident, well-oiled religious machine. That

[41] Maryknoll, N.Y.: Orbis, 2003 (1978).

in-betweenness forced him to rethink the whole meaning of what Christians call *salvation*, much in the same way my experience among "unchurched postmoderns" has affected me. He explains, "I was to learn that any theology or theory that makes no reference to previous missionary experience, which does not take that experience into account, is a dead and useless thing...praxis must be prior to theology...In my work [theology would have to proceed] from practice to theory. If a theology did emerge from my work, it would have to be a theology growing out of the life and experience of the pagan peoples of the savannahs of East Africa" (21). Similarly, I have become convinced that a generous orthodoxy appropriate for our postmodern world will have to grow out of the experience of the post-Christian, post-secular people of the cities of the twenty-first century.[42]

After some time among the Masai, Donovan described, with some disillusionment, the version of Christianity he and other Western, Euro-American missionaries had imported into Africa: "an inward-turned, individual-salvation-oriented, un-adapted Christianity" (8). He became so disillusioned with this approach that he felt the need to move away from the term *salvation* altogether. One paragraph in his book especially intrigues me:

> "Preach the gospel to all creation," Christ said. Are we only now beginning to understand what he meant? I believe the unwritten melody that haunts this book ever so faintly, the new song waiting to be sung in place of the hymn of salvation, is simply the song of creation. To move away from the theology of salvation to the theology of creation may be the task of our time (14).

As I first read that paragraph, almost with tears, I thought: *maybe*

---

[42] By *post-Christian*, I really mean *post-Christendom*, i.e., people who live after the collapse of Christendom—the official or unwritten alliance of church and state.

his faint, haunting "unwritten melody" was actually exactly what the hymn of salvation should be. Perhaps our "inward-turned, individual-salvation-oriented, un-adapted Christianity" is a colossal and tragic misunderstanding, and perhaps we need to listen again for the true song of salvation, which is "good news to all creation."

So perhaps it's best to suspend what, if anything, you "know" about what it means to call Jesus "Savior" and to give the matter of salvation some fresh attention.

Let's start simply. In the Bible, *save* means "rescue" or "heal." It emphatically does *not* automatically mean "save from hell" or "give eternal life after death," as many preachers seem to imply in sermon after sermon. Rather its meaning varies from passage to passage, but in general, in any context, *save* means "get out of trouble." The trouble could be sickness, war, political intrigue, oppression, poverty, imprisonment, or any kind of danger or evil.

God, throughout the Hebrew Bible (which Christians call, perhaps unwisely, the Old Testament), repeatedly saves from danger and evil, so to say that *God saves* means that *God intervenes to rescue.* God compassionately and miraculously steps in, gets involved, intervenes, and protects his people from their enemies and themselves. God does so in three primary ways.

Sometimes *God saves by judging.* To speak of judgment as a form of salvation surprises people who have religious baggage and don't actually read the Bible, but only hear it filtered by sermons or theological systems. They assume that judgment is something bad or awful. But in the biblical context, judgment is generally a good thing. It means the coming of truth and justice into our deceived and oppressed world. If some bad and dishonest people are out to deceive or oppress others, God brings justice by bringing judgment—the natural consequences of their bad actions—on the evildoers so they are incapacitated and can't fulfill the additional

evil they intended. If others are misjudging you, God comes as
your vindicator, your justifier.[43] God tells the truth, which exposes
the lies of your misjudgers. Over and over again, biblical writers
anticipate the day when God will come to judge evil, to expose
it and permanently incapacitate it while vindicating good. They
speak of this as a profound and joyful kind of salvation. Take Psalm
98, for example. The psalm crescendos line by line, culminating
in the last three lines:

> Sing to the LORD a new song,
> for he has done marvelous things;
> his right hand and his holy arm
> have worked salvation for him.
> The LORD has made his salvation known
> and revealed his righteousness to the nations.
> He has remembered his love
> and his faithfulness to the house of Israel;
> all the ends of the earth have seen
> the salvation of our God.
>
> Shout for joy to the LORD, all the earth,
> burst into jubilant song with music;
> make music to the LORD with the harp,
> with the harp and the sound of singing,
> with trumpets and the blast of the ram's horn—
> shout for joy before the LORD, the King.
>
> Let the sea resound, and everything in it,
> the world, and all who live in it.
> Let the rivers clap their hands,
> Let the mountains sing together for joy;
> Let them sing before the LORD,
> **for he comes to judge the earth.**

---

[43] It is essential to distinguish between judging in this sense and prejudiced judgmentalism, which are forms of injustice deserving to be judged.

He will judge the world in righteousness
and the peoples with equity.

Sometimes, though, it's a little more complicated. What if *we* are the ones who have done evil, and we see the just consequences of evildoing coming on *us*? In this situation, God saves by judging... *and then by forgiving.* So often the danger or evil we face is self-created, self-inflicted, self-sabotaging—and we keep doing it because we are self-deluded and self-deceived through denial. By judging our evil, by naming it for what it is, by penetrating our denial and self-delusion, God begins saving us.

But God goes further. The consequences of our bad behavior loom over us, we hear God's judgment and realize we've done something stupidly wrong and we have second thoughts about what we've done. As we repent, as we become truly sorry, as we have a change of heart, God goes further by forgiving us, thus bringing salvation in an even fuller sense. Salvation is what happens when we experience *both* judgment *and* forgiveness, *both* justice (exposing the truth about our wrong) *and* mercy (forgoing the negative consequences we deserve). Without both we don't end up with true salvation.

We often refer to this saving judgment as God "convicting" us of our sin and our need for repentance. Again, without it there is no true salvation. Forgiveness without conviction is not forgiveness: it is irresponsible toleration. It doesn't lead to reconciliation and peace; it leads to chaos. (Ask any third-grade teacher who tolerates her rowdy students but never convicts them by naming and addressing their misbehavior.) Conversely, judgment without mercy is not salvation, but condemnation. It doesn't lead to reconciliation and peace: it leads to alienation. The Good News of salvation is that God sent Jesus not to condemn but to save: to save by bringing justice with mercy, true judgment with true forgiveness. First by exposing our wrong (judging) so we can face our wrong and turn from it...and then by forgiving our wrong, God intervenes and breaks the chain of cause and effect, of offense and alienation, so we're truly saved—liberated, rescued—from the vicious cycle (a.k.a., mess) we created.

The third way God saves is implied in the first two, and it is familiar territory from the previous chapter: *God saves by teaching or revealing.* For example, imagine an ignorant or careless young farmer who doesn't know about soil conservation. He plants the same seed year after year, never letting fields lie fallow. He never replenishes the soil with fertilizer from his cattle. He ignores erosion by rain and wind. What will happen to him? Each year his yield will decrease, and he'll slowly starve. Imagine his sagely grandmother helping the young farmer understand how to care for the land. She teaches him how to leave fields fallow, how to rotate crops, how to fertilize, how to terrace and plant windbreaks to avoid erosion. By teaching her grandson, she saves him from starvation.

To say that Jesus is Savior is to say that in Jesus, God is intervening as Savior in all of these ways, judging (naming evil as evil), forgiving (breaking the vicious cycle of cause and effect, making reconciliation possible), and teaching (showing how to set chain reactions of good in motion). Jesus comes then not to condemn (to bring the consequences we deserve) but to save by shining the light on our evil, by naming our evil as evil so we can repent and escape the chain of bad actions and bad consequences through forgiveness, and so we can learn from Jesus the master-teacher to live more wisely in the future.

To recap: we live in danger of oppression and deception, so Jesus comes with saving judgment. When God shines the light of justice and truth through Jesus, the outcome is surprising: the religious and political leaders often turn out to be scoundrels, and the prostitutes and homeless turn out to have more faith and goodness than anyone expected. Through parable, through proverb, through invective ("Woe to you!"), and most powerfully through the drama of his life story culminating in his death and rising, Jesus, wherever he goes, shows things to be what they really are—bringing a saving judgment-with-forgiveness (or justice-with-mercy) to all who will accept it.

This is a window into the meaning of the cross. Absorbing the worst that human beings can offer—crooked religiosity, petty political systems, individual betrayal, physical torture with whip and thorn and nail and hammer and spear—Jesus enters into the center of the thunderstorm of human evil and takes its full shock on the cross. Our evil is brutally, unmistakably exposed, drawn into broad daylight, and judged—named and shown for what it is. Then, having felt its agony and evil firsthand, in person, Jesus pronounces forgiveness and demonstrates that the grace of God is more powerful and expansive than the evil of humanity. Justice and mercy kiss; judgment and forgiveness embrace. From their marriage a new future is conceived.

Then, because we are so often ignorantly wrong and stupid, Jesus comes with saving teaching, profound yet amazingly compact: *Love God with your whole heart, soul, mind, and strength,* Jesus says, *and love your neighbor as yourself,* and that is enough. After his death and rising, Jesus sends his Spirit to continue the process of teaching us, creating a community across generations and around the world that is learning to live life to the full.

I am a Christian because I believe that, in all these ways, Jesus is saving the world. By "the world" I mean planet Earth and all life on it, because left to ourselves, un-judged, un-forgiven, and un-taught, we will certainly destroy this planet and its residents. And by "the world" I specifically mean human history, because again, it was and is in danger, grave danger, ultimate danger, self-imposed danger, and I don't believe anyone else can rescue it.[44]

---

[44] For more on this subject, see Chapter 5.

Some people I know once found a snapping turtle crossing a road in New Jersey. Snapping turtles are normally ugly: gray, often sporting a slimy coating of green algae, trailing a long, serrated, gator-like tail and fronted by massive and sharp jaws that can damage if not sever a careless finger or two. This turtle was even uglier than most: it was grossly deformed due to a plastic bottle top, a ring about an inch-and-a-half in diameter that it had accidentally acquired as a hatchling when it, too, was about an inch-and-a-half in diameter. The ring had fit around its midsection like a belt back then, but now, nearly a foot long, weighing about nine pounds, the animal was corseted by the ring so that it looked like a figure eight.

My friends realized that if they left the turtle in its current state, it would die. The deformity was survivable at nine pounds, but a full-grown snapper can weigh 30. At that size the constriction would not be survivable. So, they snipped the ring. And nothing happened. Nothing.

Except for one thing: at that moment the turtle had a future. It was rescued. It was saved. It would take years for the animal to grow into more normal proportions, maybe decades. Perhaps even in old age it would still be somewhat guitar-shaped. But it would survive.

A ring of selfishness, greed, lust, injustice, fear, prejudice, arrogance, apathy, chauvinism, and ignorance has similarly deformed our species. When I say that Jesus is Savior, I believe he snipped the ring by judging, forgiving, teaching, suffering, dying, rising, and more. And he's still working to restore us, to lead us, to heal us. Jesus is still in the process of saving us. Because I have confidence in Jesus as Savior, I'm seeking to be part of his ongoing saving work, sharing his saving love for our world.

Like Vincent Donovan, I used to believe that Jesus'

primary focus was on saving *me* as an individual and on saving other "me's" as individuals. For that reason I often spoke of Jesus as my "personal Savior," and I urged others to believe in Jesus in the same way. I still believe that Jesus is vitally interested in saving me and you by individually judging us, by forgiving us of our wrongs, and teaching us to live in a better way. But I fear that for too many Christians, "personal salvation" has become another personal consumer product (like personal computers, a personal journal, personal time, etc.), and Christianity has become its marketing program. If so, salvation is "all about me," and like Vincent Donovan, I think we need another song.

As well, when I thought of Jesus only as my personal Savior, I was primarily focused on Jesus saving me from hell after I died. That's what I needed a personal Savior for.

Growing numbers of people share Vincent Donovan's (and my own) discomfort with this self- and hell-centered approach to salvation for a number of reasons:

1. Can't seeking my personal salvation as the ultimate end become the ultimate consumerism or narcissism? In a self-centered and hell-centered salvation, doesn't Jesus— like every company and political party—appeal to me on the basis of self-interest so that I can have it all eternally and can do so cheaply, conveniently, easily, and quickly? Doesn't this sound a bit shabby?

2. Doesn't being preoccupied with our own individual salvation put us in danger of being like selfish people on the Titanic who were scrambling for the life rafts, more concerned about themselves than others? Doesn't it make us less concerned about the possibility of saving the whole ship? Doesn't it reinforce exactly the kind of "sanctified self-centeredness" that the real Jesus would

have condemned?

3. Doesn't the very importance of my personal salvation pose a kind of temptation—to want heaven more than I want good; to want escape from hell more than I want true reconciliation to God or my neighbors? An overweight man was concerned about his weight, so he had a stomach bypass surgery, after which he continued to eat unhealthy foods. In the end he died sooner from a heart attack than he would have died from obesity. Couldn't this approach to salvation tempt us to be like this man? By wanting thinness more than he wanted health, he ended up with neither—this is the danger of wanting personal salvation above all.

4. And doesn't the preoccupation with hell tempt us to devalue other things that matter? In other words, isn't hell such a grave "bottom line" that it devalues all other values? It so emphasizes the importance of life after death that it can unintentionally trivialize life before death.[45]

No wonder many people feel that "accepting Jesus as a personal Savior" could make them a worse person—more self-centered and less concerned about justice on earth because of a preoccupation with forgiveness in heaven. Again, although I believe in Jesus as my personal savior, I am not a Christian for that reason. I am a Christian because I believe that Jesus is the Savior *of the whole world.*

In my adolescent years, I embraced the personal Savior/personal salvation approach, but that was only because

---

[45] I have broached the subject of hell in *A New Kind of Christian* and *The Story We Find Ourselves In* (Jossey-Bass, 2001 & 2003). I hope to address the subject more thoroughly in the third book of that trilogy, as yet untitled, with a release planned for 2005. I am not denying the place and importance of hell in Christian theology. I am suggesting that the tail has been wagging the dog for too long. In fact, the dog is in danger of becoming a walking, barking, jumping tail. Radical rethinking is needed.

I never heard this better understanding (or perhaps because in adolescence, enlightened self-interest is the highest motivation available). Through the years, as I read the Bible and pondered the meaning and message of Jesus, and as I learned the ways of Jesus through spiritual practice, I became less and less comfortable being restricted to the "personal Savior" gospel. More and more I shifted my reasoning for being a Christian to a belief that Jesus is the Savior of the world in the ways we have considered in this chapter.[46]

This does not mean that all of us benefit in every way we possibly can from the saving love of Jesus. That gap—between the benefits we could enjoy and those we are presently enjoying—is in part what fills my life with passion and urgency and is what inspires me to write and preach and live as I do.

I mentioned earlier my agnostic Jewish friend who asked me, "What's the deal with Jesus?" When I offered him an explanation not unlike what I've shared in these chapters, he said, "I could believe in a Jesus like that. If I believed in God, I think I could believe in that Jesus." I hope you can and will. I do, and it has made all the difference.

In the ways we've considered in these chapters, Jesus needs to be saved from Christians who have slimmed him down or fattened him up or otherwise converted him into our own image. Can we trust Jesus to save himself from the mess we've made of his name, and in so doing, save Christianity? If not, there is no orthodoxy to be generous about.

---

[46] The "personal Savior" gospel arose in part to solve an important problem: when Christianity was seen as the civil religion of the West, people considered themselves Christians simply because they were German or Danish or Italian or American. They saw themselves as generic Christians without personal commitment. The "personal Savior" gospel arose, in part at least, to encourage personal commitment: one made a personal commitment by believing in Jesus as their personal Savior. Sadly, like most solutions (including those offered in this book), the "personal Savior" solution then went on to create new problems. By the way, I wholeheartedly affirm the necessity of personal commitment in Chapter 13.

PART TWO: THE KIND OF CHRISTIAN I AM

CHAPTER 5

WHY I AM MISSIONAL

The term *missional* arose in the 1990s, thanks to the Gospel and Our Culture Network (www.gocn.org). It was popularized by the Network's important book called *The Missional Church* (Darrell L. Guder, et al., Eerdmans, 1998).

The term, as I understand it, attempts to find a generous third way beyond the conservative and liberal versions of Christianity so dominant in the Western world. The conservative version is preoccupied with the "personal Savior" gospel we discussed in the previous chapter, and the liberal version has lost something vitally important in their engagement with modernity (see Chapter 8).

The term also reflects the important impact of missiology (the study of missions) on Christian theology in recent decades. Thinkers such as David Bosch of South Africa and Lesslie Newbigin of India and England and Vincent Donovan of Tanzania and America began to convince people that, rather than seeing missiology as a study within theology, theology is actually a discipline within Christian mission. Theology is the church on a mission reflecting on its message, its identity, its meaning.

In addition, the term probably reflects a kind of post-colonial embarrassment about the term *missionary*, which has too often been associated with a colonial version of Christianity that inadvertently (one hopes) exported (and imposed) Euro-American culture right along with the gospel of Jesus.[47]

A story from my publishing life illustrates what is unique about missional Christian faith. My first book was entitled *Reinventing Your Church*. (I wasn't thrilled with the title, but that's another story.) Several years after its initial release, I suggested to my publisher that we re-release the book under a new title, and that I be allowed to add one chapter and revise some others. My publisher kindly agreed, and we reverted to the title I had originally hoped for, *The Church on the Other Side*.

I especially wanted to revise the chapter on mission. I'm a bit embarrassed to say this now, but in the early edition I defined the church's mission as "more Christians and better Christians." I thought I had been very forward-thinking to join the two with "and," rather than to prefer one over the other. But something didn't sit right with me about that mission statement. I rewrote it as follows: "To be and make disciples of Jesus Christ," a phrase I believe I picked up from my friends at International Teams. Since *Christian* can mean just about anything, and because *disciple* can't mean just about anything, I felt this was an improvement, and the *being* and *making* covered *better* and *more*. But this was still horribly individualistic. So I tweaked it further: "To be and make disciples of Jesus Christ *in authentic community*." A step in the right direction, but there was something still missing.

---

[47] It should be added that what we so soundly condemn as colonialism is often the flip side of what we enthusiastically praise as acts of justice and compassion. For example, when Mother Teresa found a culture that avoided caring for the dying on the streets of Calcutta, she "interfered" with that culture, motivated by her own more compassionate values. Similar "impositions" of alien values stopped widows from being immolated with their husbands' corpses in India, girls' feet from being bound and deformed in China, and female genital mutilation in parts of Africa and the Middle East (although this practice is still highly common and tolerated). These issues are more complex than they are made to appear in a lot of casual conversation.

Then I added six words: "To be and make disciples of Jesus Christ in authentic community *for the good of the world.*" That last phrase brings the essence of missional into the equation.

It says that Christians are not the end users of the gospel. It says that the gospel of Jesus is not "all about me." Two diagrams may help show the difference between Christianity as we know it and missional Christianity.

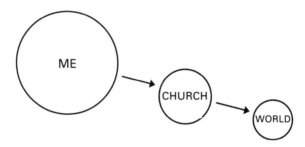

In this diagram, my largest concern is me, my soul, my personal destiny in heaven, my maturity, and my rewards. Occasionally, after "winning" people based on personal self-interest, churches can entice people to care a little about the church—but is it any surprise that people "won to Christ" by self-interest come to the church asking, "What's in it for me?"

Is it any surprise that with this understanding of salvation, churches tend to become gatherings of self-interested people who gather for mutual self-interest—constantly treating the church as a purveyor of religious goods and services, constantly shopping and "trading up" for churches that can "meet my needs" better? Is it any surprise that it's stinking hard to convince churches that they have a mission to the world when most Christians equate "personal salvation" of individual "souls" with the ultimate aim of Jesus? Is it any wonder that people feel like victims of a bait and switch when they're lured with personal salvation and then hooked with church commitment and world mission?

The following diagram shows a radically different alternative:

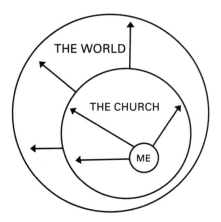

In this diagram, Jesus comes with saving love for the world. He creates the church as a missional community to join him in his mission of saving the world. He invites me to be part of this community to experience his saving love and participate in it.

This missional approach changes everything. In fact, I don't think I realize how much it changes yet because I'm still getting used to it.

Among other things, it eliminates old dichotomies like "evangelism" and "social action." Both are integrated in expressing saving love for the world. Those who want to become Christians (whether through our proclamation or demonstration), we welcome. Those who don't, we love and serve, joining God in seeking their good, their blessing, their shalom.

This approach gets rid of distinctions like *ministry* (what we do in the church) and *mission* (what we do outside it), since ministry is for mission from the start. For example, I seek to develop virtues not just for my own benefit, but so I can inflict less damage and more blessing on the world. I seek to better understand Scripture not just for my own sake, but so I'll be better equipped to serve God and my neighbors.

It also gets rid of terms like *missionary* and *mission field,* since now every Christian is a missionary and every place is a mission field.

Perhaps most profound and yet most troublesome, it gets us beyond the us-them thinking and in-grouping and out-grouping that lead to prejudice, exclusion, and ultimately to religious wars. It opens up a third alternative beyond exclusive and universalist religion. Exclusive religion says, "We're in, and you're out." Good news for us, bad news for you. Understandably, universalist religion reacts and says, "Everybody's in!" That's good news for everyone at first blush until you ask, "Why is there so much injustice then? Why are so many sad, cruel, harassed, and helpless? If everybody's in—is this as good as it gets?" Saying that "everybody's in" can too easily lead to complacency about injustice here and now and can create a kind of nice, relaxed, magnanimous apathy.[48] This magnanimous apathy may be better than the narrow antipathy often associated with exclusive religion, but I think we need a better alternative.

Missional Christian faith asserts that Jesus did *not* come to make some people saved and others condemned. Jesus did *not* come to help some people be right while leaving everyone else to be wrong. Jesus did *not* come to create another exclusive religion— Judaism having been exclusive based on genetics and Christianity

---

[48] There are new "everybody's in" proponents who share my distaste with the effects of a hell-oriented gospel and who are also seeking to avoid the magnanimous apathy I speak of here, including Philip Gulley and James Mulholland, *If Grace Is True: Why God Will Save Every Person* (Harper, 2003), to be followed by a book in progress, *If Love Is True.* Although my conclusions may differ from theirs in some ways, we share a strong conviction that the exclusive, hell-oriented gospel is not the way forward.

being exclusive based on belief (which can be a tougher requirement than genetics!).

Missional faith asserts that Jesus came to preach the good news of the kingdom of God to everyone, especially the poor. He came to seek and save the lost. He came on behalf of the sick. He came to save the world. His gospel, and therefore the Christian message, is Good News for the whole world.

The idea that the Christian message is universally good news for Christians and non-Christians alike is, to some, unheard of, strange, and perhaps heretical. To me, it has become natural and obvious. Let me explain.

Jesus was a Jew and so saw himself as one of Abraham's descendants. Abraham's original contact with God involved a kind of identity statement or mission statement: *I will bless you,* God said, *and I will make you a blessing to others. I will make your name and nation great,* God said, *and through you, all nations will be blessed.*

Lesslie Newbigin, one of the theologians who has helped me most (and whose first name often misleads people regarding his gender), used to say that the greatest heresy (false, destructive, divisive belief) in monotheism results from taking the first half of God's call to Abraham (I will bless you, I will make your name and nation great) and neglecting or rejecting the second half (I will make you a blessing, all nations will be blessed through you). Do you see the tragic difference? Any form of Christianity that takes the first part of God's call to Abraham more seriously than the second is not missional, as I'm using the term here.[49] Neither is it generous or truly orthodox!

---

[49] In my book *Finding Faith*, I call this truncated understanding "bad monotheism."

One of my mentors once said to me, "Remember, in a pluralistic world, a religion is valued based on the benefits it brings to its nonadherents." This surprised me, and I thought about it for days. Many people think the opposite of what my mentor said: that religions offer benefits to adherents and catastrophic threats for nonadherents. This offer/threat combination motivates people, they assume, to become adherents out of fear of catastrophe and desire for benefits. I think that the missional way is better: the gospel brings blessing to all, adherents and nonadherents alike.[50] For example, if Jesus sends people into the world to love and serve their neighbors, their neighbors benefit, and so do the people sent by Jesus, since it is even better to give than to receive. Or imagine a medical analogy: if followers of Jesus are like hospital employees, the sick who come to them benefit by their care, and the hospital employees benefit by being part of the hospital staff, which is rewarding in many ways.

How did he do it? The Gospels tell us. He selected 12 and trained them in a new way of life. He sent them to teach everyone this way of life. Some would believe and become practitioners and teachers of this new way of life, too. Even if only a few would practice this new way, many would benefit. Oppressed people would be free. Poor people would be liberated from poverty. Minorities would be treated with respect. Sinners would be loved, not resented. Industrialists would realize that God cares for sparrows and wildflowers—so their industries should respect, not rape, the environment. The homeless would be invited in for a hot meal. The kingdom of God would come—not everywhere at once, not suddenly, but gradually, like a seed growing in a field, like yeast spreading in a lump of bread dough, like light spreading across the sky at dawn.

---

[50] I'm *not* saying it brings *equal* benefits to both. Nor am I saying that all Christians avail themselves equally of the benefits.

It wouldn't be easy. Suffering, misunderstanding, even martyrdom were guaranteed. But the resurrection of Jesus gave this missional band confidence that death was only a comma, not a period, and that God's good and kind desires would prevail. They could be steadfast and immovable, knowing that their labors were "not in vain" (I Corinthians 15:58).

But what about heaven and hell? you ask. *Is everybody in?*

My reply: Why do you consider me qualified to make this pronouncement? Isn't this God's business? Isn't it clear that I do not believe this is the right question for a missional Christian to ask? Can't we talk for a while about God's will being done on earth as in heaven instead of jumping to how to escape earth and get to heaven as quickly as possible? Can't we talk for a while about overthrowing and undermining every hellish stronghold in our lives and in our world?

It is important to let this missional understanding sink in before you seek an answer to that preoccupying question. We must rejoice that God cares for the whole world and set our hearts to join God in caring. Does trying to fit what I'm saying into one of your categories distract you from considering a whole different way of categorizing?[51]

Imagine you are driving down a country road, on a journey west from New York to Los Angeles. You find yourself at a flashing red light somewhere in South Florida. You can turn left, turn right, or go straight. The road to the left heads east toward Boca Raton. The road to the right leads west toward Naples. The

---

[51] Even though I don't like the way this whole question is framed, or the way it can distract us from other important matters, and even though I bluster in these paragraphs against it, yes, it's still an important question, and if you want to explore varying answers to "the hell question," here are several good resources: William Crocket, ed., *Four Views on Hell* (Zondervan, 1997); Randolph Klassen, *What Does the Bible Really Say About Hell* (Herald, 2001); Philip Gulley and James Mulholland, *If Grace Is True: Why God Will Save Every Person* (Harper, 2003).

third road leads south toward Key West, through the Everglades. None of the roads leads in the general direction of Los Angeles. What do you do? Which road do you take? *What are you doing in Florida anyway?* The fact that you have to choose between these three destinations means that you are already far off track! But you have to go somewhere, so what do you do?

Here's what you do: you admit that you've been lost for a long, long time—like for the last 750-plus miles. You whack yourself in the forehead for not realizing this sooner, and then you make a U-turn and head back north until you find I-10, which will send you west toward the City of Angels.

This is how I feel when I'm offered a choice between the roads of exclusivism (only confessing Christians go to heaven), universalism (everyone goes to heaven), and inclusivism (Christians go to heaven, plus at least some others). Each road takes you somewhere, to a place with some advantages and disadvantages, but none of them is the road of my missional calling: blessed in this life to be a blessing to everyone on earth.

One signpost tells me that some people aren't ever going to be blessed, so I should just rejoice that I am one of the blessed— meaning I can retire in Naples, Florida, and enjoy the blessings of golf on the Gulf. One signpost tells me that everybody is already blessed, so I can watch the sun rise each morning from the beach in Boca Raton. The other signpost tells me that maybe some are blessed and maybe they aren't, which means I proceed straight ahead into the swamp and feel confused, not knowing what to do.

But my mission isn't to figure out who is already blessed, or not blessed, or unblessable. My calling is to be blessed so I can bless everyone. I'm going to Los Angeles!

Recently I received an e-mail saying, "I heard a rumor

that you're a universalist. Is that true?" Since I don't offer my exclusivist friends their expected answer to "the hell question," I can see why this rumor would spread. Rumors like this make me want to be an exclusivist who believes that only universalists go to heaven—after all, they have the highest opinion possible about the efficacy and scope of the saving work of Jesus! Or else I could be an inclusivist who believes that all but exclusivists are going to heaven. But no, that's ridiculous. Anyway, I'm going to Los Angeles. The old universalism pronounces that the Good News was efficacious for all individual souls *after* death, in heaven, beyond history. Inclusivism says the gospel is efficacious for many, and exclusivists say for a comparative few. But I'm more interested in a gospel that is universally efficacious for the whole earth *before* death in history.

Vincent Donovan expresses this beautifully in *Christianity Rediscovered*, where he writes: "This is universalism in the true sense...the outward thrust of Christianity from me to my neighbor to stranger to enemy to all the tribes and nations of the earth." Just imagine if every Christian child could learn that this is what it means to be a missional Christian: to join Jesus in expressing God's love for the whole world, to follow Jesus in his mission of saving love for the world. More important to me than the hell question, then, is the *mission* question.

I've been a Christian for many years, but I've been a missional Christian for only a few—although perhaps I actually was one long before I realized it. Perhaps the same is true of you.

CHAPTER 6

WHY I AM EVANGELICAL

A couple of years ago, Dr. Robert Webber wrote a book called *The Younger Evangelicals*, in which I was identified as a leader among younger evangelicals.[52] I thought this was either (a) an honest mistake, (b) an overstatement, (c) a premature assessment, (d) evidence of Robert Webber's generosity, or (e) evidence for how hard up younger evangelicals must be for leadership to have to settle for a middle-aged, bald introvert with a small Buddha belly and without proper credentials. But in spite of this questionable element, the book did a wonderful job of explaining why many younger evangelicals don't want to be identified with an older generation of Evangelical leaders whose names I won't mention.

Shortly after the book came out, a friend called from Florida and asked if I was offended by my name's inclusion in the book. I wondered: *I might be embarrassed, or maybe honored, but why would I be offended?* He explained without my asking: "I would think that you

---

[52] Robert Webber, *The Younger Evangelicals* (Baker, 2002). Many of us hope that "the emerging church" movement will be less focused on singular celebrity personalities or figureheads than recent movements have been. This seems to be the case, as new generations of creative, gifted, young, and-as-yet unrecognized leaders (many of them women and many of them non-white) are emerging across the globe. They are far better leaders than I, and my greatest honor will be encouraging and preparing the way for them. See www.emergentvillage.com for examples.

wouldn't want to be associated with that label, you know, *Evangelical*, with all its negative connotations."

My friend is right: the word *Evangelical* can have some pretty negative connotations. But it's a word I would rather not abandon, if I can help it. In fact, I am happy and honored to consider myself an evangelical.

First, though, I should explain why I was careful not to capitalize the term in the previous sentence. "Big E" Evangelical refers to a segment of the church that I love and from which I hail, but which I don't think I understand so much anymore, and in which I may not actually be wanted anymore. Since my Evangelical/ evangelical parents tried to teach me good manners, which include both (a) not barging into homes or parties where you're not wanted and (b) not outstaying your welcome where you were previously wanted, I am nervous about calling myself an Evangelical of the Big-E type. That's why in this chapter and book, I will limit myself to the more modest "small e" evangelical.

"Big E" Evangelical, as some use the term (especially in the U.S.), increasingly refers to "the Religious Right." That group would probably not want me in their company, and I can't blame them, as I'd be nothing but trouble, asking pesky questions that they don't have time for. In contrast, evangelicals include both political conservatives and liberals, and those who, like me, don't fit in either category.

As used by others, *Evangelical* sometimes means "Fundamentalists of a slightly less narrow-minded and arrogant attitude," which is, I suppose, a small step in the right direction. The word *fundamentalist* (both "Big F" and "small f" versions) invites another whole set of definitions, from "violent" to "bigoted" to "pure" to "minimalist," which will be explored in a later chapter. Suffice it to say that I would heartily like to be included among any group making even small steps in the right direction, especially fundamentalists, as long as that label means "adhering to fundamentals," and as long as *fundamentals* itself means "loving God and loving neighbors" above all.

(If *fundamentalist* means other things—such as requiring belief in a foundationalist epistemology, assenting to something like a dictation theory of biblical inspiration, upholding a sectarian and elitist approach to non-Fundamentalist Christians, and identifying judgmentalism and anger as fruits of the Holy Spirit, then there's little chance I'd be welcome in their company, which is probably for the best. *And if the previous sentence full of technical religious jargon went over your head, thank God and don't worry about it.* See Chapter 12.)[53]

More positively, *Evangelical* generally refers to people who (a) highly respect the Bible (so that for them, *biblical* is a favorite adjective, being a broad synonym for *good* or *right*), (b) emphasize personal conversion (often associated with terms like being *saved* or *born again*), (c) believe that God can be known and experienced with something like intimacy (expressed in terms like *having a personal relationship with God*), and (d) want to share their faith with others (by being *evangelistic*).[54] These values will be affirmed in various ways throughout the book and are held with equal sincerity by evangelicals.

When I say I cherish an evangelical identity, I mean something beyond a belief system or doctrinal array or even a practice. I mean an attitude—an attitude toward God and our

---

[53] For those prone to stereotype, it's important to remember that people have no choice about which religious tradition they are born into. As a result, kind, wonderful, Christ-like people can be found in surprising places. I have met, for example, some of the most magnanimous, tolerant, and spiritually vibrant Christians in fundamentalist circles—confounding every stereotype. That's where they were born, and they've felt called to stay and improve their heritage rather than leave it in protest—a noble calling, you'll have to agree. And I've found narrow, exclusive, judgmental Christians in "liberal" circles. Labels must be used with a wince, and I wince at having to use them here.

[54] See my book *More Ready Than You Realize: Evangelism as Dance in the Postmodern Matrix* (Zondervan, 2002) for more on evangelism.

neighbor and our mission that is *passionate*. When evangelicals (at their best) sing, they *sing*. When evangelicals pray, they *pray*. When evangelicals preach, they *preach*. When evangelicals decide something is worth doing, they *do* it. They don't tend to establish committees to study the feasibility of doing it. They don't ask permission from the bureaucracy to do it. They don't get a degree that qualifies them to do it. They *just do it*—and with passion.

True, this evangelical passion gets them in trouble from time to time. For example, *passionate* can easily degenerate into sentimental or cheesy or hotheaded or hardheaded or softheaded, and too often it has done so. But if I have a choice between the kind of trouble that comes from too much passion or the kind that comes from too little, my choice will be easy.

Evangelical passion leads to evangelical courage, perhaps even daring. My grandfather, Robert McLaren, had that kind of passion and courage. He was a banker, a Scot who emigrated to Canada. He felt a call from God to go to Africa at the age of 21 in 1914. That meant he went to missionary training school— not to learn highfalutin' missiological theory (a subject I have great interest in, by the way), but to learn to pull teeth, perform emergency surgery, deal with malaria, deliver babies, and survive in the jungle. He went to Portugal to learn Portuguese, and then he went to Angola where he spent 40 years of his life preaching and planting churches. His courage inspires me today.

My other grandfather, Stephen Smith, stayed closer to home—Rochester, New York. He was a simple guy with an eighth-grade education who worked on an auto assembly line and in a piano factory (that became a plywood airplane factory during World War II). He became a committed follower of Jesus in young adulthood and was soon part of a new local church in which he served for decades as an elder or lay minister. Unqualified? Undereducated? Those thoughts never crossed his mind. He loved the Lord and wanted to serve the Lord however he was able. Even in his old age, he kept a handwritten list of people—sick people, relatives, missionaries around the world—for whom he prayed after breakfast every morning, another demonstration of his evangelical passion. His passion still touches my life; my name was on his after-breakfast prayer list.

From crossing oceans as missionaries to crossing town to volunteer in a skid-row mission to crossing the street to serve humbly and faithfully in a local church, evangelicals have a passion that drives them to action; their emotion puts them in motion. And this emotion goes right to the heart of what it means to follow Jesus: loving God and loving others. Yes, I know that when evangelicals start acting like Evangelicals, they can become less loving and more judgmental, less involved and more isolated, less compassionate and more critical, less passionate and more anxious, less generous and more controlling. But that shift is a betrayal of evangelical faith, not a consequence of it. When evangelicals are being true to their identity, they do whatever it takes to express their love for God and God's love for their neighbors—however unconventional and innovative their methods might be.

In this way, evangelicals are surprisingly liberal. True, Evangelicals are (these days at least) temperamentally conservative in their theology and often in their politics. But evangelicals are traditionally liberal in their methodology, caring little for the constraints of "we've always done it that way before"—although those discouraging words are sometimes heard on the evangelical range.

Historically, from George Whitefield and the Wesley brothers leaving their proper pulpits to preach with passion out in the fields, to Charles Fuller pioneering the new technology of radio, to Bill Bright and James Kennedy adapting door-to-door sales techniques for use in evangelism, to Jim and Tammy Faye

Bakker and Pat Robertson filling the airwaves with born-again programming, to Larry Norman and Love Song adventuring into Christian rock, to Rick Warren and Bill Hybels reorienting the local church toward evangelistic outreach, to uncounted Web sites proclaiming the Word on the Internet—evangelicals are bold and liberal methodologically. Their passion and purpose drive them!

That's why you'll find evangelicals passionately at work around the world—including every dangerous and difficult place they can get themselves into. They have a mandate from Jesus to get out and make a difference. They love Jesus and they're not going to let anything stop them. I love that, and that's why I want to substitute "they" with "we" in the previous sentences.

Sure, I think Evangelicals have painted themselves into a lot of corners—theologically, politically, socially. But evangelical passion for spiritual experience, for spiritual understanding, for mission is precious. If it could be bottled, one quart of it would be worth five libraries full of religious books (including mine) and all the religious broadcasting networks in California and Texas. Even though it can't be bottled, it can be acquired because, ultimately, "it" is the Spirit of Jesus, and Jesus gives himself freely to all who ask. Both Evanglicals and evangelicals know that.

I realize that this understanding of *evangelical* differs from what many people think of when they hear the word. That's why my friend Dave Tomlinson uses the term *post-evangelical* instead.[55] *Post* is an apt prefix, really. It doesn't mean "anti" or "non." It means coming from, emerging from, growing from, and emphasizes both continuity and discontinuity. Interestingly, non-Evangelicals are also using the prefix in a similar way (post-liberals, for example). Is it possible that post-evangelicals, post-liberals, and others who

---

[55] Dave's book *The Post-Evangelical* is a very important contribution to the conversation about Christian faith and the emerging postmodern culture (emergentYS, 2003).

share a sense of continuity and discontinuity with the Christianity of recent memory could come together in mutually beneficial ways for the journey ahead? Could a convergence of postmodern Christians from various traditions bring new life and hope, both to Christianity at large and to the world? I hope so. If it happens, let the evangelicals bring the passion!

The term *evangelical* etymologically means "pertaining to the Good News." In that light, this whole book, which represents an attempt to rediscover what the Good News is and means in these strange times, can be seen as an evangelical project.

Perhaps Robert Webber's "younger evangelicals" is a gentle way of saying "post-evangelical." Either way, I was honored by my association with both terms—*evangelical* and *younger*—not at all offended. At the end of the day, I hope *evangelical* can become an inclusive and positive term, rather than a sectarian and restrictive one—an essential element of a generous orthodoxy.

CHAPTER 7

WHY I AM POST/PROTESTANT

The word *Protestant* has two potential meanings, as different from one another as dark beer and fresh-squeezed orange juice. Like dark beer and fresh-squeezed orange juice, each meaning has value, and some people have a taste for each, though probably not both at the same meal.

Protestant as *Protest*

The dominant meaning of *protestant* relates to the verb it contains: *protest*. Protestants began in the fifteenth and sixteenth centuries— first as a succession of disorganized and often erratic uprisings within the Roman Catholic Church, and then as a concerted and far-reaching revolution (called the Reformation) outside of Catholicism. The Protestants protested many problems in the Roman Catholic Church, especially confusion about how people are saved.

Regarding the latter concern, as we discussed in previous chapters, the *meaning* of salvation wasn't questioned; the *means* of salvation was the issue. By what means do people get to heaven? Catholics often (not always) taught that Jesus was the Savior, but that Christians needed to merit the salvation Jesus offered. How? By means of good works, good deeds, sacrifice, penance, and religious observance. This soon degenerated into a system whereby the church secured people's generosity and loyalty by threatening to withhold the means of salvation from them unless their cooperation was full and complete. Salvation was dispensed in return for gifts or services rendered.

In its crassest form, through purchasing "indulgences" from the church, people could buy their way into heaven through giving money—a masterful fundraising strategy if ever there was one. If you gave a large sum of money to the church, the teaching said, this good deed would merit grace from God, and God would allow you or someone you love (like expensive airline tickets, indulgences were transferable) to enter heaven with few or no purgative sufferings after death.

Not all Catholics believed this, of course, but enough did that there was real substance to the protests of people like Martin Luther, Ulrich Zwingli, Martin Bucer, John Calvin, and others. Eventually, nation-states of Northern Europe in the sixteenth and seventeenth centuries were forced to choose. Would they maintain loyalty to the Roman Catholic Church, or would they break away in protest over indulgences and about 94 other issues? Protestantism was born.

Through the Reformation, Christianity has flowered in a hundred new ways. New freedoms have been discovered beyond the limits of old hierarchies. New options have been experimented with that never would have been considered within old regimes. I am glad to be part of this heritage. But I'm not completely proud of it. Because although the Protestant Reformation did much good (imagine if it never happened!), it unleashed a lot of problems, too, including the following:

After protesting Catholic excesses, Protestants started protesting each other. Whenever a Protestant group manifested a problem—complacency, confusion, weak leadership, whatever—a subgroup would arise from within and protest those failures. Then they would break away, often damning the group which they left, proclaiming themselves the truly reformed, truly protestant, truly pure, truly right, truly true, and so on. The race was on: who could out-protest everyone else? The most cantankerous personality types often rose to prominence in a milieu like this, which, spiritually speaking, is disastrous. The existence of thousands of denominations today is in part the fruit of this Protestant dividing frenzy. (It is also the fruit of immigration patterns.)

This protest frenzy created a kind of market economy for religion, where religion was commodified. This competitive Protestant religious market eventually spawned a kind of infomercial mentality, where each group advertised its unique features, seeking loyal customers for their religious products and services. Some proclaimed their version of Christianity the purest. Others, the simplest. Others, the deepest. Others, the most austere. Others, the most relaxed. Others, the most uniform. Others, the most diverse.

The unfortunate side effects of this Protestant free-market religious competition included distortion (unique features being exaggerated out of all proportion) and arrogance (each group legitimized its own existence by downgrading others and proclaiming its superiority, like different brands of oven cleaner). Our arrogance, if you haven't noticed, is not an enhancement to the spiritual life.

In addition, Protestant groups tended to take for granted the features they had in common, which led to an epidemic of majoring on minor issues—sometimes to the point of forgetting what the major issues (such as "the point" or "the mission") ever were.

Protestants have paid more attention to the Bible than any other group, but sadly, much of their Bible study was undertaken to fuel their efforts to prove themselves right and others wrong (and therefore worthy of protest). If the Bible does not yield its best resources to people who approach it seeking ammunition with which to lay their brethren low, then Protestant Christianity has at times done a grave disservice both to the Bible and to Protestants themselves. How many Protestants can't pick up the Bible without hearing arguments play in their heads on every page, echoes of the polemical preachers they have heard since childhood? How much Bible study is, therefore, an adventure in missing the point?

Of course, not everyone joins the latest protest and departure. Those who endure the departures of their more-Protestant-than-thou brothers and sisters must eventually stop protesting and start defending themselves against the protesters. When more and more people are left in the defending mode, even though they have the name of Protestant, they're really more defenders than protesters. And if you're in the defending mode long enough, you're bound to become defensive, another trait that isn't all that helpful for spiritual vitality.

Meanwhile, the Roman Catholics haven't cooperated very well, because although at times they acted defensively in response to Protestant protest, in recent years they've pretty much agreed that the original Protestants were right about a lot of things. The average Roman Catholic today sees indulgences the same way Protestants will someday see their schmaltzy religious broadcasting or pop-atonement theology (what Dallas Willard calls "the gospel of sin management"): with embarrassment.

The average Roman Catholic today (at least, among those I meet) is increasingly clear about God's grace being a free gift, not something that can be earned or merited. It's hard to keep protesting against people who admit they aren't perfect. In fact, *your outrage as protester at their past failures compares unfavorably with their present humility in admitting past failures.* The Roman Catholic Church's recent scandals have only intensified her acknowledgement that she has some problems and needs reform. Increasing numbers of Roman Catholics show a welcome and healthy alternative to either angry protest or defensiveness: humility and repentance.

We Protestants have come darn near to selling indulgences ourselves (have you watched religious TV lately?). And the message of grace (that salvation is a gift, not earned, not merited, but given freely), which we felt the Roman Catholics had lost, has been buried under a thousand other agenda items for us. Or it simply became something else to argue about.

So what happens when Protestants get tired of protesting? What happens when they want to protest their own protesting? If they simply form another elite sect that protests Protestant protesting, they're still stuck in the cycle, doomed to become the next Protestant sideshow, super-Protestants, nothing more. Is there an alternative? I think there is, and it is found in the other meaning of Protestant.

Protestant as Pro-Testifying

What if we were to redefine protestant as pro-testifying, *pro* meaning "for" and *testify* meaning "telling our story"? What if Protestants switch their focus from protesting what they're against to telling the story about what they're for?

Do we even know what we're for? So many of us are sure about what we're against, but in the process of being against so much, we've either forgotten what we're for or become for things not worth being for. What are we here for? Simply by asking that question, we begin to move beyond the Protestant ethos that we're protesting in this chapter.

Perhaps this kind of pro-testifier would be better called post-Protestant, since the first definition is so dominant. Either way—this to me is truly wonderful—both Catholics and Protestants and Eastern Orthodox, too, can come together as pro-testifiers or post-Protestants now, because together we are reaching a point where we acknowledge not just "their" failures, but "ours." In so doing, we realize that (a) we aren't superior to one another, and (b) we have a lot to learn from the very people we've been protesting and defending against. Most importantly, we can come together searching for what we are for, something nearly everyone forgets.

One of the most fascinating and vigorous sectors of protesting Protestantism has been "restorationism"—a belief held by a succession of groups through church history that, by finally getting the last or lost detail right, they now represent a full-fledged restoration of "New Testament Christianity."

Having been raised in one such group, and having spent a lot of time with many wonderful people in other restorationist groups as well, I can tell you this: if you are part of a restorationist group, the group dynamics of your group will be nearly identical to those of every other restorationist group. Change the details— mode or meaning of baptism, church structure, administrivia of worship or piety (day of week, style of service, clothing or dietary scruples, etc.), doctrinal fine print (a unique interpretation of at least one verse from Revelation, for example, that highlights your group as eschatologically significant)—and you could be in any super-Protestant restorationist setting.

Fortunately, beneath these squabbles over distinctives, one nearly always finds an idealism among restorationists, a belief that Christianity should and can be better than its common manifestations. This is a good thing and needed—an important contribution (along with the less helpful static) restorationists bring to the table.

In restorationist circles (Churches of Christ, Seventh Day Adventists, Plymouth Brethren, et al.), one often finds a beautiful, sincere, childlike desire to follow Jesus whatever the cost and however lonely the road. This positive and often courageous desire can be a bridge to the pro-testifying definition of Protestant (if the overemphasis on the last and lost details or distinctives can be dropped). My friend Samir Vesna, a brilliant former-Communist Croatian Seventh Day Adventist pastor (how's that for a unique accumulation of adjectives?), offers a beautiful example of how restorationists, and Protestants in general, can move from being Protesting Protestants to pro-testifying a generous orthodoxy.

Restorationists (and other Protestants gone defensive) often refer to themselves, Samir says, as a *remnant*. This remnant language is common in the Bible. For those who need consolation for small numbers, it's an attractive blanket to wrap up in: we're not small because we're ineffective, or lazy, or ingrown, or otherwise unattractive; we're small because we're a *faithful remnant*! Everyone else has compromised. They're taking the easy way. We're the few, the committed, the faithful, *the proud*. (Oops.) Anyway, Samir has seen a lot of this remnant thinking in restorationist territory; he sees how destructive it is.

He was preaching the stories of Moses in Exodus, where God seeks to "renegotiate the contract" with Abraham's descendants in light of their repeated unfaithfulness. God says that he will abandon the Israelites at large and will let Moses become the patriarch of a new people of God. In other words, Moses represents the remnant; he's the only faithful one left. What does Moses do?

In a stunning move, Moses says, "God, blot me out. Reject me. Don't reject the people." This loyalty wins God's heart, and on Moses' behalf, God relents from rejecting the Israelites. (This same pattern is seen in Paul in Romans 9 through 11, and of course, in Jesus' whole life and death.)

Samir asked his friends with a remnant mentality: *What is a truly faithful remnant like?* Its members do not turn inward in elite self-congratulation, smugly casting a critical eye of disdain on the rest. No, the faithful remnant "after God's heart" turns its heart others-wise, outward, toward the unfaithful, in loyalty and love. True faithfulness bonds the hearts of the faithful to their unfaithful neighbors.

Could this new understanding of the *faithful remnant* help restorationists, and Protestants in general, move from protest to pro-testifying?

What might "post-Protestant Christianity" be like? People like you and me can, with God's help, be the ones to help answer that question in the coming decades, not just by what we say but by how we live—and especially how we love our neighbors.

The faithfulness of a faithful remnant is not crabbed and constricted; it is loyal, magnanimous, and generous. That is something to pro-testify about.

CHAPTER 8

WHY I AM LIBERAL/CONSERVATIVE

Today I spoke at a large youth workers' convention (youthspecialties. com). My friend Mark Oestreicher introduced me in a very kind way. "How many of your would call yourselves liberal?" he asked, and a smattering of hands clapped and a few voices cheered. (Liberals are generally a refined and restrained lot.)

"How many of you would call yourselves conservative?" he then asked, and there were more and louder claps and hoots from across the audience.

Then he asked, "And how many of you wish there could be a third alternative, something beyond the confining boxes of liberal and conservative?" To my surprise the room erupted with applause and cheers. Then Mark very kindly said that I was a pilgrim in search of that third alternative. (Then I got up to speak, and my talk proved much less interesting than his introduction.)

In the conservative circles I grew up in, *liberal* was like "red" or "commie" in the 1950s or like "terrorist" in the 2000s. It was a label that ended your career, acceptance, and respect. It still does. It's no surprise then that among liberals, the term *conservative* possesses parallel excommunicating properties.

A short history lesson may help orient you to understand this theological polarization. The Protestant Reformation was, among other things, Christianity going "post-medieval," or "modern." It was one facet of a massive transition taking place in Western civilization roughly between 1500 and 1700, a transition that gradually ended the medieval world and gave birth to what is called the modern world.

Philosophically, a profound shift was occurring, a shift in how we humans understand how we understand. In other words, how do we know that we know truth? If you asked a medieval person, his answer would almost certainly have included the words *the authorities*. We know the truth because the authorities are given, by God, truth that they convey to us. Our job is to trust them because they are God's channels of truth. This form of truth we might call social-relational; we know truth by being in a right relationship to God-given authorities. How do we know the authorities are right? Because they tell us so, on God's authority. How do we know that they're right when they say they're right on God's authority? The medieval Catholic answer was, "Never ask that question."

But what happens when you truly believe the authorities are wrong? Perhaps they're wrong about matters of science (as Copernicus and Galileo thought) or perhaps (as Luther and Calvin thought) about matters of faith. You have only one choice if you are going to retain your intellectual integrity: you must distrust the authorities. But what do you do instead?

The modern answer: *think for yourself.* Do research. Enter into argument. Perform, in some circumstances, your own experiments. Reflect on your own experience. Find truth as an individual, without the authorities. Martin Luther's famous individualistic statement, uttered before the Catholic authorities with whom he disagreed, expresses this shift perfectly: "Here I stand."[56] That sentence might be understood as the first statement uttered in the modern world.

The earliest Protestants didn't lose a source of authority altogether, though. They transferred the fulcrum or center of authority from the church to the Bible (which the coincidental— or providential—invention of an improved printing press facilitated greatly). But the Bible requires human interpretation, which was a problem. Fortunately, the modern "I" thought itself qualified (through reason, study, education, scholarship, methodology, technique) to interpret. (And unlike the church authorities, the Bible didn't fight back, threaten with torture, or excommunicate.)

But perhaps you can see the next challenge coming: *what happens when the "I" sees problems with the Bible?* How do "I" know the Bible is always right? And if "I" am sophisticated enough to realize that I know nothing of the Bible without my own involvement via interpretation, I'll also ask how I know which school, method, or technique of biblical interpretation is right. What makes a "good" interpretation good? And if an appeal is made to a written standard (book, doctrinal statement, etc.) or to common sense or to "scholarly principles of interpretation," the same pesky "I" who liberated us from the authority of the church will ask, "Who sets the standard? Whose common sense? Which scholars and why? Don't all these appeals to authorities and principles outside of the Bible actually undermine the claim of ultimate biblical authority? Aren't they just the new pope?"

Protestant Christians responded in two ways to these

---

[56] Len Sweet suggests that the postmodern parallel may be "there we go," with *there* meaning into mission and into the future, with *we* emphasizing the communal dimension of the Christian way, and *go* evoking our call to mission and ministry in God's world. See *A Is for Abductive* (with Brian McLaren and Jerry Haselmeyer, Zondervan, 2003).

questions. Some essentially said, "Never, ever ask this kind of question. The Bible is the ultimate authority, and the modern 'I' is qualified to seek to understand it and interpret it (but not question it) using standard principles of interpretation, and that settles it. There are no contradictions in it, and it is absolutely true and without error in all it says. Give up these assertions, and you're on a slippery slope to losing your whole faith." This response was at the heart of *conservative* Protestant thinking.

For others, this response seemed like another version of medieval Catholicism, substituting a paper pope for a flesh-and-blood one, substituting Bible scholars and teachers for cardinals and bishops, simply changing the place where people were told, "Never ask that." These Protestants said that free inquiry must be encouraged, not discouraged. This was, in broad terms, the *liberal* Protestant response.

Both conservatives and liberals had serious problems as the years went on. Conservatives couldn't agree on what the infallible, inerrant Bible meant and constantly labeled the interpretations of their fellow Protestants grossly errant. Liberals, listening to their shrill, quarrelling voices (which were easy to find on religious broadcasts), often said, "See? The Bible can be used to prove anything." What good is it, liberals would ask conservatives, to have an inerrant Bible if you have no inerrant interpretations and if, as time goes on, the errant interpretations multiply and divide rather than move toward agreement? Not only that, but conservative biblical interpretations, it seemed, had been used to justify some ethically and scientifically dubious causes (slavery, male chauvinism, horrific treatment of aboriginal peoples, abuse of the environment, identifying the mentally ill as witches, explaining away fossils and other findings) and to oppose some credible investigations (paleontology, evolution, cosmology, psychology).

Meanwhile, liberals had another set of problems. Just as conservative biblical interpretations could "prove" almost anything, liberal free inquiry could question anything. Their questioning and research could arrive at conclusions that left the Christian faith severely—some would say fatally—wounded, depleted, and drained of content. When the Bible's trustworthiness was questioned, then the divinity, resurrection, and existence of Jesus were questioned; even the existence of God was suspect. What was left to believe in? Had liberal Christianity self-destructed? Had Christianity become a wrapper with no contents, an excuse to gather and hear exhortations to be nice folks, good citizens, and safe drivers? What happens when the methodology of free inquiry that unleashed your movement now turns on your movement and threatens to suck the life out of it?

Liberal—or "mainline"—Protestantism had become the civil religion of America in the first half of the twentieth century. It was liberal Protestants who were invited to the White House, quoted by the press, asked to give invocations at public events, and so on. Power proved tempting, however, and as a result, liberal Christianity seemed increasingly domesticated, tame, and sycophantic. Even in the 1960s, when many liberal Christians rediscovered their passion by fighting for Civil Rights and against the Vietnam War, too often their rhetoric seemed like a Christianized version of leftist politics, and their spiritual understanding seemed to be less virile than their political ideologies.[57] Many of them seemed to know a lot about marching in demonstrations and registering voters (good things, to be sure) but little or nothing about, say, prayer.

What did liberals and conservatives do in the face of these serious problems? Among other things, they did something very

---

[57] The words "too often" in the preceding sentence do not mean *always*! Happily, there were powerful exceptions to this generalization.

human: they compared their own best to their counterpart's worst. They focused on their counterpart's weaknesses and failures and didn't think much about their own: "At least we're not loosey-goosey like those anything-goes liberals" or "At least we're not rigid and unthinking like those blind, reactionary, bourgeois conservatives." Name-calling can become a pretty engaging activity for a pretty long time, as any playground or political campaign can demonstrate. A lot of energy was (and still is) spent on name-calling, self-congratulating, and so on.

They kept busy with other, more profitable things too, of course. Conservatives, confident in the message of the Bible, spread their understanding of it on radio and TV and through books and personal witness. They planted churches, formed parachurch ministries, published books, wrote music, and presented concerts and other evangelistic events. Around the world they won millions of converts, not seeming to care that they were marginalized in the public square back home. (Actually that marginalization back home may have helped fuel their exploits abroad.) Liberals, still confident in at least some of the ethical teachings of Jesus, addressed social and ethical problems with gusto and courage as they thought best.

During the first half of the twentieth century in the U.S., liberal Christianity served as the civil religion of America, and conservatives were marginalized. For a number of reasons (which we can't explore here), a power shift happened in the 1960s and 1970s. By the 1980s the liberals were sent to the backseat, and the conservatives were soon riding shotgun, basking in their new role as the civil religion of America. (My friend Diana Butler Bass suggests that liberals are still suffering from a power hangover, and conservatives from a power buzz.) Meanwhile, beginning in the 1960s, the liberal Protestant denominations began to decline, and many conservative groups began to grow (much of their growth resulting from defections from the liberals). This change of fortunes created a great deal of backslapping and pride among conservatives, with corresponding hand-wringing, defensiveness, denial, or malaise among the liberals.

Why were conservatives growing in numbers and influence?[58] Conservatives were sure it was because they were true to the Bible and were uncompromising in their faith. Their counterparts were declining, conservatives believed, because liberals had compromised with the high culture of modern rationalism. They had put the human authority of individual reason above God's authority in the Bible, losing their message and mission. Liberals, of course, had a mirror-image explanation: conservatives grew because their faith was self-centered and self-serving, compromised with the "low culture" of middle-class racism, greed, and apathy, pandering to the fears and prejudices of the masses, cowardly and willfully ignorant in the face of the facts of science. If liberals had sold out to leftist politics at the expense of their spiritual vigor, conservatives were doing the same with the ideology of the right.

Globally, liberals had to admit that Christianity had swung decidedly conservative in the twentieth century.[59] Liberals, it has been said, favored the poor, but the poor favored the conservatives (especially the conservative Pentecostals). With increasing numbers both in the West and beyond, conservative Christianity entered the twenty-first century with momentum and confidence.

I think conservatives and liberals were both right and wrong and were each in their own way trying to do what they felt was right. After all, modernity was no Sunday school picnic for the

---

[58] Dean M. Kelley's famous book, originally published in 1977, *Why Conservative Churches Are Growing* (Mercer Univ. Press, 1995), explores this question in detail. His thoughtful answers (relating to demands of membership and social strength) differed from the popular answers given in this paragraph.

[59] See Philip Jenkins, *The Next Christendom* (Oxford Univ. Press, 2002).

Christian faith in any of its forms. In their struggle with modernity, Christians found two ways of surviving: liberal and conservative. Surviving is sometimes heroic, sometimes desperate; there were signs of both heroism and desperation among both liberals and conservatives.

The best of liberal and conservative Christians were, then, truly heroic, but in different ways. Liberals were heroic for tackling tough issues often several decades before the conservatives. For example, in terms of science and learning, they tackled issues like evolution and the age of the earth long before their conservative counterparts. Ethically, they were concerned about racial reconciliation in the 1950s and 1960s in America, while conservatives often opposed them, finally getting at least superficially concerned in the 1990s (largely through the influence of the Promise Keepers movement). Liberals took action on the issue of women in ministry decades before most conservatives began to rethink their position.[60] The same could be said about stewardship of the earth, concern for the poor, sensitivity to the plight of Palestinians, and a questioning of unconditional support for Israel. And although the debate has been agonizing, liberals have blazed the trail in seeking to treat homosexual and transgender persons with compassion. Conservatives may follow in their footsteps in this issue just as they have in others, several decades down the road, once the pioneers have cleared the way (and once their old guard has passed away).

---

[60] While liberals have heroically taken the lead (along with Pentecostals) in celebrating the equality and giftedness of women, their ecclesiastic systems in recent decades have too often been so confining, ineffective, inflexible, bureaucratic, and oppressive that most of their congregations have been in decline. Women have often been sent in as hospice workers to care for dying congregations, a tendency that (a) only reinforces stereotypes about women as caretakers, not leaders, and (b) makes work satisfaction, much less professional success, a pretty dim hope. This is not to invalidate the real value of hospice pastors who help congregations die with dignity. Yes, this is a needed work and calls for a needed kind of leadership. My complaint is that it is all too often the only kind of leadership offered to women. At any rate, I don't want to give the impression that women leaders are being treated especially well in any sector of the church, just less poorly in some places than others. This footnote doesn't do justice to the magnitude of the problem it summarizes; I hope others will make more of this problem than I am able to do here. See the emerging women's leadership initiative at www.emergentvillage.com.

While liberals have pioneered in the area of science and ethics, conservatives have been heroic in other ways, especially related to individual conversion and basic discipleship. Millions of people are dedicated Christians at the beginning of the twenty-first century who wouldn't be if it weren't for the conservative missionary advances of the nineteenth and twentieth centuries. Through Sunday school curricula, parachurch organizations, and small group programs, not to mention Christian radio and television pioneered by conservatives, millions of people have not only become Christians, but have also sent down roots into Scripture and made a beginning, at least, in spiritual disciplines and devotional habits. Conservative leadership in these areas has been truly heroic.

Both liberals and conservatives have shown signs of desperation as well. Certain facets of conservative Pentecostalism and liberal traditionalism, for example, have characteristics of withdrawal from reality. (Much more could be said about this, but it is hard to do so without sounding uncharitable, cynical, and ungenerous.) At least some facets of the Church Growth movement, in which I participated and from which I learned much, will probably look like desperate measures from a vantage point farther down the road.

Modern skepticism, pluralism, consumerism, individualism, and narcissism drove both sides to desperation—and understandably so. For all its advances and conveniences, modernity proved a largely inhospitable environment for the spiritual life of human beings—in both its liberal and conservative expressions.

Now, as we gradually leave modernity and enter the postmodern world, the trouble doesn't end for either liberals or conservatives.[61] To the degree they've defined themselves (a) in reaction to modern issues and (b) in polarization to one another, and to the degree they do not wake up and engage with emerging postmodern issues and challenges, they both become relics—stuck in the past rather than moving into the future. To the degree they preoccupy themselves with the question of who's right, to the exclusion of considering whether they are truly good (as in "bearing good fruit"), they're destined to fade, wither, fail. To the degree that they have sold their spiritual birthright for a political ideology, they must repent; neither left nor right leads to the higher kingdom.

As we've seen, much of the polarization between liberals and conservatives has come from comparing "our" best with "their" worst ("our" worst often accurately critiqued by "them" and "their" worst by "us.") But neither of us understood "their" best very well, and thus both we and they violated Jesus' dictum about not judging.

When I imagine what a generous orthodoxy can become, I realize I must seek to honor both conservative and liberal heroism. And when I do, I want to consider myself both liberal and conservative. I must learn from their mistakes, and when I do, I don't want to be boxed in either category. Instead they can look up for a higher way and look ahead to the new fields of opportunity and challenge that stretch from here to the horizon, where the terms *post-conservative* and *post-liberal* may be helpful for a while, and then the whole polarizing vocabulary can be, I hope, forgotten.

Beyond modernity the prospects for liberal/conservative reconnection and convergence are better than ever. I'd like to modify a well-known parable about liberals and conservatives to make that convergence at least a little more imaginable.

---

[61] Nancey Murphy's helpful book *Beyond Liberalism and Fundamentalism* (Trinity Press, 1996) makes this point powerfully and clearly, as does Stanley Grenz and John Franke's *Beyond Foundationalism* (Knox, 2000).

A Parable

Once there was a village along a river. A famine struck the village, and then a plague began to spread. The situation was desperate, and a group of brave men and women was chosen to seek help from a sister city many days' travel upstream. They hiked upstream through the trackless gorges and pathless ravines that bordered the river, and finally, after great struggle, reached the city.

The people of the city provided food and medicine along with canoes to carry the cargo back to the village. The band of brave travelers set off, determined and confident, yet under great pressure. If they failed in their journey or arrived too late, thousands in their village would die—their families, friends, and neighbors. One day as they paddled along, intent on their mission, they heard a frightening roar ahead of them. As they rounded a bend in the river, their hearts sank as they saw a stretch of raging rapids before them.

"We can't make it," one said. "We need to portage around the rapids."

"No," another said, "we can make it, but we'll need to throw all nonessential baggage overboard. We'll have to travel light. Besides, you know the terrain on land. It's impossible to carry all our gear and cargo over that terrain. And even if we could carry it all, we would have to make many, many trips, and our progress would be so slow. We would arrive too late to save our village."

The debate continued: "But it's too dangerous! What if our canoes tip over? Then we'll drown, and our friends and families will die too." A loud argument followed, some arguing for portaging and others arguing for running the rapids.

In the end, the party split in two. Those who were going to run the rapids left all the gear they felt they could spare on the shore and shoved off. As they moved through the rapids, the raging waters grew even rougher and more dangerous than they anticipated. In fear they began jettisoning more of what little remained of their cargo. Some canoes made it safely through the rapids. Some were swamped entirely, their vessels and cargo lost, and some of the travelers barely made it to shore, where they were rescued by their waiting companions.

Meanwhile, those who had remained ashore upstream began the long and tedious process of repacking and carrying their gear and canoes over land, many miles downstream, to a place where the waters were smoother and they could launch their canoes. They were determined to carry not only all their own cargo, but also the provisions the other party had (foolishly, in their opinion) left behind. Nothing could be lost because the village was in desperate need.

When those who rode the rapids made it below the dangerous stretch of the river, they made camp, exhausted yet exhilarated by the thrill of running the rapids. But then a frightening realization began to hit them: they had survived the raging waters, but they now lacked sufficient provisions to complete their mission. So what if they made it to the needy village? Now they had next to nothing to offer and would only add mouths to feed. They had thrown so much overboard that now their whole mission was in danger of failure in spite of their heroic success through the rapids. They set up a temporary camp and discussed their options for hours on end. While their situation was not immediately dangerous since they had some of their provisions left, their prospects for ultimate success were grim, and a feeling of despair began to set in when they thought of the village. They were paralyzed, and days passed as they sat around their temporary camp, their progress stalled.

Many miles upstream, their counterparts were having troubles of their own. The terrain was so difficult, and progress was so slow that this party on foot became frustrated. The air was filled with arguments. "Let's just give up the journey and set up permanent camp here. We'll never make it. We should just stop here. We might as well just save ourselves," some would say. Others would urge them to keep moving, giving rousing speeches about the need for courage and strength and perseverance. But there was no trail, the terrain was brutal, and their loads were heavy and awkward.

Eventually, many travelers were so exhausted by carrying the heavy cargo that they simply couldn't take another step. Should the stronger ones leave these tired comrades behind, or should they stay and wait until they regained their strength? Eventually their progress slowed to a stop, and they set up a temporary camp, filled with uncertainty about their future—and their village's future as well.

The next day they tried to go a little farther, but soon they were stalled again, *exhausted, arguing, aching, blistered, and afraid. After a few days, they were so sore, sick, and tired that they decided to make camp until they could think of a better way forward. At least they had plenty of provisions. But their sense of adventure was gone; they were just holding on. And a kind of despairing concern for their village was always on their minds.*

The parable, I think, describes the story of liberals and conservatives at this point in history—both stymied, but in different places and in different ways. What kind of ending can you imagine? Can you imagine the two parties somehow reuniting and moving on together again? Is there any other alternative?[62]

As I've said, the terms *post-evangelical* or *post-conservative* and *post-liberal* are already in use, and I wonder if they represent the hope of a reunited rescue party. Having survived in different ways the rough waters of modernity, they are now facing a new challenge: working together to save the village which we call planet Earth, and which God calls "beloved creation."[63]

Maybe there's a place beyond the current polarization, a place that is both orthodox and generous.

---

[62] My preferred ending would involve the rapids runners traveling back to find and aid their portaging brothers, who have provisions needed by both the rescuers and the village that they are seeking to save—but who lack the strength the rapids runners possess. This story could also serve to describe Catholics and Protestants.

[63] George Lindbeck, a post-liberal leader, was quoted in *The Nature of Confession: Evangelicals and Postliberals in Conversation* (Timothy Phillips, Dennis Okholm, eds. InterVarsity Press, 1996) as follows: "...if the sort of research program represented by postliberalism has a real future as a communal enterprise of the church, it's more likely to be carried on by evangelicals than anyone else" (p. 253).

CHAPTER 9

WHY I AM MYSTICAL/POETIC

Perhaps you can recall this powerful moment in Carl Sagan's movie *Contact*: a scientist has entered a wormhole in space and is allowed to see what she calls "a celestial event." The beauty and grandeur of the event stun her. Awestruck, wide-eyed, she says, whispering, "Poetry! Indescribable...They should have sent a poet."

Walter Brueggemann, one of the theologians whose writings help me most, suggests that Christian theology needs a moment of awe like Sagan's scientist. In "Poetry in a Prose-Flattened World," the introductory essay to *Finally Comes the Poet*, Bruggemann describes a theological landscape dominated by theologian-accountants, theologian-technicians, theologian-scientists—but not theologian-poets:[64]

> The gospel is...a truth widely held, but a truth greatly reduced. It is a truth that has been flattened, trivialized, and rendered inane. Partly, the gospel is simply an old habit among us, neither valued nor questioned. But more than that, our technical way of thinking reduces mystery

---

[64] Brueggemann (Fortress, 1990).

to problem, transforms assurance into certitude, revises quality into quantity, and takes the categories of biblical faith and represents them in manageable shapes...There is then no danger, no energy, no possibility, no opening for newness!...That means the gospel may have been twisted, pressed, tailored, and gerrymandered until it is comfortable with technological reason that leaves us unbothered, and with ideology that leaves us with uncriticized absolutes.

What is needed, he says, is a new kind of preaching, preaching that opens "out the good news of the gospel with alternative modes of speech," that is "dramatic, artistic, capable of inviting persons to join in another conversation, free of the reason of technique, unencumbered by ontologies that grow abstract, unembarrassed about concreteness." Because "reduced speech leads to reduced lives," Brueggemann calls on preachers to explore another approach:

> To address the issue of a truth greatly reduced requires us to be poets that speak against a prose world. The terms of that phrase are readily misunderstood. By prose I refer to a world that is organized in settled formulae, so that even pastoral prayers and love letters sound like memos. By poetry, I do not mean rhyme, rhythm, or meter, but language that moves like Bob Gibson's fast ball, that jumps at the right moment, that breaks open old worlds with surprise, abrasion, and pace. Poetic speech is the only proclamation worth doing in a situation of reductionism, the only proclamation, I submit, that is worthy of the name preaching.

This non-prose world—called unreal by the rulers of this age, but real to people of faith—is the world entered by the mystic, the contemplative, the visionary, the prophet, the poet.

When I entered college, I started as a philosophy major, but soon I switched to literature. Why? Philosophy, as I experienced it in the 1970s at my large state institution, was engaged in the prose language of the scientist; the wisdom I was seeking was found in the wilder language of the poet. Catholic theologian Hans Urs von Balthasar said it like this, "God needs prophets in order to make himself known, and all prophets are necessarily artistic. What a prophet has to say can never be said in prose."[65]

This healthy poetic sensibility is illustrated beautifully in the story of Blaise Pascal, a brilliant seventeenth-century mathematician who attempted to bring prose clarity and precision to proving the tenets of faith. Just the title of his vast apologetic says volumes: *Pensées* (*Thoughts*). For modern man, truth—both mathematical and spiritual—is arrived at through prose thought, prose logic, prose rationality…not intuition, not imagination, not wonder, not awe, not worship, not reverence, not trust, not faith.

When Pascal died, *Pensées* was left unfinished. As brilliant and wonderful as Pascal's thoughts were, even more intriguing was a sheet of paper on which Pascal had written and which he secretly stitched inside his coat. Here's what he wrote:

MEMORIAL
The year of grace 1654,
Monday, 23 November…
From about half past ten in the evening until about half past midnight,
FIRE.
"GOD of Abraham, GOD of Isaac, GOD of Jacob"
not of the philosophers and of the learned.
Certitude. Certitude. Feeling. Joy. Peace.

---

[65] Hans Urs von Balthasar, *The Glory of the Lord: A Theological Aesthetics*, 1984, in Brueggemann, 1990.

GOD of Jesus Christ.

"My God and your God..."

Forgetfulness of the world and of everything,

except GOD.

He is to be found only in the ways taught in the Gospel.

Greatness of the human soul.

"Righteous Father, the world has not known you,

but I have known you."

Joy, joy, joy, tears of joy.

I have departed from him:

"They have forsaken me, the fount of living water."

"My God, will you leave me?"

Let me not be separated from him forever.

"This is eternal life,

that they might know you, the one true God,

and the one that you sent, Jesus Christ."

Jesus Christ.

Jesus Christ.

I left him;

I fled him,

renounced,

crucified.

Let me never be separated from him.

He is only kept securely by the ways taught in the Gospel:

Renunciation, total and sweet.

Complete submission to Jesus Christ and to my director.[66]

Eternally in joy for a day's excercise on the earth.

Not to forget your words. Amen.

On that night in 1654, the prose mathematician became a poet and mystic.[67]

---

[66] It is of interest to note that Pascal's mystical experience did not lead him into an isolated, individualized spirituality but drove him back into dialogue with his spiritual director.

I can use the word *mystical* to describe his experience, but only with hesitancy because to many people, *mystical* is still a debased word, sub-rational, maybe a little crazed. They prefer analytical prose to mystical poetry. But *mystical* really is a wonderful word, suggesting ways we partake of mystery, mystery beyond the grasp of reasonable prose.

In Chesterton's *Orthodoxy*, mysticism is celebrated as essential not only to orthodoxy, but also to sanity itself. With hyperbole, but not without reason, Chesterton claims—

> Imagination does not breed insanity. Exactly what does breed insanity is reason. Poets do not go mad; but chess players do...Perhaps the strongest case of all is this: that only one great English poet went mad, Cowper. And he was definitely driven mad by logic, by the ugly and alien logic of predestination. Poetry was not the disease, but the medicine...He was damned by John Calvin...Poetry is sane because it floats easily in an infinite sea; reason seeks to cross the infinite sea, and so make it finite. The result is mental exhaustion...The poet only asks to get his head into the heavens. It is the logician who seeks to get the heavens into his head. And it is his head that splits... The madman is not the man who has lost his reason. The madman is the man who has lost everything except his reason...Materialists and madmen never have doubts... Mysticism keeps men sane. As long as you have the mystery you have health; when you destroy mystery you create morbidity (12-13, 15, 21, 24).

For Chesterton, mysticism has a kind of clarity and precision that reason cannot have, and poetry can take us places prose never can:

---

[67] Pascal's "Memorial" can be found in many places on the Internet.

Like the sun at noonday, mysticism explains everything else by the blaze of its own victorious invisibility...We are conscious of it as a kind of splendid confusion; it is something both shining and shapeless, at once a blaze and a blur. Detached intellectualism is...all moonshine; for it is light without heat, and it is secondary light, reflected from a dead world. But the Greeks were right when they made Apollo the god both of imagination and of sanity; for he was both the patron of poetry and the patron of healing... The circle of the moon is as clear and unmistakable, as recurrent and inevitable, as the circle of Euclid on the blackboard. For the moon is utterly reasonable, and the moon is the mother of lunatics and has given to them all her name (26).

C. S. Lewis, writing midway between our day and Chesterton's, was in many ways the literary disciple of Chesterton. Lewis is renowned for his highly reasoned apologetic work; his logical prose is far more beloved than his poetry. But his prose is far more poetic than many realize (try to find a paragraph in *Mere Christianity* or *Miracles* that isn't built around a strongly imaginative metaphor or two, for example), and it suggests a man with imaginative and mystical sensitivities no less powerful than Pascal's.

Take this passage, for example, from *Perelandra* (New York: MacMillan, 1944), one of his science fiction/fantasy novels. An earthling has visited Venus and is seeing a view—*vision* is probably a better word—of the sky, with commentary from an extraterrestrial/angel. Gradually the vision of creation unfolding above the man and angel begins to resemble a dance:

He thought he saw the Great Dance...and that part of him which could reason and remember was dropped farther and farther behind that part of him which saw. Even then, at the very zenith of complexity, complexity was

eaten up and faded, as a thin white cloud fades into the
hard blue burning of the sky, and a simplicity beyond all
comprehension, ancient and young as spring, illimitable,
pellucid, drew him with cords of infinite desire into its
own stillness. He went up into such a quietness, a privacy,
and a freshness that at the very moment when he stood
farthest from our ordinary mode of being he had the
sense of stripping off encumbrances and awaking from a
trance, and coming to himself...Then his consciousness
was engulfed (219, 222).

This kind of writing depends on something beyond mere
rationality. It depends on imagination and vision, and these are
portals into the mystical, where "consciousness is engulfed" by
something beyond itself.

There long have been Christian traditions recognizing
the profound importance of mysticism and poetry, and the
corresponding limitations of rationality and prose, including
the *via negativa*—the negative way—and the *hesychastic* tradition,
which discovers God in silence. Both traditions remind us of the
limitations of language when talking about God, a subject so great
that no words can do it justice.[68]

This rebuke to arrogant intellectualizing is especially apt
for modern Christians, who do not build cathedrals of stone and
glass as in the Middle Ages, but rather conceptual cathedrals of
proposition and argument. These conceptual cathedrals—known
popularly as systematic theologies—were cherished by modern
minds, liberal and conservative, but late modern thinkers like
Karl Barth understood their limitation and temptation:

---

[68] For more on these Eastern approaches to the experience of God, see Kyriacos Markides, *The
Mountain of Silence* (Image, 2002). And while we're on the subject of words, Chesterton's are worth
noting: "The long words are not the hard words, it is the short words that are hard. There is much
more metaphysical subtlety in the word 'damn' than in the word 'degeneration'" (*Orthodoxy* 134).

> My lectures at the University of Basel are on "Systematic
> Theology." In Basel and elsewhere the juxtaposition of
> this noun and this adjective is based on a tradition which
> is quite recent and highly problematic. Is not the term
> "Systematic Theology" as paradoxical as a "wooden iron"?
> One day this conception will disappear just as suddenly as
> it has come into being.[69]

At the heart of the theological project in the late modern world was
the assumption that one could and should reduce all revealed truth
into propositions and organize those propositions into an outline
that exhaustively contains and serves as the best vehicle for truth.
If not on the scholarly level, this assumption ruled supreme in
the minds of many rank-and-file Christians. But just as medieval
cathedrals now serve more as history/art museums than houses
of worship, Barth anticipated the day when the common sort of
systematic theology would become a historical artifact. Prose
abstractions just don't contain or convey God's truth as well as
we thought they did. This is obviously true of our "theological"
jargon—words like *omnipresent, omniscient, omnipotent, immutable, impassible,*
and so on.

I need to add, hastily and sincerely, that many of my best
friends are systematic theologians, and I think the new systematic
theologies they produce and celebrate will be wonderful,
magnificent, and inspiring—perhaps better called "systemic" than
systematic, because their work will have the beauty and symmetry
and dynamic of a living organic system rather than the stiff order
of a lifeless, rigid, mechanistic outline. This emerging approach
has been described as *coherent* (hanging together, making sense when
its many parts are integrated), *contextual* (sensitive to its cultural
and historic situation), *conversational* (never attempting to be the last
word, and thus silence other voices, but rather inviting ongoing

---

[69] From the foreword to *Church Dogmatics* (Westminster John Knox, 1994).

dialogue in the search for truth), and *comprehensive* (relating to all of life).[70] It will be the friend, not the enemy, of the kind of poetic sensibility we are exploring in this chapter.

As soon as we speak of the limitations of systematic theology, we must acknowledge the limitations of even our poetic language—our images, metaphors, similes. Do we think can they fully contain God, either?

For example, to say that God is judge is to poetically portray God via the image of a human judge. But judges have different roles in different societies—so what kind of judge is God like? It's worthwhile to realize that judges didn't develop in human society until the last few millennia; could it have been said that God was like a judge before judges existed? And more, while God is like any particular model of judge in some ways, God is also unlike that judge in many others.

So we reach for another metaphor to correct the first, and we say that God is also a father, or a friend, or a shepherd, or a vinedresser, or wind, or storm, or fire, or water, or a rock. Each metaphor enlightens, but taken too far, or taken in the wrong way, can mislead. (Is God cold and uncaring like a rock? Shapeless and conforming like water?) We must, therefore, never underestimate our power to be wrong when talking about God, when thinking about God, when imagining God—whether in prose or in poetry. Romano Guardini, chaplain to Pope John XXIII in the Second Vatican Council era, captured the challenge of trying to speak of God and divine truth:

> [When one] attempts to convey something of God's holy otherness he tries one earthly simile after another. In the

---

[70] Thanks to John Franke for help and insight on the emerging contours of postmodern systematic theology. His upcoming and as yet untitled book (from Baker) on theological method will explore this subject in more detail.

end he discards them all as inadequate and says apparently
wild and senseless things meant to startle the heart
into feeling what lies beyond the reaches of the brain.
Something of the kind takes place here: "Eye has not seen
nor ear heard, nor has it entered into the heart of man,
what things God has prepared for those who love him"
(1 Cor. 2:9). [These realities beyond understanding] can
be brought closer only by the overthrow of everything
naturally comprehensible. Flung into a world of new logic,
we are forced to make a genuine effort to understand.[71]

Now there is no need to swing to an opposite extreme, to say that
since even metaphors can mislead, we might as well give up on
language altogether. C. S. Lewis caught the needed balance—that
language can be a window through which one glimpses God, but
never a box in which God can be contained—in a dense but brilliant
poem called "A Footnote to All Prayers." The poem begins:

> The one whom I bow to only knows to whom I bow
> When I attempt the ineffable Name, murmuring Thou

Then he compares himself to Phaedius, a classical Greek sculptor
famous for his majestic sculptures of the gods:

> And dream of Phaedian fancies and embrace in heart
> Symbols (I know) which cannot be the thing thou art.
> Thus always, taken at their word, all prayers blaspheme
> Worshipping with frail images a folk-lore dream...

Lewis goes on to say that people deceive themselves in prayer,
thinking that their images or thoughts of God *are* actually God,
and compares all our prayers to arrows aimed wide of their target
(but that God mercifully hears despite their bad aim). All who pray,

---

[71] Guardini (Regnery-Gateway, 1954), p. 73.

he realizes, are idolators "crying unheard/To a deaf idol" if God takes the words of their prayers absolutely literally. He concludes by begging God to "take not...our literal sense" but rather to translate our limping metaphors into God's "great,/unbroken speech."

A generous orthodoxy, in contrast to the tense, narrow, controlling, or critical orthodoxies of so much of Christian history, doesn't take itself too seriously. It is humble; it doesn't claim too much; it admits it walks with a limp. It doesn't consider orthodoxy the exclusive domain of prose scholars (theologians) alone but, like Chesterton, welcomes the poets, the mystics, and even those who choose to say very little or to remain silent, including the disillusioned and the doubters. Their silence speaks eloquently of the majesty of God that goes beyond all human articulation. And it welcomes the activists, the humanitarians, the brave and courageous and compassionate, because their actions speak volumes about God that could never be captured in a text, a sermon, an outline, or even a poem.

This mystical/poetic approach takes special pains to remember that the Bible itself contains precious little expository prose. Rather it is story laced with parable, poem interwoven with vision, dream and opera (isn't this the best contemporary genre to compare to the book of Job?), personal letter and public song, all thrown together with an undomesticated and unedited artistic passion. Even Paul, who, at the hands of lawyers like Luther and Calvin comes out looking (we shouldn't be surprised) like a lawyer—and who at the hands of prose scholars comes out sounding like a prose scholar—needs to be reappraised in this regard. Have you noticed how he resorts to poetry in Romans 11, Philippians 2, and Colossians 1?[72]

---

[72] See Brian Walsh and Sylvia Keesmaat's brilliant exposition, *Colossians Remixed: Subverting the Empire* (Intervarsity Press, 2004).

Yes, this element can be pushed too far, straining both generosity (by asking us to condone every vision or dream proclaimed by an array of kooks, nuts, and charlatans) and orthodoxy (by asking us to ignore doctrinal nonsense promoted in the name of mystical experience). Kyriacos Markides describes the needed balance well:

> Christianity, a Catholic bishop in Maine once told me, has two lungs. One is Western, meaning rational and philosophical, and the other Eastern, meaning mystical and otherworldly. Both, he claimed, are needed for proper breathing...Both the mystical and the rational approaches to God were part of the early church. They were only set asunder by subsequent historical developments.[73]

Perhaps this balanced approach means that serious theologians in the years ahead will more often, along with their scholarly work, write poetry, or make films, or compose music, or write plays and novels—not as their avocation, but right along with their primary theological vocation.[74] Can we celebrate this kind of artistic play as the serious work of generously orthodox Christians?

I used to be embarrassed that I work as a pastor and write books on theological topics, yet have no formal training in theology, having snuck into ministry (as I said in Chapter 0) through the back door of the English department. Even though I've been on a seminary's board of directors, even though I am adjunct faculty at several seminaries, and even though I have spoken to many seminary presidents and faculty and have deep respect for the work of seminaries—and, in fact, have received an honorary doctorate from a respected seminary (Carey Theological College

---

[73] *The Mountain of Silence* (Image, 2002), p. 235-236.

[74] For example, by viewing *The Truman Show* and *Bruce Almighty*, one could make a case that even comedic actor Jim Carrey and his directors are serious practitioners of theology.

in Vancouver, BC)—I myself have never taken a single for-credit seminary class.

Even though I am unapologetically pro-education, believing that our need is not for less education for Christian leaders, but rather for better, deeper, broader education, I'm not so embarrassed by my lack of "proper credentials" anymore. In fact, I can see God's guidance in it. My graduate training was in literature and language, which sensitized me to drama and conflict, to syntax and semantics and semiotics, to text and context, to prose and to poetry. It gave me a taste, a sense, a feel for the game and science and art and romance of language. It helped me to see how carefully chosen and clear, daring words can point to mysteries and wonders beyond words. It prepared me to see how a generous orthodoxy must be mystical and poetic.

There's mystery and poetry in everything, really, if we have eyes to see, ears to hear: in botany, in biology, in history, in architecture, in medicine, in mathematics, even in astronomy— as Carl Sagan's movie *Contact* made so clear. In fact, as we learn a generous orthodoxy, we become more and more prepared to see the mystery and poetry everywhere, to hear it, to feel it, and to sing.

CHAPTER 10

WHY I AM BIBLICAL

A friend of mine recently confessed that he was unhappy with my theological direction over the last few years. I asked what concerned him, and he replied, "Well, *I* still have a high regard for the Bible." I told him I was stung by his remark because it implied that I didn't. He apologized, and the sting didn't remain for long, but I think some of my other friends feel the same way.

I have spent my entire life learning, understanding, reappraising, wrestling with, trusting, applying, and obeying the Bible, and trying to help others do the same. I believe it is a gift from God, inspired by God, to benefit us in the most important way possible: equipping us so that we can benefit others, so that we can play our part in the ongoing mission of God. *My regard for the Bible is higher than ever.*

True, I grew up being taught that the Bible was an answer book, supplying exactly the kind of information modern, Western, moderately educated people want from a phone book, encyclopedia, or legal constitution. We want to know exactly when the earth was created (4004 B.C. or thereabouts) and how (instantaneously, during six 24-hour periods), along with when it will end. (Back in the 1960s, we "knew" the Bible taught that the world would end within about 25 years...oops. We also "knew" from the Bible that it would end through a conflict between the United States/Israel representing God versus the Soviet Union/China representing the devil. Oops again.)

We wanted a simple, clear, efficient, and convenient plan for getting to heaven after death. Between now and then, we wanted clear assurance that God didn't like the people we didn't like, and for the same reasons we didn't like them. Finally, we wanted a rule book that made it objectively clear, with no subjective ambiguity, what behaviors were right and wrong for all time, in all places, and among all cultures, especially if those rules confirmed our views and not those of people we considered "liberal."

Although I was taught that the Bible fulfilled these modern-Western-moderately-educated desires, I no longer see the Bible this way. But that doesn't mean I have a lower regard for the Bible. Although I value it differently than I used to, and a little differently perhaps than my friend does now, I still, with my friend, value the Bible more than I can adequately explain. I hope I do so in the way the Bible itself tells me to.

If you consult the Bible itself, inquiring for what kinds of claims are made in the Bible about the Bible, a few pivotal passages come to mind, especially one from a letter written by the early church leader, Paul, to his younger protégé, Timothy, in about AD 67. In it Paul, suffering alone in a cold prison, urges Timothy to remain true and strong: "But as for you, continue in what you have learned and have become convinced of, because you know those from whom you learned it, and how from infancy you have known the holy Scriptures, which are able to make you wise for salvation through faith in Christ Jesus" (2 Timothy 3:14-15). What a fascinating phrase to describe the holy Scriptures: *able to make you wise for salvation* through faith in Christ Jesus!

Then Paul adds these oft-quoted words: *"All Scripture is God-breathed and is useful for teaching, rebuking, correcting and training in righteousness, so that the man of God may be thoroughly equipped for every good work"* (2 Timothy 3:16-17).

What is meant by *God-breathed* or *inspired*? God's breath is associated, from the first verses of the Bible, with creativity and life-giving vitality. In Genesis 1, again and again, God breathes out (metaphorically, of course: we're not saying God has lungs, vocal cords, air to vibrate them—remember Chapter 9!): "Let there be..." And God's creative breath gives permission to whatever possibility (light, trees, fish, people) to become actual...actually come into being. In this primal, sacred narrative, the creative breath of God is associated with God's life-giving Spirit (the linguistic connections between Spirit and breath or wind are profound), who first moves over the chaos of the waters so they yield their creative possibilities and eventually teem with life, and who then enters humanity, making each person "a living soul," or a living person.

To say Scripture is God-breathed is, then, to elicit this primal language of creation. Think of the difference between a corpse and a living, breathing body, and you'll understand the difference between a bunch of words and words vitalized with God's breath. But even understanding this, how do we understand the interaction between God's breath or impulse and the human impulses that produced the Scriptures, including this letter of Paul? After all, it was very obviously written by one human being to another, in a certain time and place, dealing with certain situations and needs, bearing all the marks of Paul's humanity, including his personal opinions (e.g., 1 Corinthians 7:12) and biases (e.g., Titus 1:12-13).

Let me offer this analogy. I am a human being with a name (plus an assortment of numbers that certify me as a citizen, driver, credit-card holder, phone owner, etc.). Like every other human,

I am both a creation of God and a pro-creation of parents who, in partnership with friends and teachers and authors and culture in general, helped make me all I am today. The way God willed to create the "me" I am today, then, like every other human, is through a complex synergy of biology and community and history (plus my own will, choices, and the like). These parental origins, these organic means, these social and historical contexts, do not decrease in any way the reality of God as my ultimate Creator, the One who through all these many instrumentalities says, "Let there be a Brian," and here I am. In the same way Scripture is something God has "let be," and so it is at once God's creation *and* the creation of the dozens of people and communities and cultures who produced it. One doesn't decrease the other. One doesn't lessen the other. One doesn't nullify the other.

The Christian community at its best through history has always had a deep feeling and understanding for this integrated dual origin of the Scriptures. In differing language (developed to counteract different misunderstandings and threats from within and without) the Christian community in its Catholic, Protestant, and Orthodox forms has sought to hold on to both dimensions of the origin of Scripture. Not to hold them in balance or dynamic tension (because they aren't really in opposition!), but to hold them together as friends, as partners, as colleagues.

Sometimes, however, we have turned *Creator-and-creation-in-partnership* into a dynamic tension, and sometimes we have sought to resolve the tension by leaning one way or the other. Often we have treated the Bible as if God dictated it, with no organic participation at all (no personality, no community, no culture, no historical context). By analogy, it is as if Jesus were to blink into existence as a full-grown man, with no mother Mary, no belly button, no stepfather Joseph, no Cousin John or Aunt Elizabeth, no second-temple Judaic culture, no context of the Roman Empire in the background with its thrones and swords and crosses.

At other times we have acted as if the personalities of authors, the influences of communities and cultures, the domination of historical forces completely explained the Bible, edging God out of the equation entirely. As if (by analogy) Jesus were just another cog in the machine of humanity, with no God-with-us to be found at all. Seen in this light, Scripture became for us an embarrassment, a bunch of words, primitive, superstitious maybe, not very useful for anything except understanding ancient religious mythology.

By the way, this implied analogy between the Scriptures and Jesus is dangerous, but John's Gospel, in referring to Jesus as "the Word of God," seems to make some room for it. Also by the way, "the Word of God" is never used in the Bible to refer to the Bible. It couldn't since the Bible as a collection of 66 books hadn't been compiled yet. (If you want a feel for the richness of the phrase "Word of God," ask the Lutherans; it's a secret that their tradition seems to know without knowing that it knows.)

At our best moments, we've enjoyed Scripture and profited by it with the effortless joy of riding a bicycle, where our momentum in mission meant that we didn't need to think about balancing at all. We're enjoying the exhilaration of speed and wind and scenery too much to be self-conscious. Between our best and worst moments, we're like a novice bicycle rider who must constantly talk to himself: am I leaning too far to the left? To the right? At our worst moments, we give up riding altogether and spend our time critiquing other riders—*he leans too far left, she too far right*, and so on. So when we're moving ahead in mission, we probably can't explain how we do it as well as we do it—because it's a matter of feel, of instinct. Our explanations seem a lot clumsier than our riding.

Just as it's nearly impossible to balance a bicycle when it's not moving, we're most likely to crash in our dealing with Scripture if we're not moving forward in our mission. Perhaps the best way to use Scripture is not to concentrate on our use of Scripture at all but rather to focus on our pursuit of mission. Then we will need Scripture to do what it was intended to do. This is exactly where Paul goes next in his letter to Timothy.

The Bible, he says, is good for equipping people to do good works. It does so specifically through teaching (telling you what is true and right), rebuking (helping you see where you've gone wrong), correction (guiding you on how to get on the right track again), and training in justice (educating you in the skills of staying on the right path).

Interestingly, when Scripture talks about itself, it doesn't use the language we often use in our explanations of its value. For modern Western Christians, words like *authority, inerrancy, infallibility, revelation, objective, absolute,* and *literal* are crucial. Many churches or denominations won't allow people to become members unless they use these words in their description of Scripture. Hardly anyone realizes why these words are important.[75] Hardly anyone knows about the stories of Sir Isaac Newton, Rene Descartes, the Enlightenment, David Hume, and Foundationalism—which provide the context in which these words are so important. Hardly anyone notices the irony of resorting to the authority of extrabiblical words and concepts to justify one's belief in the Bible's ultimate authority.[76]

Oddly, I've never heard of a church or denomination that asked people to affirm a doctrinal statement like this: *The purpose of Scripture is to equip God's people for good works.* Shouldn't a simple statement like this be far more important than statements with words foreign

---

[75] It should be noted that I am not saying these words are "bad" or not important, nor am I denying they have value and validity, but I am saying that they are important *within certain contexts* and that many use them without deeply understanding those contexts.

[76] Again see Franke and Grenz, *Beyond Foundationalism* (Knox, 2000) and Nancey Murphy, *Beyond Liberalism and Fundamentalism* (Trinity, 1996).

to the Bible's vocabulary about itself (inerrant, authoritative, literal, revelatory, objective, absolute, propositional, etc.)?

It's no surprise then that biblical Christians have thrived when we've used the Bible with the goal of becoming good people who, because we follow Jesus, do good works in God's good world. And we have languished and wandered when we have used the Bible as a weapon to threaten others, as a tool to intimidate others and prove them wrong, as a shortcut to being know-it-alls who believe the Bible gives us all the answers, as a defense of the status quo —none of these being the use Paul the apostle wanted Timothy, his protégé, to make of the Scriptures. Sadly, sometimes the very people who most love the Bible have been those who have used it for these other purposes, sometimes to the neglect of its essential purpose.[77]

But again, think about what truly biblical Christians (Protestant, Catholic, Orthodox, liberal, conservative, charismatic, whatever) have done when they have understood the profitable purpose of Scripture. Instructed by Scripture, they have left the comforts of home and country and gone to every corner of the world, spreading the Good News of Jesus in word and deed. They have built hospitals and schools to heal bodies and strengthen minds. They have given money to needy people around the globe, many of them voluntarily living at 90 percent of their means or far below that, so that they could always give away the first 10 percent. They have crossed racial, ethnic, and class barriers, seeing all people as brothers and sisters. They have chosen to suffer rather than betray their faith or make others suffer. They have produced art both lofty and down-to-earth, from Handel's "Messiah" to "Amazing Grace" and from a European cathedral to a Shaker kitchen chair. And no less important, they've done

---

[77] Deuteronomy 29:29 clearly affirms a similar intended purpose for the Torah, the first five books of the Hebrew Bible, as do Psalm 119 and the book of Proverbs.

their work as teachers, farmers, bricklayers, nurses, scholars, mechanics, sellers, public servants, scientists, homemakers, cab drivers, and cooks with a special sense of purpose, love, and joy. Their "good works" included doing "good work" from day to day— whatever they did on the farm, in the office, in the home, in the classroom, or at the factory was seen as part of their holy, sacred vocation in God's creation.

Why? Since they understood the real purpose of Scripture, they let Scripture equip them for good works in our needy world. Their words and deeds together have qualified them to be bearers of good news. Sure they have never been perfect, but they have often been wonderful. That's why I am proud to be a biblical Christian in the tradition of St. Francis, Mother Teresa, Billy Graham, my grandparents and parents, and thousands like them.

I need to be forthcoming, though, and admit that the Bible has not only been an inestimable blessing to me: it has also been a problem. The more I learn from Jesus, the more I cringe when I read passages in Exodus or Joshua where the God of love and universal compassion to whom Jesus has introduced me allegedly commands what today we would call brutality, chauvinism, ethnic cleansing, or holocaust. I ache when biblical passages are used to reinforce an escapist, deterministic, or fatalistic view of the future, to assert the subjugation of women by men, or to justify a careless attitude toward our beautiful God-given planet. When I introduce the Bible to my friends outside the church, these things jump out at them, and they wonder how "a nice guy" like me could be so excited about what seems to them a barbaric book.

I try to explain that the problem isn't the Bible, but our modern assumptions about the Bible and our modern interpretive approaches to it. I try to explain that there is a better way to understand and apply the Bible, a largely new and unexplored way that can be summarized like this: *We need to reclaim the Bible as narrative.*

The Bible is a story, and just because it recounts (by standards of accuracy acceptable to its original audience) what happened, that doesn't mean it tells what should always happen or even what should have happened. The following diagram clarifies this point:

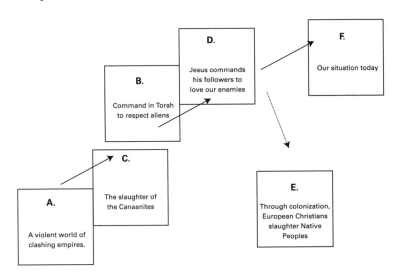

We must begin with a recognition of (A) how violent the world of the ancient Middle East was. The violence of the Jews entering Canaan in 1400 B.C. (C) was not extraordinary; it was typical of their day. And so we ask: in that context was God commanding the people to do, *not what was ideal or ethically desirable for all time*, but what was necessary to survive in that world at that point? Was there a viable alternative at the time for a group of wandering, homeless, liberated slaves seeking a homeland? In other words, assuming history is real and not a simulation, not a chess game in which God plays both sides, not a video game moving to the pressure of God's thumbs on a controller—if God is going to enter into a relationship with people, then God has to work with them as they are in their individual and cultural moral development. And back in those days, that meant that any group of people, if they were to survive, had to fight.

Two analogies might be helpful here.

1. I am an American. My nation was founded on land theft and countless broken treaties, on the suppression, exclusion, ethnic cleansing, and near eradication of the people who inhabited this land (Native Peoples). And having stolen the land, my forefathers prospered on the subjugation and enslavement of another people (African slaves). Now, my country dominates the world and sees American self-interest as its "prime directive." Everything I know of God tells me that God was outraged by the atrocities of my European ancestors and brokenhearted for the victims, and that God remains outraged by American arrogance today. But what is God to do? Forever curse Americans, refusing to assist them, refusing to respond when we sing "God Bless America"? Should God forsake American children and grandchildren to a hundred generations because of the original American holocaust? Wouldn't God's blessing of a nation so conceived imply an endorsement of the atrocities that were and are committed?

And which country or people group does not have similar violence in their heritage, in history or prehistory? All of our genes descend from people like the conquerors of Canaan. In fact, all *Homo sapiens* may, some conjecture, exist today because we brutally wiped out *Homo neanderthalenis*. If God blesses anyone, he must bless the violent and the children of the violent because there is no one else to bless. This is not an excuse, but it is reality. We can't remove ourselves from this equation. There is no other raw material with which for God to work but this ugly, violent, primitive raw material. If God wants a nonviolent and kind humanity in the future, God must enter into heartbreaking relationship with violent and cruel humanity in the meantime—just as parents, if they want a beautiful and mature adult child in 20 years, must begin now with screaming, crying, illiterate, selfish babies who lack bladder and bowel control.

2. Consider our civilization today. Imagine (it's not hard) that a thousand years from now, in a world ravaged by side effects of the industrial revolution (global warming from fossil fuels, extinction of species, destruction of rain forests, pollution of water and air, nuclear contamination or catastrophe, etc.), our descendants look back on our era as the most destructive in human history. "How could God ever have blessed people who drove automobiles, who heated their homes with energy derived from fossil fuels or nuclear energy, who through their taxes funded the creation of horrific weapons?" they'll ask. "Wasn't God's blessing of them a sign of approval of their destructive ways?" We would protest: *But we didn't know! We didn't know how much damage we were doing. We were just trying to survive. It's how people lived in our day.* And perhaps God would protest as well, "I didn't approve of all they did, but I loved them, and I wanted them to survive so that you could survive now, a thousand years later."

According to the Torah, while God is commanding the destruction of Canaan, God simultaneously commands (B) that once it was subdued, the Jews should treat their neighbors and aliens with respect and kindness. God never commands them to build a divinely sanctioned empire that will conquer all their neighbors and destroy or assimilate them; after all, they had been the victims of empire themselves in Egypt. Instead God strictly limits violence and leads the Jews to create a society that was a step above that of their neighbors ethically.

And then Jesus comes with a new command (D) that fulfills and supersedes all Torah: to love one another, and especially to love one's enemies—to forgive, not to inflict revenge, to give, not to take or even grasp what you already have. What if God could never have gotten to D without first working with people from A, through B and C?

We have to face, sadly but honestly, the reality that in many circumstances such as (E), people who ostensibly follow Jesus Christ have violated the plotline of our story, have reversed the flow of the narrative. They have acted regressively, as if (C) were intended as an expression of God's desire for all time, honoring Moses above Jesus (D), denying where they are in the unfolding narrative (F). They have kept the ethnic cleansing card in their back pocket, and they have thus become perpetrators and victims of tragically bad literacy, confusing the genre of ancient biblical narrative with the modern genres of political constitution or moral dictionary or religious blueprint. As a result, they have preferred to read the Bible as a *timeless* document rather than a *timely* one.[78]

We now can look back at the narrative flow of the Bible (covering about 2,000 years from Abraham through the apostles) *and* the narrative flow of how we Christians have read it (2,000 years to the present). We see great leaders—such as St. Francis, Gandhi (who sought to follow the way of Christ without identifying himself as a Christian), and Martin Luther King, Jr.—whose reading and application of the Bible advanced the narrative trajectory (a useful term from Stanley Grenz). And we can see the powerful and ironically named Pope Innocent III of the Fourth Crusade, or the Conquistadores in Latin America, or

---

[78] If I were a non-Christian, the first question I would want to ask a Christian neighbor would be this: "Do you still keep the ethnic cleansing card in your back pocket?" I wouldn't feel safe in his neighborhood until I knew the answer.

the Protestants persecuting alleged witches and Anabaptists and Catholics, or the churches of the United States and South Africa justifying racism and apartheid—whose reading and application have hijacked the trajectory and at times threatened to crash it into the ground. And we, too, have a choice today: will our readings betray the way of Christ in our day, or will they set our course toward God's dreams? Will we let the story continue in and through us, along its intended trajectory, toward God's undying, embracing dream called the kingdom of God?

This narrative approach does not lessen the agony one feels reading the conquest of Canaan with the eyes of one taught by Jesus to love all, including enemies. But it helps turn the Bible back into what it is, not a look-it-up encyclopedia of timeless moral truths, but the unfolding narrative of God at work in a violent, sinful world, calling people, beginning with Abraham, into a new way of life. This isn't the deterministic progress of Marxism or capitalism; this is the struggle of common people in the journey of faith, hope, and love. And it challenges us: to be truly biblical does not mean being preoccupied with some golden age in the ancient world and God's word to people back then. It means learning from the past to let God's story, God's will, and God's dream continue to come true in us and our children.

But this is a whole new way of approaching the Bible, you say. This is a whole new concept of being biblical. Orthodoxy has a deeply different feel in this light—less rigid, more generous. Yes, I think you're right.

CHAPTER 11

WHY I AM CHARISMATIC/CONTEMPLATIVE

As I explained in Chapter 1, my life was deeply and forever enriched by association with charismatic (or Pentecostal) Christians in my late teens and early 20s. I learned that the Holy Spirit is alive and active, a constant companion and source of empowerment and courage. One of my early spiritual mentors played an invaluable role in my experience with the Spirit of Jesus.

I had met some Pentecostals who seemed to have something I wanted and needed (joy and confidence, both springing from a robust spiritual vitality), along with some other things I was better off without (a tendency to exaggerate, to push too hard, to gloss over problems and pretend that things were better than they were). I had been taught to be suspicious of Pentecostals/charismatics, so I asked my mentor Dave what he thought. He told me the story of a couple (John and Elizabeth Sherrill) who had set out to debunk and disprove Pentecostal experience, but ended up experiencing it themselves and recounted their findings in a book.[79]

Dave also said that I should expect a mix of good and

---

[79] *They Speak with Other Tongues* (Chosen, 1999).

bad among charismatics and quoted a verse from Paul's writings: "Test everything. Hold on to the good. Avoid every kind of evil" (1 Thessalonians 5:21-22). Then he added, "My policy is to say to God, *Give me all you've got!* So if God wants me to speak in tongues, I'll sing like a tweety bird. I don't want to quench the Spirit at all. I want to experience everything God has for me."

This good advice gave me freedom to be a person of the Spirit whether or not I affiliated specifically with churches or organizations with a Pentecostal/charismatic label. Through the years I have found that the Spirit doesn't respect labels much, nor for that matter does the Spirit work on my timetables, produce miracles on demand, guide me to a blissfully happy and trouble-free life, or exempt me from the mistakes by which all humans seem to learn most of what they really know. But the Spirit of Jesus is real, active, powerful, present, and wonderful. Of this I am deeply confident.

Sometimes I'm talking with someone—offering pastoral counsel or just talking with someone I meet on a plane or in a restaurant—and a kind of wisdom or insight comes to me, wisdom that I can't explain or claim as my own. The person receiving this wisdom feels touched, perhaps almost frightened, as if somehow a deep secret of their deepest heart has been addressed. I feel like a conduit, a channel, a receiver who shares what I receive from beyond myself. Sometimes the opposite happens. I'm in a conversation with a brain overfull of opinions, but something stops me, tells me to hold my tongue, keep my opinions to myself.

Sometimes I know I should give away a sum of money to someone in need, and I know that not doing so would be missing a great opportunity to do good. I don't hear an audible voice, but I know I have been spoken to. Sometimes I'm praying, and I feel a confidence rise up in me that what I'm asking for will truly happen, and this confidence gives me courage to take risks I would not normally take. Sometimes I'm preaching or preparing to preach, and I feel a boldness wash over me like a brisk wave in the surf, and I know I'm being empowered by the Spirit of God.

I have my Pentecostal/charismatic friends to thank for teaching me to expect and welcome these experiences, and to understand their true source. They taught me to grow to the point where one of these "sometimes" is taking place, or is about to take place, or has just taken place nearly all the time.

If charismatics gave me my high school diploma in the ways of the Spirit, it was from Catholic contemplatives that I entered an undergraduate degree in the liberal arts of the Spirit.

I think it's safe to say that many charismatics believe that the Spirit of Jesus can be experienced *one step beyond the normal.* In other words, Jesus is always present, but one must take a step of faith to experience him. I think this is very often true; no one should expect the Holy Spirit to help them walk on water if they refuse to step out of the boat. So if you're sitting, you need to stand. If you're standing, you need to clap. If you're clapping, you need to dance. If you're dancing, you need to shout, and so on. This can be very exciting, and it can help one leave behind needless inhibitions and have a lot of good, clean Pentecostal fun "in the Spirit."

But it can also become a kind of treadmill where one has to work harder and harder to "work up" an experience of the Spirit. What was once exciting can become fatiguing. I have felt that fatigue at times and have sensed it in others (especially charismatic worship leaders, who are expected to deliver high-voltage Spirit experiences on a weekly basis to millions of "charismatic consumers" around the world—a tough assignment, cruel, really—for too many reasons to go into here).[80]

---

[80] I address this topic further in *Adventures in Missing the Point* (emergentYS, 2003), pp. 202-214.

Along the way I read and met Catholic contemplatives who helped me learn a lesson from this fatigue. They believed no less fervently than charismatics that the risen Jesus is present in Spirit and can be experienced. But rather than locating that experience one step *beyond* the normal, they located it in the very *center* of normalcy. Instead of jumping and shouting, they typically recommended sitting in silence, walking calmly, or in some other way relaxing and quieting one's soul.

One Catholic named Brother Lawrence called this realization "practicing God's presence." I began to experiment with this practice early in my spiritual journey. My goal was to learn to realize that Jesus (via the Holy Spirit) was my companion at every moment (even now as I sit on an airplane over the North Sea, returning home from the UK) and to open myself to the sense of being accompanied at all times. This practice became, I think, the single most important spiritual discipline in my life (along with regular church involvement and tithing). No wonder that one of the names Jesus gave to the Holy Spirit was Comforter or Companion, and no wonder the early apostles spoke of "walking in the Holy Spirit."

Through the years I have noticed that among the people most dedicated to missional activism, you find either (a) people burned out because of the difficulty of the task, or (b) people who have best learned to undergird their activism with contemplation, with quiet resting, with finding God in the center of normalcy— including the normalcy of struggle and hard work. Contemplation isn't only for passive, withdrawn people, but also for active, involved ones. A Catholic philosopher, Josef Pieper, has helped me a great deal in this regard.[81]

---

[81] Josef Pieper, *Happiness and Contemplation* (St. Augustine's Press, 1998). Thanks to Nick Howard for introducing me to Pieper.

Pieper, whose writings resonate with profound insight from Aristotle and Aquinas, seems at first glance the polar opposite of a charismatic. But an essential commonality brings them together: *joy*. Pentecostals and contemplatives both agree that joy and serenity are true hallmarks of spiritual vitality. Both understand that God, through the Holy Spirit, is with us, surrounding and filling us. They know that God is of all beings the most happy, so that in God's presence is fullness of joy.

Catholic contemplatives, it seems, have had an easier time with joy than non-charismatic Protestants, preoccupied as they tend to be with modern rationality, abstract theory, and depressing topics such as total depravity. Listen in this regard to what was said about Ignatius of Loyola by his disciples in the sixteenth century:

> We often saw how even the smallest things could make his spirit soar upwards to God, who even in the smallest things is the Greatest. At the sight of a little plant, a leaf, a flower or a fruit, an insignificant worm or a tiny animal, Ignatius could soar free above the heaven and reach through into things which lie beyond the senses.[82]

The charismatic/contemplative approach forms one spiritually in a way that enriches daily life. It can also prepare space in one's soul, I believe, for extraordinary experiences of God —"favors of God" as the medieval mystics would call them.

I can recount one such story from a few years back. I was walking in a park near my home, as I often do, savoring the colors and textures of the leaves, responding to the unique "personalities" of different kinds of trees that overarched the pathway, noticing the birds and butterflies as my fellow creatures. This is not at all unusual for me; this is how I "live and move and have my being"

---

[82] Quoted in Karen Armstrong, *A History of God* (Ballantine, 1993) p. 285.

in God—to walk as a creature among creatures in God's wonderful
creation, with my heart open to the Creator, practicing God's
presence with me.

But on this occasion, for a period of about 20 minutes,
I felt that every tree, every blade of grass, and every pool of water
become especially eloquent with God's grandeur. Somehow they
seemed to become transparent—or perhaps *translucent* is the better
word—because each thing in its particularity was still utterly visible
and unspeakably important: the movement of the grass in waves
swayed by the wind, the way the goldfinches perch just so on a purple
thistle plant. These specific, concrete things became translucent
in the sense that a powerful, indescribable, invisible light seemed
to shine through. The beauty of the creations around me, which I
am always careful to notice, seemed on this day to explode, seemed
to detonate, seemed to radiate with glory.

An ecstasy overcame me that I can't describe. It brings tears
to my eyes as I sit here and type. It was the exuberant joy of simply
seeing these masterpieces of God's creation…and knowing myself
to be among them. It was to be one of them, and to feel and know
that "we"—all of these creatures, molecules, and phenomena—were
together known and loved by God, who embraced us all into the
ultimate "We."

In this experience, as in many others, I felt a tinge of fear
along with the joy—fear that my physical being could not contain
the joy I felt, that I was about to split or explode or come undone.
I was simply silent, walking normally although a bit slower than
usual. But I could never have shouted loud enough or danced
outrageously enough to express the joy that I contained, that I
received, during that walk.[83] I cannot express it now.

---

[83] I realize that what I am describing here and what I describe in Chapter 9 are much the same.

Because of experiences like this over the years, I know that contemplatives and charismatics are talking about the same thing. Simply *seeing* things in a new light—this is what contemplation is. Pieper describes it better than anyone I have read. He refers to the diaries of poet Gerard Manley Hopkins in which common flowers and other natural phenomena are described with loving precision:

> What are the words of the message which has come to him from the heart of flourishing creation? We are not told. For this, too, is part of the nature of contemplation: that it cannot be communicated...This passionate precision of sensual description is a demonstration of the intensity with which the gaze of earthly contemplation respects the visible aspects of objects in this world, and tries to preserve them. It would also seem that veneration for concrete reality is kindled by the contemplative impulse which seeks the divine meaning underlying all beings. G. K. Chesterton, considering his life in retrospect, said that he had always had the almost mystical conviction of the miracle in all that exists, and of the rapture dwelling essentially within all experience. Within this statement lie three separate assertions: that everything holds and conceals at bottom a mark of its divine origin; that one who catches a glimpse of it "sees" that this and all things are "good" beyond all comprehension; and that, seeing this, he is happy. Here in sum is the whole doctrine of the contemplation of earthly creation (87-88).

This insight into true "having" intensifies, by the way, the tragedy of consumerism: one acquires more and more things without taking the time to ever see and *know* them, and thus one never truly enjoys them. One has without truly having. The consumer is right—there is pleasure to be had in good things, a sacred and almost unspeakable pleasure, but the consumer wrongly thinks that one finds this pleasure by having more and more possessions instead of by possessing them more truly through grateful contemplation. And here we are, living in an economy that perpetuates this tragedy. An outrage! A pity.

I believe this is why I have never been very attracted by money or wealth, and why it has always been a sincere pleasure for me to tithe and give away money. Since I was introduced to the practice of God's presence, which in turn led me into the contemplative way, I have nearly always felt so rich, so blessed, so sincerely full of "enough" that it was hard to get excited by an advertisement or sales pitch. What more could I need? (If any of my books begin to sell very well, of course, I will have new temptations in this regard, for which I request the prayers of my readers in advance.)

I feel (not every single moment, but often) that I am carrying around this hilarious secret: that I actually own all things, that all things are mine—because I am Christ's, and Christ is God's, and God allows me to have things in the way that matters most. Not by having them in my legal possession (which has many downsides, including upkeep and taxes!), but by having them in my spiritual possession by gratefully seeing them, gratefully knowing and cherishing them.[84] Those weren't legally *my* goldfinches or *my* sycamore trees or *my* rocky-bottomed streams in the park that day, but did anyone on earth possess them as fully as me that day? (Besides, how significant is legal possession in the long run anyway?)

Without this charismatic/contemplative posture, I can't imagine what my life would be. And I don't think that a generous orthodoxy can consider this path an optional pursuit. I believe it is on this robust, overflowing charismatic/contemplative pathway that one gains the joy and serenity to be generous. Listen to

---

[84] I Corinthians 3:21-23

Pieper once more:

> A man drinks at last after being extremely thirsty, and,
> feeling refreshment permeating his body, thinks and says:
> What a glorious thing is fresh water! Such a man, whether
> he knows it or not, has already taken a step toward that
> "seeing of the beloved object" which is contemplation. How
> splendid is water, a rose, a tree, an apple, a human face...
> Who among us has not suddenly looked into his child's
> face, in the midst of the toils and troubles of everyday life,
> and at that moment "seen" that everything which is good,
> is loved and lovable, loved by God! Such certainties all
> mean, at bottom, one and the same thing: that the world is
> plumb and sound; that everything comes to its appointed
> goal; that in spite of all appearances, underlying all things
> is—peace, salvation, *gloria*; that nothing and no one is lost;
> that "God holds in his hand the beginning, the middle,
> and the end of all that is" (84-85).

If one sees this, and knows this, and has this, how can one not walk
and leap and praise God?

CHAPTER 12

WHY I AM FUNDAMENTALIST/CALVINIST

Let's keep the "fun" in fundamentalist for this chapter, okay?

The term *fundamentalist* arose in the American church in the early twentieth century. It represented—this will surprise many—an attempt to reverse through tolerance some of the negative splintering effects of Protestantism described in Chapter 7.

As Protestants were frantically dividing into more and more fractious denominations, some wise people said, "Let's stop this splitting frenzy. Let's affirm the fundamentals of the faith, the essentials that bring us together. Then we can be tolerant of differences of opinion on the minor issues that currently divide us because we will have affirmed our common commitment to the essentials, the fundamentals." Five fundamentals were affirmed, to which we'll return later.

From this charitable impulse, however, came a movement that has been characterized (and no doubt caricatured) as "fightin' fundies." Now I'm not a fighter by disposition, which in part explains why I've never felt very much at home in fightin' fundamentalist circles. I am further distanced from fundamentalism by being philosophically post-foundationalist, but that's another story that others have told better than I can. What's more, the term *fundamentalist* has been hijacked by the media when referring to violent extremists, usually Islamic. So why bring up the term?

There is a sense in which we who are seeking a generous orthodoxy need some of the "fightin' fundy" spirit—carefully defined and in a measured dose. The wise preacher of Ecclesiastes might say, "There is a time for everything—a time to be laid-back and a time to be outraged; a time to be tolerant and a time to stand up and say, '*I'm not going to take this anymore.*'" The challenge for all fighters, of course, is to be sure that they find out what is now truly worth fighting against, and then to be sure that they have something that is truly worth fighting for.

For me the "fundamentals of the faith" boil down to those given by Jesus: *to love God and to love our neighbors*. These two fundamentals will not satisfy many fundamentalists, I fear. They'll insist on asking, "Which God are we supposed to love? The God of the Baptists or Brethren, the God of the Calvinists or Methodists, the God of the Muslims or Jews?" I'll respond by saying, "Whichever God Jesus was referring to." Then, still unsatisfied, they'll probably ask, "What exactly do you mean by love? And who is my neighbor?" At that point I'll probably mutter something incoherent about Samaritans and walk away.

Not because these questions are *unimportant*, but because they are so important. But that line of approach (definitions and schools of theology, arguments and delineations and lines of reasoning) won't bring us to good answers.

No, Jesus has taught us that the way to know what God is like is not by determining our philosophical boundary conditions/definitions/delineations before departing, but rather the way to know is by embarking on an adventure of faith, hope, and love, even if you don't know where your path will lead (think of Abraham, Hebrews 11:8). The way to know God is by following Jesus on that adventure. One doesn't learn what God is like in a library or pew and then begin to love God in real life. One begins to love God and others in real life. In the process one learns what God is like—and one might be driven to the library and pew to learn more. Anyone who doesn't embark on the adventure of love doesn't know God at all, whatever he can say or define or delineate, for God is love.[85]

So with those fundamentals of love, what is worth fighting against and for? So much. But unfortunately, so much of what we're currently fighting against ("we" meaning the church in America for starters) isn't the real enemy, and so much of what we're fighting for isn't the real prize. Largely we're fighting to get something back—a lost status as the civil religion of the West, control (political, too often) over things that are out of our control, a privileged position as the favored religion of the Empire, protection of the middle class from the lower and upper classes, and so on. These are futile fights.

We're also focused on fighting symptoms like abortion, promiscuity (hetero or homosexual), divorce, and profanity. We might add terrorism to the list. But these are not the disease. These are in many ways the symptoms of the very disease that we inadvertently tend to support, aid and abet, defend, protect, baptize, and fight for—a system sick with consumerism, greed, fear, violence, and misplaced faith (in the power of the Economy and the State and its Weapons).

Closely related to a generous fundamentalism is the subject of Calvinism. There are many forms of fundamentalism (in the broad, journalistic sense of the word)—Baptist, Lutheran, Pentecostal. In fact, probably any movement can have a

---

[85] See 1 John 4:7-12 for more details on this kind of fundamentalism.

fundamentalist pole: I know I've met a fundamentalist liberal or
two through the years. But the fundamentalist pole of Calvinism
has exerted an especially strong influence in my life, in the
religious life of America, and indeed across the world.

Calvinism as practiced today has less to do with John Calvin
(1509-1564), the great Swiss reformer, than it has to do with some
of Calvin's successors a hundred years later. It is usually associated
with an understanding or misunderstanding of predestination.
Although scholarly understandings of predestination are finely
nuanced, the "on the street" version generally asserts that God is
the chess player, and we are the pieces, and we go where we are
moved. If God wants to take us off the chessboard and put us in
the oven, there we will go, and there's nothing we can do about it.
If God wants us to be cool in heaven forever, we will, and again,
there's nothing we can do about it.

This view of reality folds much (not all) of today's
Calvinism into a broader way of thinking called Determinism,
which says that ultimately, our freedom is an illusion, and that
we're just puppets of one sort or another. (A teenager recently
described his view of God in innocently deterministic terms: God
is the video game creator and player, and we're characters in a
game God plays for personal entertainment. Being "good" means
not resenting that we're jerked around in this way.) Whether
it's God who makes us puppets, or whether it is genes, physics,
socioeconomics, or psychosexual aggression, it doesn't matter
much to me. I have little time for determinism. If it's true, then
I can't help but not believe it, because after all, I have no choice.
(And if you believe it, ditto.)[86]

---

[86] Chesterton's orthodoxy was similarly impatient with determinism, especially scientific
determinism: "The Catholic church believed that man and God both had a sort of spiritual
freedom. Calvinism took away the freedom from man, but left it to God. Scientific materialism
binds the Creator Himself; it chains up God as the Apocalypse chained the devil. It leaves
nothing free in the universe" (*Orthodoxy*, 137).

Again I think Calvin's actual interest in determinism is overrated; he wasn't creating it but rather was reflecting a widely held belief that went back at least to Augustine. But after Calvin's death, I think a terrible convergence occurred, something like the Perfect Storm, when the massive low-pressure system of theistic determinism (Calvin-the-next-generation via Beza & Co.) synergized with the strengthening hurricane of mechanical determinism (Sir Isaac Newton) and then drew strength from the high-pressure system of rationalistic philosophy (Descartes and others). The perfect storm produced a whole new landscape where mechanisms were seen as the ultimate reality, and where God was promoted to chief engineer, controlling the whole machine. I do not believe in this modern mechanistic God or this closed, mechanistic universe. I do not believe that this universe is a movie that's already "in the can," having been "produced and shot" already in God's mind, leaving us with the illusion that it's all real and actually happening. I find it hard to imagine worshiping or loving a deterministic, machine-operator God.[87]

Yet I have great respect and love for the Reformed churches, which trace their lineage back to Calvin. Many Reformed Christians today, like me, value Calvin but not determinism. These Reformed Christians have been an inspiration to me since my late teenage years. When I was growing up, there was anti-intellectualism rampant in Evangelical Christianity. At that time it was mostly in the Reformed churches (Presbyterian, Christian Reformed, etc.) that one found much intellectual vigor and life of the mind. Reformed writers and speakers like Francis Schaeffer, R. C. Sproul, Ravi Zacharias, Os Guinness, J. I. Packer, and others gave me a challenge and permission to think, and, forever

---

[87] This in no way discounts the deep love many strict Christian determinists have for God. My experience with sweet and kind Christian determinists tells me this: they are willing to accept what is to me the most unflattering portrait that can be painted of God from the Bible and still love that God. I admire their love, even if I don't believe their portrait is flattering to its Subject.

grateful, I made use of that permission.

In terms of intellectual rigor, I believe that Reformed Christianity is the highest expression of modern Christianity, which is a sincere compliment—and a gentle warning, too. If we are moving beyond modernity in general, then the forms of Christianity that have most successfully adapted themselves to the assumptions and thought patterns of modernity are in the most trouble. For this reason, I suspect that Reformed Christianity is in for a major identity crisis in the next few decades, with some of its number entrenched in modernity, and with others—resourced by the robust faith and thought of their forebears—helping lead the way for life, thought, and ministry in the emerging culture.

I believe Reformed Christianity has in its own trunk at least three of the resources needed to forge a new and more generous, nonmechanistic identity. (It will find other needed resources by consulting fellow Christians, including those it has tended to snub and critique, among them Anabaptists, Pentecostals, and Roman Catholics.) First, it has the bold example of the young Calvin (which is often overshadowed by the teachings and temperament of the older Calvin). Consider this.

Calvin became a pastor when he was 18, and he had written his first edition of the entire *Institutes of the Christian Religion* by the age of 25. This young man must have sensed that, with the Protestant rejection of the Catholic establishment, a dangerous vacuum existed. What would be needed to replace the role of a huge and often corrupt medieval establishment? Not another huge and corrupt establishment, but instead a lean and pure intellectual system: a logically rigorous system of doctrine that would effectively reindoctrinate Catholics (and perhaps Lutherans?) while indoctrinating the next generation of young Calvinists. Seeing the need, Calvin stepped in and produced it in six short years, between the ages of 19 and 25.

What would a brilliant, bold young Calvin do today, I wonder? Now we have a different problem. We have no shortage of establishments (including Reformed ones) and no shortage of lean and mean doctrinal systems. Would a young Calvin today correctly identify a completely different need and boldly meet it with similar skill and passion? I believe he would.

So I suppose there are two ways for Reformed Christians to honor Calvin and the other Reformers down the road:

1. *To faithfully defend and promote their post-medieval formulations through all time.* Reformed theologian Dr. John Franke calls this "the conservative distortion of so closely equating Reformed theology with the events, creeds, and confessions of the sixteenth and seventeenth centuries as to virtually eliminate, in practice if not in theory, the reforming principle of the tradition, thus betraying a central commitment of its formal character." [88]

2. *To follow their example in seeking to construct formulations of faith that are as fitting to our postmodern times as theirs were to their post-medieval times.* [89] This is the path a new generation of Reformed/Reforming Christians will take.

The courageous, bold, innovative example of the young Calvin is the first great resource that the Reformed churches have, a resource augmented by other often underappreciated examples, such as that of Martin Bucer, who among his other virtuous deeds hid and protected Anabaptists rather than executing them (see Chapter 13).

---

[88] Franke's excellent essay *Reforming Theology: Toward a Postmodern Reformed Dogmatics* originally appeared in Westminster Theological Journal, 65 (2003), 1-26. It is also available at www.emergentvillage.com.

[89] These ideas were first expressed in a conversation in *Books and Culture* in 2002. You can read the whole conversation at www.christianitytoday.com.

Beyond the examples of Calvin and his fellows, Reformed Christians also have one of the slogans of the Reformation in their trunk—a priceless asset in these times: *semper reformanda,* or *always reforming.* Strictly speaking then, *Reformed Christian* is a misnomer; *reforming Christian* would be more accurate, as John Franke of Biblical Seminary writes:

> Reformed theology is always reforming according to the Word of God in order to bear witness to the eternal truth of the gospel in the context of an ever-changing world characterized by a variety of cultural settings: *theologia reformata et semper reformanda*...Accordingly, the process of reformation from the Reformed perspective is not, and never can be, something completed once and for all and appealed to in perpetuity as the "truly Reformed" position. In the words of Jürgen Moltmann, reformation is not "a one time act to which a confessionalist could appeal and upon whose events a traditionalist could rest."[90]

The idea of continual reformation is essential for any understanding of a generous orthodoxy. To illustrate, a few years ago I came up with a simple book idea that turned into *The Church in Emerging Culture: Five Views.*[91] The idea for the book grew out of this simple matrix:

---

[90] See Franke's essay *Reforming Theology: Toward a Postmodern Reformed Dogmatics* at www.emergentvillage.com.

[91] EmergentYS/Zondervan, 2003.

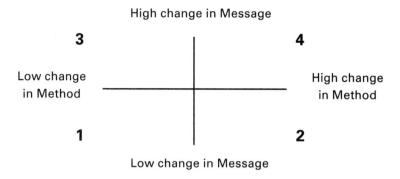

Method in the matrix means media, techniques, tools, forms, structures—everything from seeker-sensitive services to televangelism to ancient liturgy to denominations to nondenominations to hymnody to sermon styles to candles to the lectionary. *Message* means what is communicated through these tools or media.

The matrix makes a number of questionable assumptions, including whether method/form/medium and message/content/ substance can actually be separated. But the belief that they can be separated is so widespread among modern Christians that we (Len Sweet and our friends at emergentYS) felt the matrix still worked to get people thinking, even if that thinking eventually deconstructs the original assumptions. We found five representatives to speak to each of these quadrants (with two in Quadrant 1, one representative holding the methodology and message at their level of development in the Patristic period, and the other in the early Reformation period).

To the surprise of some of my friends, I chose to represent Quadrant 4 (they expected I'd choose Quadrant 2), believing that our message and methodology have changed, do change, and must change if we are faithful to the ongoing and unchanging mission of Jesus Christ. In other words, I believe that we must be *always reforming*, not because we've got it wrong and we're closer and closer to finally "getting it right," but because our mission is ongoing and our context is dynamic. From this viewpoint "getting it right" is beside the point; the point is "being and doing good" as followers of Jesus in our unique time and place, fitting in with the ongoing story of God's saving love for planet Earth.

In my chapter, I explained it like this: If Jesus fulfills his vocation and succeeds in his earthly mission, the world is forever different. We must never underestimate or forget what Jesus did, but neither can we stop there, because Jesus sent us into the world to continue his mission, affirming (he said this, not I) that he was leaving even greater works to his followers (John 14:12). So Jesus, by succeeding in his mission, creates a new situation for the apostles to move into. He tells them to do something that he had never done before—to leave Judea and Samaria and go into "all the world."

When they do this, they are confronted with a new problem: should they let Gentiles into this new Way? If they do, another problem arises—the problem that preoccupies Paul in his epistles: how can we bring these two deeply separated and bitterly distrustful communities (Jews and Gentiles) into one community of love in Christ? Paul and his peers succeed, and they do so to such a degree that the Way of Christ spreads like wildfire among Gentiles. Which creates new problems: would Christianity become a subset of Greek philosophy? Would the Roman Empire see this new, growing movement as a threat and seek to wipe it out? If the Roman Empire decides to legitimize the new movement, what new problems would that create?

Each of these new challenges and opportunities requires Christian leaders to create new forms, new methods, new structures—and it requires them to find new content, new ideas, new truths, new meaning to bring to bear on the new challenges.

These new messages are not incompatible with the gospel of the kingdom Jesus taught. No, they are inherent in it, but previously undiscovered, unexpressed, perhaps unimagined. Jesus' original message was pregnant with all that they would need, but there was much, Jesus said, that they could not yet bear to hear, and so Jesus would send the Spirit of truth to guide them into all truth as they needed it and were ready to bear it.

The new dimensions of the message are examples of the Spirit of truth doing what Jesus promised he would do: continuing to guide them into new, previously unknown truth, truth that had been hidden in Christ all along, but had not yet been bearable, needed, seen, or discovered. I can't see church history in any other way, except this: *semper reformanda*, continually being led and taught and guided by the Spirit into new truth. Again, Franke says it well:

> The expression of Christian thought has taken shape and has been revised in the context of numerous social and historical settings. It has also developed in the process of navigating a number of significant cultural transitions: from an initially Hebraic setting to the Hellenistic world; from the thought-forms of Greco-Roman culture to those of Franco-Germanic; from the world of medieval feudalism to the Renaissance; from the Renaissance to the Enlightenment; and from the developed world to the third world. Currently, theology is grappling with the challenges raised by the transition from a modern to a postmodern cultural milieu. Throughout this ongoing history Christian theology has been shaped by the thought forms and conceptual tools of numerous cultural settings and has shown itself to be remarkably adaptable in its task of assisting the church in extending and establishing the message of the gospel in a wide variety of contexts. At the same time, theological history also provides numerous

examples of the inappropriate accommodation of Christian faith to various ideologies and cultural norms. This checkered past confirms the vitality of Christian theology while warning of the dangers of too closely associating it with any particular form of cultural expression (*Reforming Theology* at www.emergentvillage.com).

Reformed Christians have a third resource hidden in their trunk, a resource that all fundamentalists share: a legacy of horrible mistakes, misjudgments, and even atrocities. There was a strange confidence and certainty that Calvin's system gave his followers, and that confident certainty, while comforting and productive, also proved dangerous at times. It allowed Calvin himself to oversee the execution of fellow Christians for disagreeing with his system, playing the same brutal power and coercion games that Protestants protested (and still protest) among Catholics. That confidence also allowed many early Calvinists who settled America to assume that they were "elected" by God through "manifest destiny" to steal the lands of the Native Peoples. It allowed some of the settlers of the 13 colonies to assume that God had given the African races to them for use as slaves. It helped their descendants to continue an ethic of racial superiority long after slavery ended. Similarly, it allowed the settlers in South Africa to create and defend apartheid. There's so much more we could say, but the point is made: Calvinist confidence energized them to do much good and much otherwise.

If Reformed Christians can truly be "always reforming," learning from these tragic mistakes will augment their legacy of confidence with a new legacy of repentance and humility. From that new legacy, a kinder, gentler Calvinism will yield rich resources for a more generous orthodoxy for years to come.[92]

But what of Reformed distinctives? Many Calvinist Christians have used a clever acrostic to summarize their unique doctrinal emphases: TULIP, which stands for total depravity, unconditional election, limited atonement, irresistible grace, and perseverance of the saints. Believing as I do that doctrinal distinctives are a lot like cigarettes, the use of which often leads to a hard-to-break Protestant habit that is hazardous to spiritual health (and that makes the breath smell bad), I'd propose a slight revision to the old acrostic for Reforming Reformed Christians:[93]

> **T = Triune Love**: For many zealous Reformed folk, the metaphor of God as judge seems to predominate over all other metaphors, and the divine attribute of sovereign will is favored over all other attributes so that God's relation to creation is seen primarily in terms of legal prosecution (as judge) and absolute control (as naked will). If, however, we allow a different metaphor—of community—to become more prominent in our thinking (speaking of the Divine Community of Father, Son, and Spirit), then the attribute of love emerges as a more primal essence of God's being. (After all, before creation God had no evil to judge and nothing to control, yet God existed without boredom, according to our creeds, in an eternal, dynamic, glorious and holy fellowship of love.)
>
> **U = Unselfish Election**: As we saw in Chapter 5, the great missiologist Lesslie Newbigin claimed that the most stubborn heresy in the history of monotheism is the belief that God chooses people for exclusive privilege,

---

[92] Richard J. Mouw of Fuller Seminary is a sage leader pioneering a "kinder, gentler Calvinism" that seeks to move beyond the problems addressed here. See his upcoming Zondervan release, *Calvinism and the Las Vegas Airport: Making Connections in Today's World*, where he writes, "I have learned so much from other Christian traditions that I have come to think of myself as an *eclectic* Calvinist. I draw freely from other traditions in fleshing out my theology. I do not see my Calvinism as locking me into a closed system of thought that must resist at all costs any outside theological influences" (Chapter 11).

[93] To clarify: my complaint is not with doctrine (the essential teaching of the church) nor with doctrinal distinctives (specific teachings that various denominations hold which make them distinct from other groups), but with an *overemphasis* on (or *preoccupation* with) doctrinal distinctives.

not for missional responsibility. A Reforming Reformed tradition would grasp this powerful insight and preserve the Reformed emphasis on election—but not the exclusive election that, like a popular credit card, offers elite privileges to possessors. Rather a Reforming Reformed faith would see election as a gift that is given to some for the benefit of all others. To be chosen means to be "blessed to be a blessing," to be healed to heal, to be chosen to serve, to be enriched to enrich, to be taught to teach. This reformation in the Reformed understanding of election would be truly revolutionary and, I think, liberating.

L = Limitless Reconciliation: Instead of speculating on the limited scope of legal atonement (as the original "L" in the acrostic did), a Reforming Reformed faith would concentrate on the *missio dei* of relational reconciliation, a reconciliation that never isolates divine from human relational healing, and therefore always prays to be forgiven by God *as we forgive others*, that always loves God *and neighbor*, and that never, ever asks the question, "Who is my neighbor?" to contract the scope of love. Because God's heart moves God to come to us in Christ, as neighbor to all, and so moves us to become peace ambassadors of Christ to all.

I = Inspiring Grace: Rather than picturing God's grace as a dominating, almost mechanistic force that cannot be resisted, a Reforming Reformed faith would view God's grace as a passionate, powerful, personal desire to shower the beloved with healing and joy and every good thing. Having received this grace freely and fully, the Reforming Christian would thus be inspired by grace to freely extend that grace to others in an overflow of good works, yielding a truly generous orthodoxy.

P = Passionate, Persistent Saints: With firm conviction that the gospel is a story of triune love, unselfish election, limitless reconciliation, and inspiring grace, Reforming Christians would be indefatigable in their attempts to live and share the gospel, resilient after failure, persevering in adversity, persistent over centuries and across generations. Rather than a grim endurance, they would have an unquenchable hope, confident that God will never fail to fulfill a promise, and be passionate to join God in expressing saving love for our world until every promise comes true.

Reforming in this way, the Reformed faith of today would be both revolutionized and revolutionary, a nightmare to some, a dream for others. Be that as it may, I would hope that these are already in fact the true colors of the best of the Reformed tradition.

Fundamentalists (whose circle overlaps with the Reformed circle) could, if they wanted to, similarly reform their list of five fundamentals. Their five fundamentals (alas, with no acrostic to make them memorable) were chosen largely because they represented battle lines with theological liberals in the nineteenth and early twentieth centuries: the virgin birth, the inerrancy and verbal plenary inspiration of the Bible, penal substitutionary atonement, the bodily resurrection of Jesus, and the imminent return of Jesus. Of the five, only two (virgin birth and bodily resurrection) were rooted in the creeds (three if you include the return of Jesus, but the word *imminent* is not an element of the creeds). So the five taken together were fundamental *not* for the general practice of the Christian faith, but rather for resisting modern liberalism. Now that the Goliath of modern liberalism has shrunk to a "mini-me" of its original size, perhaps fundamentalists can launch a new project: to discern which elements truly are fundamental or essential for the practice of vibrant Christian faith—beyond defending against (or reacting to) modern liberalism. I probably won't be asked for help in this project (if it is ever launched), but if I were, you can guess what my answer would be.

I should add briefly that fundamentalists and Calvinists share two traits that I hope will be dropped by any who wish to participate in a generous orthodoxy. The first is a fondness for reductionism, epitomized by their love for the Latin word *sola* (only), seen in what are often called Reformation mottoes: sola Scriptura, sola fide, sola TULIP, sola the five fundamentals, etc. The belief that truth is best understood by reducing it to a few fundamentals or a single "sola" insight is, to me, at least questionable if not downright dangerous. Isn't truth often best understood in a conversation, a dialectic (or trialectic), or a dynamic tension? Isn't it subverted by a tendency to "sola-ize"? It wasn't just a rock singer back in the 1970s who crooned "one is the loneliest number." The wise preacher of Ecclesiastes said two are better than one, and three better still. Reductionism isn't all it's cracked up to be.[94]

Finally, harsh rhetoric has too often characterized Calvinists in particular and fundamentalists in general. Calvin himself lacked the bitter, bullying, and often profane polemics of Luther (who fortunately had virtues even more robust than these vices). But Calvin's descendants (among others) sometimes seem to believe they have been granted an exemption from 1 Corinthians 13 or Ephesians 4 or Colossians 3 in the defense of Calvinist theology. The generous or ungenerous way they critique this chapter (which no doubt deserves critique) will illustrate to what degree they will uphold this trait or relax it—that word *relax* perhaps being the best word on which to end a fun-filled chapter like this.

---

[94] Someone might accuse Jesus of being reductionistic when he boils down the 10 (or however many) commandments to the two of loving God and neighbor. (In Galatians 5:14, Paul goes even further, reducing all the commandments to one: love.) However, Jesus' new commandment of love—as anyone who practices it knows—is far more expansive and demanding than any list, no matter how long. So this is actually a deepening and expansion of, not a reduction of, the Law.

CHAPTER 13

WHY I AM (ANA)BAPTIST/ANGLICAN

How do you know if something is true? According to the traditions of science, you pursue a three-phase protocol. First, you perform an experiment. (Let's call this the *practice* or *experimental* phase.) Second, you observe the results, collect the data, and make observations. (Let's call this the *experience* or *observation* phase.) Then you present your practice and experience to the community of scientists for verification or falsification. Will the same practice yield the same experience time after time for other truth seekers? (Let's call this the *discernment* or *validation* phase.)[95]

Something similar happens, I think, in the world of spirituality. First, you engage in spiritual *practices* like prayer, Bible reading, forgiveness, and service. Then you see what happens; you remain open to *experience*. Finally, you report your experience to others in the field of spirituality for their *discernment*, to see if they confirm your findings or not.

Over the last few decades I have undertaken this kind

---

[95] For more on this process see Ken Wilber, *The Marriage of Sense and Soul: Integrating Science and Religion* (New York: Broadway Books, 1998), chapters 11-12.

of three-step process in regard to the Anabaptist and Anglican approaches to Christian faith. I came along, not as a member of either tradition, but as someone ready to test their practices and reported experiences, to see if my experience would validate theirs. Before I share my findings, I need to explain a good bit of church history and theology, beginning with Anabaptism.

If Lutheran describes the followers of Luther, and Reformed the followers of Calvin, Anabaptist describes the more radical members of the Reformation who were often hated, regularly persecuted, and sometimes killed by both Lutherans and the Reformed.

Many people are unfamiliar with the term *Anabaptist*, although they will have heard of the Amish, the Mennonite Brethren, or perhaps the Church of the Brethren, all of whom are Anabaptists. More people are familiar with the term *Baptist* than *Anabaptist*, and may wonder what the difference is. Here in the United States, it's probably "Southern Baptists" they hear about most, partly because Southern Baptists comprise the largest Protestant denomination in the country, and partly because several colorful Southern Baptists have a way of getting on the TV evening news pretty often, though seldom in a positive light (which doesn't seem to bother them at all).

Many Baptists in the United States and the United Kingdom trace their heritage to Smith and Helwys, two Separatist English pastors who did "the Protestant thing" in regard to both Anglicanism and Congregationalism (see Chapter 7) in about 1625. This self-understanding identifies Baptists as a twig of the Separatist branch, which is itself an offshoot of the Protestant limb, which diverged from the Roman Catholic trunk of the Christian tree in the early 1500s. Other Baptists in these English-speaking countries tell quite a different story about their origins.

But in Europe, in contrast to most Anglo-American understandings of Baptist heritage, non-English speaking Baptists generally see themselves as part of the Anabaptist movement. *Ana* means "again," so Anabaptists, the name would suggest, not only baptize, but they "baptize again." If you're not confused yet, keep reading, because nearly all Christians baptize (the Salvation Army doesn't, and neither do Quakers), even though they aren't all called Baptists. And Anabaptists don't always baptize *again*; nowadays once—after infancy—is generally enough.

Consider this table:

	A. Baptize as a Saving Act	B. Baptize as a Symbolic Act
X. Baptize adults (or believers)	I	3
Y. Baptize infants (or children of believers)	2	4

Column A sees baptism as an essential act, a saving act. It is part of what makes a person a Christian, and without it one is not a real Christian. Column B sees baptism as an important but nonessential act, symbolic of what is essential—a sincere belief and commitment in the heart, mind, and soul of the individual. Row X practices baptism for people old enough to believe and make a personal commitment—adults and older children—while Row Y practices baptism for infants, the children of people old enough to believe and make a personal commitment. (This matrix does not take into account various modes of baptism, such as full immersion, infusion or pouring, or sprinkling. The amount of water used is less significant here than the purpose of using the water.)

This matrix yields four possible positions on baptism. In Quadrant I (the rarest position among Christians today), baptism is a saving act without which one is not a Christian, and it is reserved for of-age believers only. Various groups called "The Churches of Christ" have held to this view, along with some Pentecostals, although many in these circles are moving quietly toward Quadrant 3. For Quadrant 2, baptism is a saving act, but it is typically applied to the infant children of believers. The Roman Catholics, Greek Orthodox, and some Anglicans (Episcopalians), Lutherans, and Methodists hold to this view, believing that in baptism a child is really and truly changed in their being or nature from one kind of person (non-Christian) to another (Christian).

In Quadrant 4, baptism is practiced for the children of believers, but it is seen as symbolic rather than as an essential saving act. Presbyterians and some Anglicans, Lutherans, and Methodists hold to this view. (Many of the latter seem to allow for both Quadrant 2 or 4 understandings.) Baptism in Quadrant 4 symbolizes the faith and commitment of the parents to raise their children in the Christian community, or it symbolizes the commitment of the community itself to raise the child in the faith, or it symbolizes the commitment of God to bring this child into active Christian faith as she or he matures, or some combination of the above.

In Quadrant 3, only people who have made personal commitments to believe in and follow Christ are baptized. This is seen as a decision an individual can make for himself or herself; neither his parents nor her community can presume to make any meaningful commitment on behalf of the individual.

My understanding is that the very early church held to Quadrants 3 or 4, but gradually migrated to Quadrant 2. Such a migration makes sense (whether it was right or wrong). In the early days everyone who became a Christian did so by personal choice. Over time, as more and more Christian couples had children and raised them in the faith (and as fewer and fewer of them invited non-Christians to become Christians), most new Christians in the world would be born into Christian families. And when Christianity became the dominant religion of the Roman Empire, it became harder and harder for a child *not* to be identified as a Christian as he or she grew up, since simply being in the Empire seemed to identify one as a Christian. So baptism gradually and naturally became a celebration of another citizen's birth in the increasingly Christianized empire.

In the fifteenth and sixteenth centuries, many looked around Europe and realized that virtually everyone thought of themselves as Christian, whatever their moral character, whatever their way of life, whatever their beliefs and commitments or lack thereof. Some of them became disillusioned with this nominal (in name only) or notional (in opinion only) Quadrant 2-approach to Christianity. They felt that being a Christian was radical and personal, not merely nominal or notional. They became convinced that being born and baptized in a so-called Christian environment no more made one a bona fide Christian than being born in a so-called stable would make one a bona fide horse. Many of them experienced powerful reinvigorations of faith (or perhaps "invigorations" would be a better term) that made them doubt whether they had ever been a real Christian before at all, in spite of their Quadrant 2 (or 4) baptism and residency in a so-called Christian environment.

As an expression of these changing understandings, many of them were baptized *again*—hence the name Anabaptist. Infant baptism didn't count for them anymore, so they were baptized *again* as believing adults, their baptism serving as a sign or symbol of their faith. But consider: would these Quadrant 3 people and their descendants have their children baptized in infancy? *No.* So the children of Anabaptists would *not* be baptized twice, once at infancy and again in adulthood: they would not be baptized at all unless they chose to be baptized as an expression of individual and personal faith and commitment when they reached an age where they could make their own personal decision—which would in general only happen once. So future Anabaptists wouldn't baptize *again*, in spite of their name.

For reasons you will understand from Chapter 7, I am not so interested in identifying myself as a super-Protestant who finally "has it right" about baptism. I'm less interested in how and when you were baptized than I am in why and whether you live the meaning of your baptism, whenever it happened and however much water was used to do it. But I am interested, very interested, in identifying with the Anabaptist movement that arose in the sixteenth century, the original move from Quadrant 2 to 3. Why? Seven main reasons come to mind, presented here in no order of importance.

Anabaptists emphasize personal commitment.

Anabaptists understand that although people may be born into a Christian family or culture, no one is born an automatic Christian. One becomes a Christian through an event, process, or both, in which one identifies with Jesus, his mission, and his followers. (Perhaps some readers will feel this insight applies to them very personally, right at this moment, and they would like to make this personal commitment.)

Anabaptists see the Christian faith primarily as a way of life.

While so much of contemporary Christianity is nominal (affiliating with the name of Jesus Christ but demonstrating little fruit) or notional (holding—even passionately—to notions, doctrines, or propositions about Christ, but again, demonstrating little fruit), Anabaptists have long understood that what really counts is a fruitful way of life. This is one reason why Anabaptists have been underrepresented in the academy and have relatively few major theological voices there: they would rather express themselves in care for the poor, the land, and the community than in notional arguments.[96]

Anabaptists saw the same scholastic dryness in late Medieval Catholicism that other Protestants saw. But while some other Protestants, in a kind of lateral conversion, replaced Catholic scholasticism with a new Protestant scholasticism of their own, Anabaptists steered a more radical route, seeing the whole scholastic approach itself as the problem. Anabaptists wanted a forward conversion into a different approach to Christian faith entirely: faith as a way of life in community.

Anabaptists have taken a radical posture in relation to modernity.

While an Amish man in plain clothing or a Mennonite mother capped with a prayer bonnet may appear the epitome of conformity in relation to their group, they are better seen as the epitome of nonconformity in regards to the larger culture. Imagine an Amish man wearing a Nike swoosh on his straw hat or an Izod alligator under his suspenders; the image makes the point better than anything I could say. The Anabaptists have known all along (probably more viscerally than conceptually) that modernity was a misdirected project, and although there are, to be sure, many downsides to their stance, they have represented a needed and radical counterculture, quietly proclaiming through their

---

[96] For a deeper explanation of this tendency by a notable exception to it, see William James McClendon, *Systematic Theology* (Abingdon, 1988, 1994, 2000). See also Michael King's work through Pandora Press (www.pandorapressus.com).

nonconformist ways that the land is important, community is important, the extended family is important, and that speed, style, technology, convenience, efficiency, and mechanization are not all-important, *contra* modernity.[97] No wonder Anabaptists are also called the Radical Reformation.

Anabaptists have lived and worked in the margins.

Believing as I do that modernity is slowly but surely being replaced by a new postmodern ethos—and believing that in this postmodern milieu Christians will have neither the dominating position they had through the Middle Ages nor the privileged position they had during much of modernity—I believe we have a lot to learn at this juncture from the Anabaptists, who were willingly marginalized throughout modernity. Because they rejected the idea of the state church that the early Reformers accepted, they were welcome in neither Catholic nor Protestant countries and were for some years bitterly persecuted by Protestants in Northern Europe and Catholics in Southern. As outsiders they learned to function at the margins, and they learned that the gospel functions there just as well as or better than at the centers of power, prestige, wealth, and control. Rather than lamenting that "Christendom" is over, Anabaptists have always felt, "Good riddance!" Ever since Constantine, they believe, the church has been perverted by copulation with the Empire and its seductions.

Anabaptists have made Jesus Christ central.

While some Protestants seem to let Jesus be Savior, but promote Paul to lord and teacher, Anabaptists have always interpreted Paul through Jesus, and not the reverse.[98] For them the Sermon on the Mount and the other words of Jesus represent the greatest

---

[97] A Mennonite friend of mine said, "We managed to secede from modernity until the 1960s. Then we feared we were missing something, so we jumped in with both feet. It took us about 30 years to realize that was a big mistake."

treasure in the world. Jesus' teachings have been their standard. And although they have failed in living them—as we all have—at least they've let their failure be obvious by letting the message of Christ dwell richly in their hearts.

Anabaptists seek to practice peace.

As a natural consequence of centering on Jesus' teachings, Anabaptists have consistently refused to kill their enemies.[99] Enemies should be loved and forgiven, they have taught, not killed; followers of Christ should turn the other cheek and suffer, not retaliate. This commitment has meant that they respond to the military draft as conscientious objectors, which has earned them the nickname "The Peace Churches." It has also disposed them to be against capital punishment.

While a generous orthodoxy does not assume that everyone will become a strict pacifist, it does assume that every follower of Christ will at least be a pacifist sympathizer and will agree that if pacifism is not required for all followers of Christ just yet, *it should be as soon as possible*. In other words, people holding to the vision of Jesus Christ—the kingdom of God—never believe that the ways of violence lead to peace. For them, there is no way to peace, but rather peace itself is the way to life in God's kingdom. (This is why an argument that brands pacifism as *impractical* makes little sense to Anabaptists. *Practicality* used in this way is a means of preserving the status quo, and Anabaptists believe the kingdom of God is not the status quo. For them, the only *practical* way to receive the kingdom of God is to live in peace.)[100]

---

[98] In no way does this statement imply a disregard on my part—or Anabaptists'—for Paul. Rather it locates Paul as a follower of Jesus, not his reinterpreter.

[99] This commitment to peace was no doubt intensified by the ugly anti-Anabaptist violence by Catholics and Protestants alike at the time of the Reformation, along with the violence by some early Radical Reformers (e.g., the Peasants' Revolt). Those who suffer persecution when they are outcasts sometimes become those who inflict it when they are in power, but this has not been the case with the Peace Churches, which have generally avoided both violence and dominating power.

Anabaptists have practiced "community in creation."

Community has become a buzzword in the church in recent years. Overbusy individuals hope they can cram it into their overstuffed schedules like their membership to a health and fitness club (which they never have time to use). Churches hope they can conjure it with candles, programs, or training videos. Anabaptists know that community is far more costly than that: one cannot add it to anything, rather one must begin with it in order to enter it, practice it, and preserve it. They realize that community involves proximity, and that proximity involves land, and that our ties to one another can never be separated from our ties to the land, the watershed, the local economy in which we live. They have an instinct about the deep ties between community and sexuality, community and freedom, community and economics. I suspect that Anabaptists know more than they know that they know in this regard, and I hope we all can learn from them before they forget.[101]

Anabaptists face problems, too. The cost of maintaining the values I have celebrated above is that Anabapists have tended (until recent years) to isolate from, rather than penetrate, culture. Their pacifism means that they can be uneasy welcoming in people who work for the military, or even the police, or government, or contractors who work indirectly for the military. This uneasiness has worked against creating a truly open, accepting community in many cases. And when Anabaptists do venture out of their previous isolation, they face being co-opted by fundamentalists, liberals,

---

[100] This is not the place for a lengthy debate about pacifism versus "just war" theory, a debate that I am unqualified and unprepared to engage. I would only raise this question: has any war ever yet been cancelled because of "just war" theory? See my "Sermon for President Bush" at www.anewkindofchristian.com.

[101] Wendell Berry, a member of a Baptist church, seems to understand and exemplify the Anabaptist ethos as well as anyone I've read. His *Sex, Economy, Freedom, and Community* (Pantheon, 1994) strikes me as a masterpiece, perhaps among the most provocative books written in the last 50 years.

and Evangelicals, so that their unique values are diluted. There are no easy solutions to these problems.

However they deal with these problems, what excites me most is what can happen when Anabaptists are given a place at the table (a place they would hardly presume to take, so it must be offered them; they must be invited)—the table where post-liberals and post-evangelicals and catholic Catholics and generously orthodox Orthodox gather to share the treasures of their heritages. The exchange of treasures around that table can enrich us all, and without the Anabaptists there, the party is hardly worth having.[102]

Where do the Anglicans (or in the United States, the Episcopals) fit in with all this? The Church of England faced an important decision as it watched the German Lutherans to the northeast break away from the Roman Catholics to the southeast. Which way would they go at the Reformation fork in the road? Powerful forces pulled the Church of England down both roads, but their choice was to choose neither and instead seek a *via media* or middle way. They sought both to retain what was of value from medieval Catholic Christianity and to embrace what was of value from the emerging Reformation movements.[103]

Their pursuit of a middle way bridging Protestantism and Catholicism has not been easy and has cost them dearly. The problem with being a bridge, one of my Anglican mentors once told me, is that you get walked on from both ends, and this has been the experience of the Anglicans. But by walking that middle way, they learned three essential practices, practices that I have been experimenting with since I spent a few wonderful years in an

---

[102] For more on this idea of a table of sharing, or a mutual fund of heritages, see my *The Church on the Other Side* (Zondervan, 1998, 2000), Chapter 4. That chapter is, in many ways, the precursor to this book.

[103] Yes, I know about Henry VIII and the chicanery that is part of Anglican history. Yes, I realize I'm being overly generous in not bringing up the dark side of Anglican beginnings.

Episcopal church in my mid-20s.

The practice of dynamic tension

When you choose both/and rather than either/or regarding Catholicism and Protestantism, you learn to live with dynamic tension in other areas as well. You resist the reductionist temptation to always choose only one thing over another, and you learn to hold two or more things together when necessary.

Anglicans have demonstrated this both/and beautifully in relation to Scripture. Scripture is always a factor in Anglican thinking. In Anglicans' best moments, it is their primary factor, but it is never *sola*—never the only factor. Rather Scripture is always in dialogue with tradition, reason, and experience. None of them *sola* can be the ultimate source of authority: that source is God alone, the only ultimate *sola*. In the dynamic tension of Scripture, tradition, reason, and experience, Anglicans seek to discern God's authority, and when these four values agree, Anglicans move forward with confidence.[104] When they don't agree, Anglicans seek to live with the tension and tolerance, believing that better outcomes will follow if they live with the tension rather than resolve it by rejecting one of the four values. All four—Scripture, reason, tradition, and experience—are gifts from God, and none should be rejected.[105]

---

[104] Methodism, an offspring of Anglicanism, shares these four touchstones in its DNA. In fact, they are often called "the Wesleyan Quadrilateral." Lutheranism shares a similar ethos in many ways as well.

[105] Like all of us, Anglicans sometimes fall short of their ideals, as their recent struggles over homosexuality make clear. Rather than living with the difficult dynamic tension among Scripture, reason, tradition, or experience, various factions have chosen at times to abandon one or two or three of the four, or have indulged in old-fashioned power politics to get beyond both/and to either/or. Nobody says both/and is easy.

The practice of compromise

Compromise (like *tolerance*) is a dirty word for many Christians. It suggests a lowering of standards. But it is a beautiful word (like tolerance) if you are trying to live in community with others, with Scripture, reason, tradition, and experience in dynamic tension. In this light, compromise and tolerance suggest keeping a high (uncompromised!) standard of unity and a high level of respect for your brothers and sisters who disagree with you. It acknowledges that not everyone will reach the same conclusions at the same pace on every issue. So Anglicans are practiced in compromise, in making room for one another when Scripture, reason, tradition, and experience don't line up for everyone the same way.

The practice of beauty

What keeps Anglicans together if they have so much diversity—High Church, Low Church, Anglo-Catholic, evangelical, charismatic, liberal, moderate, American, African, Asian, English? How do they function if their both/and respect for Scripture *and* tradition *and* reason *and* experience doesn't lead them to fast, easy agreements?

When conceptual agreement fails, many of them will tell you they are brought and kept together by liturgy (an orderly plan for public worship). But not just by words on a page. Rather, I believe, it is their deep appreciation for the *deep beauty* of liturgy that helps them make room for one another. Even if they disagree on what the liturgy means or requires doctrinally, they are charmed by its mysterious beauty and beautiful mystery, and that is often enough to keep them together long enough to share, evaluate, and integrate varied understandings.[106] In contrast to Christians who argue about the fine points of doctrine but show little taste for the beauty of truth, the Anglican way (as I have observed it) has been to begin with beauty, to focus on beauty, and to stay with it, believing that where beauty is, God is.

These practices—or this method—are among the greatest gifts the Anglican community brings to the church at large, as McConnell explains:

> The Via Media, in historical terms, was John Donne's phrase whose heritage dates back to Aristotle's "golden mean." It is striking that in Anglican history, the focus has been on the method, rather than a distinct theology or creed. Perhaps the most important thing about Hooker is that he wrote no *Summa* and composed no *Institutes*, for what he did was to outline method. What is distinctly Anglican is then not a theology but a theological method. [107]

Anglicans and Anabaptists alike took a different road through modernity from the rest of Protestantism. As the latter largely embraced modernity, in their differing ways and degrees Anabaptists and Anglicans withheld their full allegiance from modernity.[108] For this reason (and others) they have much to offer all who seek a generous orthodoxy beyond modernity.

As I wrote earlier, I have been experimenting for years with Anabaptist and Anglican methods and practices, Anabaptist and Anglican values and ways of living and thinking. The best of

---

[106] I haven't included Episcopal structure (which is more top-down than the structures preferred by most other Protestants) as one of the enduring values of Anglicanism. While this approach to church structure has many advantages, it also has notable downsides, which recent controversies about homosexuality have made more obvious. For example, pastors or priests (including homosexual ones) can be imposed on a congregation against the will of its people, and churches in one missional setting have to abide by decisions suitable to other missional settings—but not to their own. Of course, it's easier to diagnose these problems than to cure them.

[107] Thomas McConnell, in Paul Elmen, ed., *The Anglican Moral Choice*. London: Morehouse (1983), p. 43. The importance of the word *method* in this quote reminds us again of the Anglican roots of Methodism. See Chapter 14.

[108] Of course, there are several notable Anglicans who epitomize modernity and serve as clear counterexamples to my generalizations. I won't mention any names.

these are not exclusively Anabaptist and Anglican at all, but rather the ways of the gospel, the ways Jesus Christ taught in the Sermon on the Mount and through the example of his life.

I have been monitoring my experience (as any scientist would do), which I will report here: the more I follow this Anabaptist/Anglican path, *the more real God becomes to me, the more brilliant and revolutionary Jesus seems to me, the more precious life becomes to me, the more warmly I feel toward my neighbors.*

By learning from Anabaptists and Anglicans, my orthodoxy has become more generous. I would call the preliminary results of this ongoing experiment confirming. It is now up to you to see if you can validate this experiment in your world, in your life.

CHAPTER 14

WHY I AM METHODIST

What a great story Methodists have to tell about themselves! In 1739, Anglican priest George Whitefield (1714-1770) invited Anglican priests John and Charles Wesley to join him preaching an evangelical (see Chapter 6) gospel where it's most needed (and accepted): not from the pulpits of a church grown complacent and comfortable, but in the streets and fields, wherever the unwashed and unchurched people were. The Wesley brothers joined Whitfield—George and John supplying the preaching and Charles providing some music. This was music the common folk could relate to—down-to-earth songs, lyrics in simple but beautiful English, with a good melody and a good beat, songs with feeling, more like the songs they sang in the pub at night than the highfalutin' organ music of the cathedrals. Even after Whitfield left to travel to America, thousands came to hear John and Charles. People responded powerfully with tears, shrieks, groans, and trembling.

One reporter described the scene outside a coal mine, where the miners stopped on their way home after a day of backbreaking, low-paying, bone-wearying, lung-destroying work. The miners were probably planning to anesthetize their aching muscles and downtrodden hearts with strong drink, which might lead to wife beating and other sad outcomes. John Wesley's powerful voice caught their ears. This man has passion and compassion, they thought. They stopped and listened to someone who didn't despise them for their low-life ways. The crowd grew—dirty, weary men, black-faced from coal dust. Wesley spoke of a God who loved them and wanted to help them even though they got drunk, even though they gambled, even though they mistreated their wives and children. The reporter noticed pale, clean tracks forming on the coal-blackened cheeks of these tough men, tracks formed by tears of repentance and faith.

And it didn't stop (as so much contemporary revivalism does) with an emotional experience (plus an offering). The Wesleys organized these men into groups—small ones called bands, larger ones called classes, larger ones still called societies. In these groups, the men, and soon their wives and neighbors and friends, joined to help one another experience transformation. Within weeks, within months, within years, there were thousands of people whose lives were transformed.

For decades the movement grew, eventually disengaging from the Anglican structure in which it was born. To get a feel for the early dynamic of Methodism, imagine a group of people ascending a mountain, each one always having someone a step above and ahead of them to emulate and follow, plus someone a step behind and below to encourage and bring upward and onward:

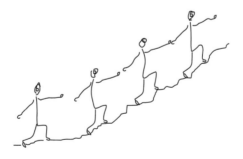

But eventually, the predictable happened, maybe like this: Imagine one of those men 10 years later, a former coal miner who has been clean, sober, and sanctified for a decade and has now become a lay preacher. He notices his teenage daughter making eyes at one of the young, single coal miners who just began attending the society meeting. He remembers what he was like back then, before he was saved and sanctified, before he left coal mining to become a grocer. The last thing he wants is for his daughter to get hooked up with a guy like that.

So at the next society meeting, he preaches a little harder than usual against sin and implies that sinners aren't really that welcome anymore. Before long the harsher rhetoric is bound to either straighten people up and get them farther up the hill or drive them away. Over time it does the latter more than the former, and frankly, that's just as well to the grocer-lay-preacher and many of his peers.

Now the focus shifts from the drunks and gamblers to the younger converts who aren't as zealous and respectable as the older ones. They're constantly pressured to either move up higher and faster or to leave altogether, with some taking either option. And pretty soon the old ascent is gone, and a plateau has replaced it:

Now instead of a progression of people at various stages of the Christian ascent, you have a high plateau of the religious and a deep canyon of the irreligious. Neither likes the other, neither understands the other, and each wishes the other would just go away. If someone in the canyon cries out to God for help, God has no one to send to help, no one who will understand, care, approach, mentor, or guide. A would-be convert has no one to look to for a model: first, because the religious are so far removed from him or her, and second, because they aren't really moving anymore anyway. Nobody is on a journey anymore; everybody is stuck in their high or low status quo.

This kind of "redemption and lift" hit the Methodists hard, and it describes what happens in many renewal movements like Methodism. It's an important cautionary tale, one that, I think, instructed the founders of Alcoholics Anonymous and encouraged them to keep the focus on the next drunk who will walk through their doors.[109]

Because of redemption and lift, the glory and genius of Methodism is largely forgotten. But it shouldn't be, because we are in a situation now that is very similar to that of Whitfield (who was a Calvinist) and the Wesleys (who weren't and so took a different path).

Luther and Calvin created Protestant intellectual systems (a kind of conceptual hierarchy) that replaced the Catholic organizational hierarchy. But nobody created a new system of spiritual formation and nurture to replace the richly developed Catholic system of spirituality that had developed during the Middle Ages. Nobody did so in the sixteenth century, and nobody did so in the seventeenth or most of the eighteenth—until the Wesleys. People had Protestant doctrine, but they didn't have tracks or pathways or methods to help them put that doctrine into practice. Without tracks or patterns or methods of spiritual formation,

---

[109] Bill Hybels of Willow Creek Community Church and Rick Warren of Saddleback Church have in our day championed this emphasis on the "seeker," the "unchurched," the not-yet-convinced-or-committed.

their piety was quickly dissipated in spiritual frustration and unfulfilled dreams of spiritual fervor. Complacency, nominalism, notionalism, and hypocrisy set in throughout the Protestant world with only a few exceptions (such as the Moravian Brethren). Not until the Wesleys did anyone do for spiritual formation what Luther and Calvin had done for doctrine: create a system to replace what had been rejected from Catholicism.

Today I think we're in a parallel situation. Modern Christianity (sadly, including many modern Methodists) moved on from the Wesleys' innovations, resulting in widespread spiritual complacency and compromise. By the 1970s a strong new spiritual formation system had been developed among conservatives, drawing loosely (and often unintentionally) from the Methodist heritage, largely by so-called "parachurch" organizations such as the Navigators, Campus Crusade for Christ, and InterVarsity Christian Fellowship.[110] Not the rosaries, feasts, and practices of the Catholics, not the bands, classes, and societies of the Methodists, but an informal system involving "quiet times," small group Bible studies, fill-in-the-blank discipleship guides, classes and curricula, revivals, retreats, rallies and conferences, and the like.

By the 1990s and certainly into the first decade of the new century, more and more conservative Protestants began feeling that these late-modern parachurch methods weren't working any more. Few realized that much of this late-modern methodology had a thoroughly modern underlying goal: to inculcate a basic systematic theology, predicated on the purely modern notions that *right thinking = right behavior*, that *more biblical content = better Christians*, that *knowledge = power*.

Meanwhile, intrepid souls like Dallas Willard, Larry

---

[110] Since the 1970s and 1980s, Howard Snyder of Asbury Seminary has been tirelessly reminding us of the resources available in the Methodist heritage, and writers like Richard Foster have also been ringing this bell with needed gusto. See Renovare.org.

Crabb, Richard Foster, and others confessed their observation: systematic theologies or biblical knowledge simply did not produce personal transformation. Many Christian leaders started searching for a new approach under the banner of "spiritual formation."

This new search has led many of them back to Catholic contemplative practices and medieval monastic disciplines (which, coincidentally, were also being rediscovered by many mainline "liberal" Protestants with great blessing).[III] The search is still in its infancy, hampered by a hard-to-shake addiction to modern thought and methodology in the church and the pressures of consumerism in the culture at large.

The search will yield (I hope, believe, and pray) a new methodism, one as catalytic and relevant to our day as the Wesleys' was to theirs. Like Wesleyan Methodism, it will emphasize the importance of small groups, spiritual friends who meet for mutual encouragement and support. Like Wesleyan Methodism, it will focus not on fill-in-the-blank answers, but on queries—questions that make one reflect, think, take stock, and pay attention to what's going on in one's own soul. Like Wesleyan Methodism, it will empower "lay" people, realizing that baptism itself is a kind of ordination to ministry and that the purpose of discipleship is to train and deploy everyday apostles. And like the earliest Methodists, it will see discipleship as the process of reaching ahead with one hand to find the hand of a mentor a few steps up the hill, while reaching back with the other to help the next brother or sister in line who is also on the upward path of discipleship.

May God save us from forgetting to reach back. Otherwise our orthodoxy will surely lose its orthopraxy (right practice), which will make it ungenerous and eventually unorthodox, too.

[III] See Diana Butler Bass, *The Practicing Congregation: Imagining a New Old Church* (Alban: 2004).

CHAPTER 15

WHY I AM CATHOLIC

Last spring I was speaking at a conference near Santa Clara, California. I like to get outdoors every chance I get. One day my early morning walk took me to Our Lady of Peace Roman Catholic Church near my hotel. Behind the church is a huge statue of Mary surrounded by a beautiful garden, which is in turn surrounded by bustling freeways.

Attracted by this little garden of peace amid the chaos of morning Bay Area traffic, I found myself sitting on a bench with Mary towering over me, looking down on me with a kind face, her arms extended. An Asian woman knelt at Mary's feet, obviously in prayer and in some anguish, her hand reaching up and resting affectionately on Mary's big toe. Sitting there, I was deeply moved by the woman's piety and by Mary's image.

How ironic, I thought, for a boy raised Protestant to be sitting there with tears in his eyes, moved by Our Lady of Peace and a humble Asian lady seeking peace. That day I became a little more Catholic and a little more catholic, too.

Many years ago our church (nonliturgical in its origins)

began using the Nicene Creed in our public worship. For the first year or two, we edited one word in the creed, changing "We believe in one holy catholic and apostolic church" to "We believe in one holy universal and apostolic church," embarrassed to use the word *catholic* for fear we would be accused (by angry ex-Catholics, for the most part) of latent papacy.

The creed—a "We-believe statement" that Christians have used for liturgical (i.e., public, worship-related) and educational purposes through the centuries—is unapologetic about the word *catholic*.[112] Eventually, I dropped my prejudice to learn what the word really means, especially in the context of that sentence in the creed.

"We believe in one...church," the creed says, and that's no easy-to-swallow statement because we're surrounded by denominations, divisions, arguments, grand polemics, and petty squabbles. That's where the "we believe" part comes in: you can only know the unity of the church by believing it, not by seeing it. When you believe it, you can see through the surface dirt and cracks to the beauty and unity shining beneath. Generous orthodoxy presumes that the divisions, though tragic, are superficial compared to Christianity's deep, though often unappreciated, unity. Perhaps the more we believe in and perceive that unity, the easier it will be to grow beyond the disunity.

To call the Christian church "holy" is to say something about its purpose, not its behavior at any given moment. The word *church* means *those called out*. *Holy* means *devoted to a sacred purpose*. Thus, the church is a community of people called out from the profane

---

[112] About creeds, Chesterton has this to say: "Whenever we feel there is something odd in Christian theology, we shall generally find that there is something odd in the truth...When one once believes in a creed, one is proud of its complexity, as scientists are proud of the complexity of science. It shows how rich it is in discoveries. If it is right at all, it is a compliment to say that it's elaborately right. A stick might fit a hole or a stone a hollow by accident. But a key and a lock are both complex. And if a key fits a lock, you know it is the right key" (*Orthodoxy*, 87).

rush and secular hassle of life to be devoted to a sacred purpose.

The one holy church of the creed is also "apostolic," which for some refers to a belief that they alone can trace their lineage back to one of the original 12 apostles. This belief has often fueled yet another kind of elitism that has undermined the *one* and *catholic* ideals of the creed in a way that is hardly *holy* in any sense of the word. But there is a more catholic understanding of the term *apostolic*: it means *missional*. The apostles were those called together to learn (as disciples) so they could be *sent out* on a mission (which is what both the Greek root for *apostle* and the Latin root for *mission* mean).[113]

From this vantage point, disciples are apostles-in-training; Christian discipleship (or spiritual formation) is training for apostleship, training for mission. From this understanding we place less emphasis on whose lineage, rites, doctrines, structures, and terminology are *right* and more emphasis on whose actions, service, outreach, kindness, and effectiveness are *good*. (That is one of those sentences that might deserve a re-read.)

In a missional/apostolic approach to Christianity, every component of our faith (worship, liturgy, creeds, theology, fellowship, spiritual formation, religious education, publishing, etc.), though in itself valid and valuable, must lead to good works, good lives, good creativity, and goodness to help our world get back on the road to being truly and wholly good again, the way God created it to be.

The difference between these two understandings of *apostolic/missional* reflects two ways of thinking about Christianity. One approach says, "Look, everybody. We're right, and you're wrong. We have the right lineage back to the original apostles, and

---

[113] See Chapter 5.

you don't. Sorry, but we're in, and you're out. There are blessings for being right and in and consequences for being wrong and out. So if you want in on the blessings and out of the consequences, you'd better join us since only we can trace our lineage back to the apostles."

The other approach says, "We're here on a mission to join God in bringing blessing to our needy world. We hope to bring God's blessing to you, whoever you are and whatever you believe, and if you'd like to join us in this mission and the faith that creates and nourishes it, you're welcome. If you've been part of the problem, we invite you to switch sides, to become part of God's solution. That's the mission we have received from the apostles. We seek to follow their example in living it radically, courageously, and generously."

What does it mean to say that the one holy apostolic church is also *catholic*? The word doesn't mean *Roman Catholic*; it means *universal*. In this way, "Roman Catholic" might seem like an oxymoron—universal except for those who don't agree with the headquarters in Rome—but it's not that simple. Actually, the Roman Catholic Church may be the most truly catholic denomination in the world, acknowledging since Vatican II that her "separated brethren" are at least brethren, higher status than some Protestant denominations will grant Catholics!

The story behind the word *catholic* might help you appreciate it more than before. All through church history and especially in the early centuries, renewal or reform movements have arisen, needed by the church. Too often these movements have seen themselves as *the new and improved* version of Christianity, even as the only legitimate version. This inflated self-image among reformers has often led to the demotion of all other rank-and-file Christians—those who don't join their reform movement—relegating them to the status of despised pretenders and compromised losers. Thus these renewal movements have often produced a kind of elitism that said, "*We're* the only ones who have it right. Everyone else who doesn't join *us* is wrong, out, sub- or non-Christian."

Against this kind of elitism others said, "No. We want you reformers to be part of us, but we aren't going to join you if it means excluding everyone else. We believe God wants the Christian church to be an accepting, welcoming community, not an exclusive, elitist community. We'll go on being the church for all the people you reject. We'll be *catholic*—the accepting, welcoming church for everyone, not just an exclusive, elite few."

There is a special pride that comes from being part of the exclusive, the elite, the prime. But to be catholic means to find another joy: the pleasure of accepting and welcoming the poor, the blind, the stumbling, the crippled, the imperfect, the confused, the mistaken, and the different. It doesn't mean that we lower our standards of authentic discipleship, rather that we raise our standards of Christ-like acceptance.

Beyond catholic Christianity, I'd like to add six things (I could name many more) about Catholic Christianity that have enriched and continue to enrich my life in Christ.

Catholicism is sacramental.

A sacrament is an object or practice that mediates the divine to humans. It carries something of God to us; it is a means of grace, and it conveys sacredness. I care little for arguments about how many sacraments there are (although I tend to prefer longer lists than shorter ones). What I really like about the sacramental nature of Catholicism is this: through learning that a few things can carry the sacred, we become open to the fact that all things (all good things, all created things) can ultimately carry the sacred: the kind smile of a Down's syndrome child, the bouncy jubilation of a puppy, the graceful arch of a dancer's back, the camera work in a fine film, good coffee, good wine, good friends, good conversation. Start with three sacraments—or seven—and pretty soon everything becomes potentially sacramental as, I believe, it should be.

Catholicism is liturgical.

Every denomination is liturgical. Some just don't know it because their liturgies aren't written down. For example, a seemingly free-form Pentecostal revival actually has a certain expected rhythm to which some deviations are perhaps allowed, but others are not. If you've been to a lot of Protestant meetings that claim to be nonliturgical, eschewing written prayers for "heartfelt" (i.e., spontaneous) ones, you soon begin to realize that (pardon my cynicism) the Lord, Father-God, is just so good, Father-God, and it's just so great just to praise his mighty and wonderful name, Father-God, glory, hallelujah, and we're just so blessed just to be here, Father-God, hallelujah, just rejoicing in his holy presence, hallelujah, and if I just hear the word *just* one more time, and if I just hear just one more religious cliché pasted to others in a long cliché train, I'm going to ruin this whole so-called spontaneous, heartfelt experience by screaming!

To have some gifted people (like the Anglicans' Thomas Cranmer or the many gifted Catholic liturgists) save us from our habitual "justs" and "spontaneous" clichés with well-chosen words, well-crafted sentences, and well-thought-out paragraphs is a great gift of liturgy.

True, liturgy led by an anemic leader with a monotone voice and a corresponding heart is a sad thing, probably no better (perhaps worse) than "just-ified" impromptu prayers. But have you experienced well-written, prayerfully planned liturgy led by gifted, enthusiastic, passionate leaders? You'll find yourself saying, "Thanks be to God!"

Catholicism respects tradition.

The Protestant Reformation separated two brothers: Scripture and tradition. The older brother tells the story that leads up to and through Christ, and the younger brother remembers what has happened since. These brothers aren't the same, but neither should they be enemies. Chesterton celebrates tradition like this:

> Tradition is only democracy extended through time. It is trusting to a consensus of common human voices rather than to some isolated or arbitrary record...Tradition means giving votes to the most obscure of all classes, our ancestors. It is the democracy of the dead. Tradition refuses to submit to the small and arrogant oligarchy of those who merely happen to be walking about. All democrats object to men being disqualified by the accident of birth; tradition objects to their being disqualified by the accident of death. Democracy tells us not to neglect a good man's opinion, even if he is our groom [butler]; tradition asks us not to neglect a good man's opinion, even if he is our father (*Orthodoxy*, 48).

One cause of the rift between tradition and Scripture seems to have been this: some treated tradition as if it were a hardened, monolithic, totalitarian regime, eliminating freedom of conscience and freedom of inquiry, like a long book of accumulated legal precedents that answer every question forever (which we noted briefly in Chapter 0). While this view of tradition gave some confidence, it felt smothering to others. Ironically, some reacted and created a kind of biblicism that was equally smothering.

Gabriel Fackre offers a different, more balanced view of tradition (which includes, by the way, the church's tradition of interpreting the Bible):

The circle of tradition is not closed, for the Spirit's ecclesial Work is not done. Traditional doctrine develops as Christ and the gospel are viewed in ever-fresh perspective. Old formulations are corrected, and what is passed on is enriched. The open-endedness, however, does not overthrow the ancient landmarks. As tradition is a gift of the Spirit, its trajectory moves in the right direction, although it has not arrived at its destination.[114]

Catholicism celebrates Mary.

Sitting there at Our Lady of Peace last spring, I recalled how we Protestants had always considered the veneration of Mary to be idolatry (Mariolatry, we called it). But that morning, hushed in the steady hum of traffic, I realized just a little, I think, of what Catholics know more deeply. By venerating Mary (not worshiping her, of course!), we come more fully to know who we are: simple humans, like Mary, called upon to bear Christ in our bodies, through our lives, to our world, whispering, "I am the Lord's servant."

Not only that, but as I sat there, I realized how impoverished my Protestant faith was with its exclusively male focus. How much we missed by failing to see the beauty of the incarnation through Mary—a beauty that magnifies the value of women, erases the shame of Eve, makes visible the importance of spiritual receptivity, celebrates the fecundity and fertility of simple submission: "Let it be to me according to your word."

I don't worship Mary, but I do honor her. Can there be anything wrong in saying of Mary what the angel said and what Elizabeth (moved by the Holy Spirit) echoed: that Mary is highly

---

[114] Gabriel Fackre, *The Christian Story: A Narrative Interpretation of Basic Christian Doctrine*, third ed. (Grand Rapids: Eerdmans, 1996), 18-19. Quoted in Franke, *Reforming Theology*, which is available at www.emergentvillage.com.

favored, the Lord is with her, and that she is blessed among women? Can there be anything wrong in saying of Mary what the Spirit sang through her: that all generations will call her blessed and that the Mighty One has done great things for her?

Catholics know how to party.

Perhaps due to its sacramentalism Catholic faith has remained so convinced of the incarnation of Jesus that it has been less likely to lapse into a grim hatred of the body and common, cultural life. Yes, paradoxically, Catholics have *ecclesiolae en ecclesia* (little churches in the big church) that sometimes practice extreme asceticism (self-denial of bodily pleasures or even comforts). One can't forget medieval hair shirts and self-flagellation, where monks and others would torture themselves physically as a kind of fleshly mortification or self-purification. And yes, there's that whole celibacy thing among priests and nuns.

But on the other hand can you imagine Lutherans or Presbyterians or Baptists creating Mardi Gras?[115] In this regard Chesterton observed: "These [Catholic] countries...are exactly the countries where there is still singing and dancing and colored dresses and art in the open-air. Catholic doctrine and discipline may be walls; but they are the walls of a playground" (*Orthodoxy*, 155).

Catholicism can't escape from its scandals.

I write these positive words about Catholicism (and catholicity) at the end of a year (2003) when the Roman Church has been in the newspapers more for its scandals and legal settlements than for its good works and good fruit. I am not insensitive to what these

---

[115] I am not condoning the drunkenness and other misbehavior associated with Mardi Gras. Many, if not most, celebrants at a New Orleans-style Mardi Gras know little or nothing about the spiritual significance of the party. I am also wondering if the tepid, bland dullness of many Protestants is as great a misbehavior.

scandals say about the state of the Roman Catholic Church.

But I am also not insensitive to the fact the Protestant and Orthodox churches have their own closets full of skeletons; they just haven't been caught. Being caught is expensive. It's painful. But it also opens the possibility for repentance. I am confident that in many quarters, repentance is happening. I don't consider the Catholic scandals to be "their" problem but "our" problem. If the Catholic Church responds to its scandals with appropriate humility and repentance, the whole world will benefit.

A generous orthodoxy is like that. It acknowledges that we're all a mess. It sees in our worst failures the possibility of our deepest repentance and God's opening for our most profound healing. It remembers Jesus' parable that wherever God sows good seed, "an enemy" will sow weed seeds. It realizes that you can't pull up the bad without uprooting the good too, and so it refrains from judging. It just rejoices wherever good seed grows.

CHAPTER 16

WHY I AM GREEN

Imagine that right now you are standing with me, thigh deep in muck.[116] Clad in hip waders, we're slogging through a spring-fed bog in northern Maryland. We're surrounded by tussock sedge, alder, jewelweed, skunk cabbage, and swamp rose. The June sun is hot, I'm sweaty, I've got six mosquito bites on the back of my neck, and my forearms are scratched and itchy from thorns of various sizes. And I'm having a great time. I'm glad to have your company here in this beautiful place.

I've done this for a couple of days almost every spring for the last dozen years. I'm out here as a volunteer with the Department of Natural Resources to do wildlife surveys. In particular we're looking for the rarest turtle in North America, *glyptemys muhlenbergii*, the little four-inch bog turtle. In the 1970s, it was found in more than 400 sites in our little state. In the 1990s, we could only find them in about half those sites. The other sites had been ditched, drained, bulldozed, polluted, invaded by non-native plants, raided by collectors, bisected by roads for turtle-smashing cars, or

---

[116] This chapter is adapted and expanded from an article that appeared in *Sojourners*, spring 2004, www.sojo.net.

otherwise made uninhabitable for these little creatures.

I don't know why I'm fascinated with turtles. They impress me as compact, resilient, unpretentious little biological units. Someone once told me they are an icon of active faith: they never get ahead unless they come out of their shell and stick their necks out. They're seldom in a hurry. If sparrows could be a kind of icon in the teaching of Jesus, I'm sure turtles can be so for me.

I once saw a television show about amphibians, cousins to turtles and other reptiles. It featured a Japanese woman who had devoted her life to studying giant salamanders. In one scene she was holding this huge, brown, slimy, fleshy, dachshund-sized blob of amphibious fierceness (these salamanders bite), and with an almost embarrassed smile she said, "I know many people think they're ugly, but I find them beautiful. I love these creatures, and I feel so lucky that I get to study them." At that moment I thought: maybe God allows each of us to join God in loving some special aspect of creation, from weather to stars to dinosaurs to rocks to antique cars to songbirds to lions to electricity to wines to motorcycles to giant salamanders. If that's the case, I get the honor of joining the Creator in appreciating turtles. You might think my Japanese counterpart and I are strange, but we actually feel quite lucky.

While my fellow volunteers and I are out here in the bogs, we also keep alert for other rare species: butterflies, birds, wildflowers, insects, amphibians. Our efforts help wildlife biologists keep track of how certain "indicator species" are doing; their status tells us how fast and how much the environment is suffering from human interference. Occasionally, there's good news, too—when we stop our mine runoff from poisoning creeks and rivers, when suburban homes stop shocking downstream ecosystems with runoff from lawn pesticides and fertilizers, when sewage treatment facilities find ways to stop raw sewage from overflowing into waterways after rainstorms.

When I meet professional wildlife biologists and other volunteers, they're surprised that a Christian pastor would be out here doing this sort of thing on his day off. They're not used to seeing mud-smeared pastors groping around in bog muck for turtles...or counting chorus frogs and Baltimore checkerspots and Indian paintbrush. I know what they're thinking: *Christians are part of the problem, not part of the solution. They read James Dobson, Chuck Colson, and Jerry Falwell, not Wendell Berry, Herman Daly, or Al Gore; they focus on the family and the military, not the environment.*[117]

Too often my environmentally concerned friends are right. But as so many species slide closer to extinction, the rare species known variously as *Christianus environmentalis* or *Disciplos verde* is making a comeback. As songwriter Bruce Cockburn said, "may their gene pool increase." I don't doubt that this love for creation will be a hallmark of the emerging generous orthodoxy. My friend Melanie Griffin, national programs director of the Sierra Club, says it like this: "In the past few years, we've seen a big increase in the number of Christians involved in actively protecting creation. They are leading stream cleanups, giving sermons about creation care, and jumping into the public policy arena. Christians bring a special energy and spirit to environmental work."

The surface causes of environmental carelessness among conservative Christians are legion, including subcontracting the evangelical mind out to right-wing politicians and greedy business interests. Too often we put the gospel of Jesus through the strainer of consumerist-capitalism and retain only the thin broth that this modern-day Caesar lets pass through. We often display a reactionary tendency to be against whatever "liberals" are for. These non-green shoots are resourced by deeper theological roots of environmental disinterest. Fortunately, other root systems are

---

[117] All the names in the latter group, by the way, see their environmentalism as an expression of their Christian faith.

spreading beneath the surface, and signs of an environmental spring are breaking through the formerly barren soil.

People who are sensitive to creation know that creation is in constant flux. Continents drift, ocean currents wobble, climates warm and cool, magnetic poles flip-flop, and bogs like this one gradually give way to wet meadows and then various kinds of forests. There's a natural succession out here under the June sun, and I think there's a kind of natural succession going on theologically for many Christians as well. Let me mention six elements of this theological succession.

The standard, stagnant theology of creation/ fall is giving way to a more vigorous theology of continual creation.

For much of Western Christianity, the doctrine of creation (a biblical term) has been eaten alive by the doctrine of the fall (not a biblical term). In other words, creation's downfall resulting from human sin has eclipsed its original glow as God's handiwork, radiant with God's glory. Make no mistake: Human sin is awful and reprehensible beyond words, and the whole earthly creation suffers because of it. But if, due to an exaggerated doctrine of the fall, God's creation loses its sacredness as God's beloved artwork, we have magnified human sin beyond sane bounds—and in fact added to its sad effects. As a result, in many circles, about the only time the word *creation* comes up these days is before *versus evolution*. The God-affirmed goodness of creation, the beauty of creation, its priceless preciousness and meaning as God's own handiwork— these values are seldom heard. Instead more discouraging words are heard—about the ruin of creation via an "ontological fall," a concept that conveniently seems to degrade God's inherently valuable handiwork into man's bargain resources for profitable exploitation. It's far easier to put a price tag on a fallen creation than on a still-sacred one.

Many of us have grown uneasy with this understanding of "the fall" (and with it, an exaggerated understanding of the doctrine of "original sin"). We are suspicious that it has become a kind of Western neo-Platonic invasive species that ravages the harmonious balance inherent in the enduring Jewish concept of creation as God's world.[118] So we are looking to the Eastern Orthodox tradition and to emerging narrative theologies where creation is still seen as sacred, "good," "very good"... and, in fact, ongoing.

When one is careful to not lose the enduring glory and continuity of creation, when one takes human sin seriously enough but no more seriously than one should, later elements in the biblical narrative (election, redemption, revelation, salvation, eschaton) are themselves understood and integrated as glorious new unfoldings of continuing creation. Creation may have been swallowed alive by a runaway, exaggerated understanding of "the fall" but, like Jonah, it's crawling back up the beach.

Seen this way, creation is revalued (i.e., redeemed) and made sacred again. It isn't relegated into the "seconds" bin at the factory as merchandise that has been ruined and devalued by an ontological accident, now marketed for a cut-rate fire-sale price to the first industrialist who comes along with cash.

No, in this view, these little bog turtles we're looking for

---

[118] In *Doctrine: Systematic Theology, Volume 2*, James Wm. McClendon rejects the concept of "'original' or inherited sin" as "a doctrinal experiment that [was] found wanting. It must be replaced with the concept of social sin, which passes from generation to generation, but requires each generation to answer to Christ not for its ancestors' but for its own fault." (Nashville: Abingdon, 1994), p. 147. Of course, one cannot lightly quarrel with Chesterton, who wrote, "Certain new theologians dispute original sin, which is the only part of Christian theology which can be really proved...If it be true (as it certainly is) that a man can feel exquisite happiness in skinning a cat, then the religious philosopher can only draw one of two deductions. He must either deny the existence of God, as all atheists do; or he must deny the present union between God and man, as all Christians do. The new theologians seem to think it a highly rationalistic solution to deny the cat" (Chesterton, 10-11). I am in no way denying sin (original, social, whatever) in the sense that Chesterton is affirming it; rather I'm suggesting we try to avoid the damage that a distortion of the doctrine has done to our understanding of the goodness of original creation and the beauty of continuing creation.

today are priceless treasures, original creations of the greatest Artist in (and beyond) history—even though they are deemed precisely worthless to someone who would want to build an interstate highway through this bog. Even this black muck squishing out between my fingers is precious, for it represents the natural recycling of organic matter of who-knows-how-many hundreds of years, decomposed leaves and grasses that now nurture the tussock sedge, the skunk cabbage, and all that depend on them.

If you see our world this way, you can't help becoming a St. Francis, a brother to the whippoorwill, a sister to the meadow vole, a friend of trees, hailing your fellow creatures in God's world in a spirit of good cheer and good, clean fun. Chesterton wisely noted how a Franciscan view of creation avoids both the profaning of creation so common in the West and the divinization of creation so common in the East:

> The essence of all pantheism, evolutionism, and modern cosmic religion is really in this proposition: that Nature is our mother...The main point of Christianity was this: that Nature is not our mother: Nature is our sister. We can be proud of her beauty, since we have the same father, but she has no authority over us; we have to admire, but not to imitate. This gives to the typically Christian pleasure in this earth a strange touch of lightness that is almost frivolity...Nature is not solemn to Francis of Assisi or George Herbert. To St. Francis, Nature is a sister, and even a younger sister: a little, dancing sister, to be laughed at as well as loved (*Orthodoxy*, 120).

Follow St. Francis and Chesterton, and you won't sell your little sister; you will seek to enjoy her, cherish her, protect her, and encourage her to become all she can be.

The eschatology of abandonment is being succeeded by an engaging gospel of the kingdom.

Evangelical-dispensational "left-behind" eschatology (the doctrine of last things or end times that expects the world to be destroyed in just over seven years or one thousand and seven years, depending on the fine print) makes perfect sense in the modern world.[119]

Understandably, Christians in the power centers of modernity (England in the 1800s, the United States in the 1900s) saw nothing ahead in the secular story of industrial modernity... nothing but spiritual decline and global destruction. Their only hope? A skyhook Second Coming, wrapping up the whole of creation like an empty candy wrapper and throwing it in the cosmic dumpster so God can finally bring our souls to heaven, beyond time, beyond messy matter, beyond this creation entirely. There is virtually no continuity between this creation and the new heavenly creation in this model; this creation is erased like a mistake, discarded like a non-recyclable milk carton. Why care for creation? Why get sentimental about a container that's served its purpose and is about to be discarded into the cosmic trash compactor of nothingness?

This pop-Evangelical eschatology made an understandable but serious mistake: it wrongly assumed that modernity was all there was or ever would be, while it rightly assessed how hopeless the future would be if modernity-without-end was indeed upon us. Just as the early Christians could not imagine the gospel outlasting the Roman Empire (unless they got the point of the apocalypse of John), nineteenth and twentieth century Evangelicals couldn't imagine the gospel outlasting modernity, the empire of Scientism,

---

[119] This eschatology or expectation regarding the end of the world has been recently popularized through the *Left Behind* series of novels.

consumerism, and individualism.

For pop-Evangelical eschatology to proliferate, it had to ignore or, better, reinterpret much written by the Old Testament prophets. Prophetic visions of reconciliation and shalom *within* history (metaphorically conveyed via lions and lambs, children and serpents, swords and plowshares, spears and pruning hooks) had to be pushed *beyond* history, either into a spiritualized heaven or a millennial middle ground—a post-historic time zone between history and eternity, so to speak. They also had to marginalize Jesus with all his talk of the kingdom of God coming on earth, being among us now, and being accessible today.

But now, as more and more of us celebrate Jesus as master-teacher as well as Savior, we are struck by the present hope of "the kingdom of God" that is so central in Jesus' message. In this kingdom, Jesus said, sparrows matter. Lilies of the field matter. Yes, people matter even more, but it's not a matter of either/or; it's a matter of degree in a realm where everything that is good matters—where everything God made matters, including that damselfly darting back and forth up above us and the little pickerel frog peering out from the ferns over there.

Increased concern for the poor and oppressed leads to increased concern for all of creation.

God sent Jesus into the world with a saving love, and Jesus sends us with a similar saving love—love for the fatherless and widows, the poor and forgotten to be sure, but also for all God's little creatures who suffer from the same selfish greed and arrogance that oppress vulnerable humans. The same forces that hurt widows and orphans, minorities and women, children and the elderly, also hurt the songbirds and trout, the ferns and old-growth forests: greed, impatience, selfishness, arrogance, hurry, anger, competition, irreverence—plus a theology that cares for souls but neglects bodies, that focuses on eternity in heaven but abandons history on earth.

When greed and consumerism are exposed, when arrogance and irreverence are unplugged, when hurry and selfishness are named and repented of, when the sacred-secular rift in our thinking is healed, the world and all it contains (widows, orphans, trees, soil) are revalued and made sacred again.

So, as the old system of church-as-chaplain/baptizer/servant-of-state-and-commerce gives way to a new prophetic role, the poor and forgotten benefit, and so do all living things. One realizes that the spirit of St. Francis and the spirit of Mother Teresa are one and the same: the Spirit of Jesus, to whom the poor and sick and the sparrows and salamanders are all precious, each in a unique way.

There is a succession in our understanding of ownership.

If a strain of liberal Christianity was once tempted to become the civil religion of socialism (which reverences state ownership), then certainly conservative Christianity has become the happy mistress of capitalism (which enshrines private ownership). No wonder, then, that many Christians defend private ownership and private enterprise as vigorously as a line in the creeds.

At this moment some are asking, "What's wrong with that?" So I ask, "Can we imagine other understandings of ownership that acknowledge, whatever land records say, that *the earth is the Lord's, and all it contains*? Can we imagine an economy based on stewardship rather than exclusive ownership?"

For increasing numbers of us who consider ourselves post-liberal and post-conservative, "sacred" words such as *private* (meaning personal and individual), *ownership* (meaning autonomous personal and individual control), and *enterprise* (meaning autonomous, personal, individual control over projects to use God's world for our purposes) seem to fly in the face of kingdom values like *communal* (meaning seeing beyond the individual to the community), *fellowship* (which means sharing, holding in common with the community, not grasping as "mine!"), and *mission* (meaning our participation in God's projects in God's world for God's purposes).

I must admit that, apart from a miracle, I see no human power capable of standing up to the expanding empire of global consumerism, which author Tom Beaudoin ominously calls "theocapitalism." But as a Christian, miracles aren't out of the question for me. It is very possible that a biblical stewardship that celebrates *God's* ultimate ownership could someday fuel a new grace-based economy—just as private ownership currently fuels our greed-based consumerist economy (or as government ownership fuels a control-based socialist economy).

An economy of stewardship doesn't see every majestic mountain as a potential site for strip-mining operations. Nor does it view forests as board feet of marketable lumber. Nor does it assess this spring-fed emergent wetland (once properly drained and bulldozed) as a lucrative site for a "housing development" (an unfitting term if there ever was one, since bulldozers and pavement *un-develop* in hours what it took God's creation centuries to *develop*).

We see everything as God's—from the spring peepers singing in the pool to my right to the aluminum used to manufacture the beer can floating by the cattails to my left. For us, whatever we "own" is really entrusted to us by God, borrowed and reverently used by us for a time, after which we must let go one way or another—either through giving and sharing or through dying and releasing our former possessions to others. Even the molecules that make up our bodies are on loan to us. One day we will give them all back, rendering an account of how we have used them through time—time also being a precious gift of which we have been made stewards.

There is a succession from local/national to global/local.

Modern Protestant Christianity has focused on the local church and the national church. Even when it was involved in "world mission," it often simply expanded its national church structures to other locales, in a kind of spiritual colonialism. But now, many factors lead Christians of all types to become less nationalistic and more global in their thinking.

These factors include the global reach (and domination) of the Euro-American economy and military, the global impact of terrorism, and the global dimensions of ecological threats such as global warming, soil depletion, and air and water pollution. Smokestacks in Japan can kill orcas in Puget Sound; smokestacks in Ohio can kill yellow perch in the Adirondacks; runoff from farms in Pennsylvania can bury oysters in Chesapeake Bay; the pet trade in the United States can deplete rare parrots in New Guinea.

This move from local/national to global/local helps us see the world in more creaturely terms and in more spiritual terms. Creatures live more essentially in local watersheds than nations. Creatures live in ecological habitats, not just political states. Lines on maps between nations and states are, in a sense, human fictions, changing fashions, revealing some truths but obscuring others, facilitating justice in some ways but frustrating it in others.

The more we root ourselves in our local environment, the more we honor our status as creatures. The more we remember that we are part of one planet, the more we acknowledge where God has situated us. The ecological problems we face will require nation-states to address them, no doubt, but the nation-states will have to take themselves less seriously while taking local environments and their interconnection in our integral, holistic (holonic) planetary system more seriously.[120]

A new understanding of neighborliness is replacing an old sense of rugged (a.k.a., selfish) individualism.

Clearly, if our thinking extends beyond "me, myself, and I" to our neighbors (human and nonhuman) as the gospel teaches us, we will realize that our neighbors downstream suffer from our water pollution, downwind from our air pollution, and downhill from our erosion. And when we consider our neighbors in time as well as space, we start thinking differently about our children, grandchildren, and more distant descendants. What toxins are we sending downstream in time to poison them?

What kind of world do we want to bequeath to those downstream from us in time? Do we want to deprive our grandchildren from seeing elephants and tigers and hummingbirds in the wild (consoling ourselves that zoos will keep a few caged ones alive, and museums will have dusty stuffed ones)? Do we want to leave them a world even less in balance than our world today? Is that neighborly? The more we as Christians follow Jesus by thinking in terms of our duty to our neighbors "downstream" in space and time, the more we will take our stewardship of creation seriously.

What exactly will we *do* differently in this emerging theological habitat, this new stage in the spiritual forest succession? That remains to be seen. But for starters, we will see differently

---

[120] For more on holonic and integral thinking, see Ken Wilber's *A Theory of Everything* (Boston: Shambala, 2001).

and care differently and value differently. If those differences catch on widely among Christians, with Christianity being the largest religion in the world, there are bound to be good effects in our world.

Ultimately, those effects will have to go beyond the important but limited conservation actions of individuals (recycling, reusing, abstaining, etc.). The effects of caring will have to change our systems—transportation systems that depend on fossil fuels and that divide and devastate our nonhuman neighbors' habitats, housing systems that maximize human impact through suburban sprawl, farming systems that rape rather than steward land, advertising systems that make us want more stuff that we don't need and that will soon fill even more square miles with rotting, rusting trash.

Even our family systems will need reconsideration. For example, we may realize that the nuclear family (of so much Christian focus) and "subatomic family" (i.e., the nuclear family further split by divorce) both require (and waste) more resources than the truly traditional family—the extended or "molecular" one. Could extended families and intentional households ever make a comeback? If they do, it will be good news for all of creation—including humans.

Those systemic changes may be a hundred years out (please God, not that long), but if our theology doesn't change our level of caring soon, they may be a thousand and seven years out, and that will surely be too late. Just caring is a good start. That's a real start. Who knows where it could lead?

Volunteering at my watershed (which, again, is the environmental address that matters more than nation, state, or zip code) is one small way to express my care for creation. My care flows from my generously orthodox identity: a creature who wants to care generously for other creatures because I am made in the image of a Creator who cares generously for us all. I hope you'll find your own ways to express care, too, whatever your environmental address, because a generous orthodoxy is a green orthodoxy.

CHAPTER 17

WHY I AM INCARNATIONAL

I have a confession to make.[121] Almost every time I tune in to religious radio or TV, I want to change my religion. I'm a preacher myself and a frequent guest on well-done radio talk shows, so I should appreciate radio and TV preachers, but somehow, hearing many of them[122] makes me want to become Buddhist, Jewish, Muslim, Hindu—anything but what I'm hearing. What is the source of my (over)reaction to religious broadcasting? I think my frustration has to do with how religious programming is funded: through voluntary donations. And raising donations for religious broadcasting isn't easy. Like many difficult things, it has become a science.

A key factor in the science of successful religious-broadcast fund-raising is fear. So listeners/viewers are told of vast left-wing conspiracies to "destroy the family" or "stamp out

---

[121] CHAPTER LENGTH ALERT: This is the longest chapter in the book. You may wish to pretend it is three chapters instead of one. Otherwise you are advised to brew a fresh pot of coffee before proceeding.

[122] If you are a radio or TV preacher reading this book, I'm sure I don't mean you. I mean those other guys whom you, too, wish would get off the air. There are plenty of exceptions to my gross (and playful) generalizations here, and my tongue keeps drifting into my cheek. By the way, many religious broadcasters belong to the "Evangelical Council for Financial Accountability"; I wonder if a sister group should be formed: The Christian Council for Theological Responsibility?

religious freedom." They are then begged to help fight against "the homosexual agenda" or "secular humanism" or "postmodernism" or "terrorism" or some other real or imagined bugaboo—by sending in their sizable tax-deductible donations, for which they will receive an exciting premium (a *genuine* mustard seed in a cube of clear plastic, for example).

The result? Funds are raised. But there is also an unintended consequence of these fear tactics. Christians who listen to fear broadcasts become afraid. Recently I received an e-mail from an intelligent young "religiously right" Christian (intelligent enough to use e-mail) who told me he expects to die as a martyr at the hands of "liberals." How many hours of religious broadcasting does it take to produce this much fear?

I know these broadcasters are good people. I know none of this is intentional. It's a systems thing. (I could easily play into a parallel systems thing by overly demonizing religious broadcasters, which I suppose I've already done.) But even so, when the fervent furnace of religion kindles sparks of fear in people's hearts, a dangerous wildfire can rage out of control, and a lot of people can get hurt—especially the people who have been characterized as threats.[123]

Christians aren't the only ones who do this, of course. Across the world, ethnic majorities and minorities, political parties, religions, clubs, genders, departments, schools of philosophy, and other gangs and tribes practice in-grouping and out-grouping with gusto and glee. Chimpanzees and dogs do it, too, showing the primal roots of the practice, although chimps and dogs lack the advanced technology to punish out-groups

---

[123] If the apostle James were here today, I think his warnings about the uncontrolled tongue (3:1ff) would begin: "Let not many of you become broadcasters, brothers and sisters." (He would probably discourage excessive religious publishing, too.) More constructively, may I encourage you to support religious programming that does not use fear and greed for fund-raising but instead earns your support based on the quality of the broadcasting itself?

as we humans do. They can bark, screech, bite, and scratch; we can imprison, torture, oppress, exclude, blacklist, intimidate, excommunicate, and impose ethnic cleansing and holocaust. The word *orthodoxy*, so central to the title of this book, is often one of the prime weapons of exclusion, conjuring inquisitions and throwing around damning labels like *heretic* and *infidel*.

My friend Neil Livingstone once told me that Jesus didn't want to create an in-group which would banish others to an out-group; Jesus wanted to create a *come-on-in group*, one that sought and welcomed everyone. Such a group came not to conquer, not to badger, not to vanquish, not to eradicate other groups, but to save them, redeem them, bless them, respect them, love them, befriend them, and embrace them.

Or, put another way, Jesus threatened people with inclusion; if they were to be excluded, it would be because they refused to accept their acceptance. If people rejected his acceptance, he did not retaliate against them, but submitted himself to humiliation, mistreatment, even crucifixion by them. Missiologist David Bosch said it like this: "...it is when we are weak that we are strong. So, the word that perhaps best characterizes the Christian church in its encounter with other faiths is *vulnerability*...The people who are to be won and saved should, as it were, always have the possibility of crucifying the witness of the gospel." [124]

You might object: But Jesus said he didn't come to bring peace, but a sword. He spoke of families being divided because of him and his message. Yes, I would respond, but if you want to see how this works, imagine these scenarios:

Imagine you're a white son of white, racist parents. One

---

[124] David Bosch, *Transforming Mission* (Orbis, 1991), p. 485. Subsequent quotes will be referenced in text.

day you come home and say, "As a follower of Christ, I think we should love African Americans and Hispanics." As a peacemaker in the way of Christ, you will create division.

Imagine you're a corporate executive in a prosperous company. You say at a board meeting, "I would like to reduce our profit margin over the next 10 years so that we can lead the industry in creating recyclable products, so we minimize damage to God's earth and so we act as proper stewards of God's creation." As a follower of Christ, you will create division.

Imagine you are a leader in a political party that prospers (again, like many organizations that need to raise funds) by creating fear of rivals. You write a memo saying, "We need to treat our opponents exactly as we would want to be treated. We need to speak truth, free not only of lies, but also of exaggerations. Our yes must be yes, our no must be no. Even if they slander us, we must not return insult for insult. In fact, we must do good to our opponents." In the name of peace, you will soon, in all likelihood, experience a sword (and in all likelihood, that sword that will cut short your political tenure).

As Chesterton writes, "Any man who preaches real love is bound to beget hate...Real love has always ended in bloodshed" (*Orthodoxy*, 143).

Real love of this sort was ultimately demonstrated by the incarnation of Christ. An early missionary in the modern Protestant missionary movement, Daniel Crawford, understood the radical nature of Christ's incarnation and its implications for all of us who are associated with Christ's name. He went from Scotland to central Africa but failed to return to "civilization" for his expected furlough. Eventually his countrymen received a letter from him explaining why he didn't feel the need to always return "home," for Africa was now his home: "I am de-nationalized—a brother to all men; Arab, African, Mongol, Aryan, Jew; seeing in the Incarnation a link that binds us up with all men." [125]

Just as Jesus' incarnation bound him, not just to the Jewish people, but to all humanity, his incarnation links his followers to all people—*including* (WARNING: here's the kicker that may put me in the same category as the imaginary scenarios above) *people of other religions.*

When I say we are linked and bound through Christ's incarnation to all people, I am not saying *all religions are the same, it doesn't matter what you believe, truth is relative,* blah, blah, blah. I am saying that because we follow Jesus, because we believe Jesus is true, and because Jesus moves toward all people in love and kindness and grace, *we do the same.* Our Christian identity must not make us afraid of, superior to, isolated from, defensive or aggressive toward, or otherwise hostile to people of other religions. Rather, the reverse.

I originally titled this chapter "Why I Am Buddhist/ Muslim/Hindu/Jewish," seeking to echo—provocatively—Crawford's words about being linked to all people.

The original title proved excessively provocative, however, if not downright misleading. So the current, less-provocative title emerged, affirming that a generous orthodoxy takes the incarnation very seriously, affirming that God's movement "us-ward" in Jesus Christ sends us on a similar trajectory "them-ward."

---

[125] F. Roy Coad, *A History of the Brethren Movement* (Vancouver, B.C.: Regent College, p. 187). Thanks to Skip Smith for this quote.

Because I follow Jesus, then, I am bound to Jews, Muslims, Buddhists, Hindus, agnostics, atheists, New Agers, everyone (*even religious broadcasters*, I was just reminded by a still, small voice). Not only am I bound to them in love, but I am also actually called to, in some real sense (please don't minimize this before you qualify it), become one of them, to enter their world and be with them in it.

In saying this, I am echoing one of Jesus' earliest followers, Paul. The apostle Paul had been a Pharisee, a member of the religious movement most unfavorable to Jesus, and the group of which Jesus was most critical. Pharisees were the elect and elite among the elect and elite. They wouldn't eat with non-Jews; they wouldn't greet them, embrace them, marry them, or even help them if they found them beaten and left to die on the road. Pharisees didn't understand the difference between love/acceptance and approval, so, lest they be accused of approving of other religions, they refrained from loving or accepting people who were part of other religions (as well as subpar members of their own).[126]

Jesus entered Paul's life, and Paul entered Jesus' way, and all this changed, to the point where Paul could say, "To the Jews I became like a Jew, to win Jews...To those not having the law I became like one not having the law...so as to win those not having the law. To the weak I became weak, to win the weak. I have become all things to all men that by all possible means I might save some. I do all this for the sake of the gospel, that I may share in its blessings" (1 Corinthians 9:20-23). Can you feel the immense, shocking, almost heretical potency of these words written by this former Pharisee? (Again, if you're familiar with them, please try not to let your familiarity blunt their impact.) The gospel, the story of God's becoming "one of us" through incarnation, propels Paul on an incarnational ministry to become "one of them,"

---

[126] Thanks to my colleague Keith Matthews and former religious broadcaster Rich Bueller (one of the best ever) for this important distinction between love/acceptance and approval.

whoever "they" are.

There are two things this incarnational ministry is not. It is not a kind of dishonest spy work, where one pretends to be something one is not, like an Internet pedophile who pretends to be a teenager so he can enter their trust, or like a network marketer who pretends to be your friend so he can add you to his down-line. And again, neither is it a kind of "everybody-is-okay/all-religions-are-equally-true" relativist/pluralist tolerance, where I smoke weed with the Rastafarians, chant with the Hare Krishnas, bow toward Mecca with the Muslims, and dance with the Pentecostals because "it's all good, it's all fun, it's all mellow, and it doesn't matter which religion (if any?) you believe as long as you're sincere, man." If you take what I'm saying and turn it into either of these approaches, you're smoking some kind of weed yourself, I think.[127]

No, a generous incarnational orthodoxy means something very different. It's hard to understand because it is quite new, but also so old (as old as Jesus' incarnation and Paul's "all things to all people") that it has been forgotten. In a sense, what I am asking for in relation to other contemporary religious cultures is that we give them the same freedom and respect my European ancestors were given many centuries ago, something I started thinking about when my children were small and we decided to homeschool them for a few years.

We weren't homeschoolers of the religious-right type, afraid that "the secular system" would pollute our kids. True, we had our doubts about the secular system, but we had equal doubts about the religious one. Our desire to homeschool flowed more from the fact that my wife and I were both educators, and we were

---

[127] Many people are rightly allergic to pluralistic relativism. Unfortunately, they think the only alternative is an even less-thoughtful approach. For a more thoughtful approach, one that goes beyond pluralistic relativism (rather than stopping short of it), see Ken Wilber's *A Theory of Everything* (Shambala, 2000), Chapter 2: "Boomeritis." See also the last paragraphs of this chapter.

excited about the prospect of giving our kids a love for learning that we feared normal institutionalized education (secular or religious) might squelch. As we searched for curricula to use, we of course had to wade through a lot of the religious-right type of curriculum because it dominates the market.

And as we did so, this struck me: the most conservative forms of religious curricula all taught extensively on the Greek and Roman gods and goddesses. Why? Because "classical" Western culture had been adopted as part of the Christian heritage. Long ago, Christians in the West had learned to appreciate and even love Greco-Roman culture; they baptized it, integrated it into Christianity's heritage. Zeus, Apollo, Athena, Pan, Dionysius, and Mercury weren't demons to be feared or idols to be destroyed—they were part of our heritage to be redeemed, with rich symbolism and profound meaning for Christians today.

Christianity had similarly embraced much of Northern European culture, finding place in our Christmas celebrations for the evergreen tree and yule log of the pagan Scandinavians, for example. In its first thousand years, then, Christianity didn't seek to replace Greco-Roman or Northern European or Celtic cultures (of my ancestors) with the culture of its own Jewish roots; rather it sought (in its best moments) to enter these cultures, redeem them, transform them, and preserve everything of value in them. The apostles reached this conclusion in relation to the "meat sacrificed to idols" controversy very early in church history. The Celtic missionary movement followed the apostolic lead especially well in this regard (though the Romanized church often did not), with far-reaching impact.[128]

---

[128] The kind of cultural redemption I'm envisioning here is not a Borg-like "resistance is futile; prepare for assimilation." It is, rather, the same kind of loving conservation known to all mothers who save (note the word) their child's drawings, report cards, baby shoes, class pictures, letters from summer camp, etc.

However, the modern missionary movement of the last 200 years did not fully follow this apostolic or Celtic path. Instead the modern missionary movement unintentionally adopted (with some happy exceptions) the Roman way, which cooperated with the spirit of its age, the spirit of colonialism, white supremacy, Eurocentrism, jingoism, and chauvinism. So now, when we think of *orthodoxy* in missions, we think of a colonial approach, which doesn't simply seek to drive the sin from the culture, but which seeks (without realizing it) to drive the culture from the people and replace it with a Euro-American Christian subculture.

What Muslims have tended to do with Arab culture, Christians have tended to do with Euro-American culture: impose it wherever they go. This is understandable for Muslims because they have (they believe) a divinely dictated sacred text and no incarnation. However, this cultural colonialism is illogical and inexcusable for Christians—who have a sacred text and one believed to be inspired, but *not dictated*, and who believe that God spoke in various times to various cultures, and then entered human culture and history lovingly, climactically, personally, and incarnationally through Christ.[129]

Many readers will remember the Taliban regime's decision to destroy with explosives ancient Buddhist statues, carved from a mountainside in the eastern part of Afghanistan (like Mount Rushmore in the United States). That's a vision of cultural replacement; annihilate the cultures associated with other religions and replace every memory and artifact of them with the trappings of the religion in power. This is exactly what Western Christianity has practiced in many less explosive but no less real ways in our history. This is exactly what I believe must change in a generous orthodoxy on the road ahead.

---

[129] It may be worth noting that many Christians have an understanding (dictation theory) of their sacred text that is more Islamic than truly Christian.

The fact is, all religions of the world are under threat—from fundamentalist Islam, but more, from the McDonaldization and Wal-Martization of the world, from global consumerism, from forces that emanate not from Arabia or Afghanistan, but from New York and Hollywood—forces that make all religions equally superfluous, trivial compared to the lust for a new car or a new pair of jeans.

All the religions of the world are under threat from reductionist ideologies emanating from our centers of modern education, whether in Boston, San Francisco, or Paris—ideologies that, often under the guise of tolerance, are intolerant of any ideology but their own. And all religions, along with everything else on earth, are under threat from weapons of mass destruction, whose buttons are fingered not only in the Middle or Far East, but also down the road from my home, in Washington, D.C., and Northern Virginia. Should the Christian faith be listed among these threats to the religions of the world? Given the chance, would Christianity eradicate every vestige of the world's other religions?

No. The Christian faith, I am proposing, should become (in the name of Jesus Christ) a welcome friend to other religions of the world, not a threat. We should be seen as a protector of their heritages, a defender against common enemies, *not* one of the enemies. Just as Jesus came originally not to destroy the law but to fulfill it, not to condemn people but to save them, I believe he comes today not to destroy or condemn anything (anything but evil) but to redeem and save everything that can be redeemed or saved.

Ah, but you say, there's the problem: there's so much evil in *other* religions. Yes, I reply, there is indeed, but not just in other religions. There is so much evil in our own, too. So I (under wise advisement, recalling Chapter 0) propose that before we seek to remove the splinters from the eyes of other religions, we concentrate on the planks in our own. I also propose (with Jesus' parable from Matthew 13:24-30 in mind) that we don't seek to root up all the bad weeds in the world's religions (including our own), but rather seek to encourage the growth of good wheat in all religions including our own, leaving it for God to sort it all out as only God can do.

Wheat in other religions, you ask? Yes.

Now, contrary to popular opinion, it is not true that all religions say basically the same things. They have much in common, but there are notable contradictions and incompatibilities, many of which become more significant as they go deeper. But in many cases (again, not all), at any given moment, different religions are not always saying different things about the same subjects; rather they are often talking about different subjects entirely. Zen Buddhism, for example, says little about cosmic history and purpose as do Judaism and Christianity (and Theravada Buddhism). Western Christianity has (for the last few centuries anyway) said relatively little about mindfulness and meditative practices, about which Zen Buddhism has said much. To talk about different things is not to contradict one another; it is, rather, to have much to offer one another, on occasion at least.

If, as a Christian, I am to love my neighbor as myself and to treat my neighbor as I would be treated, then without question one of my duties in regard to my neighbor of another religion is to value everything that is good that he offers me in neighborliness— including the opportunity to learn all I can from his religion. Another duty is to offer everything I have that could be of value to him—including the opportunity to learn from my religion if he can. This is not a compromise of my faith or his; this is a required practice of it.

The theologian/missiologist who has most helped my thinking in this regard is the South African David Bosch. Born in

1930 and killed in 1992 in a tragic car crash, Bosch (pronounced more like "Bush") was a missionary in Transkei from 1957-1971, and then served as professor of missiology at the University of South Africa. He was dean of the Faculty of Theology from 1974-1977 and 1981-1987. He served as the chair of the National Initiative for Reconciliation from 1989 until his untimely death. Fluent in Xhosa, Afrikaans, Dutch, German, and English, he played an important role in the white South African clergy's acknowledgement of the evil of apartheid, and in apartheid's remarkable end.

In the 1980s, recognized for his comprehensive understanding of the history of Christian mission, he was offered a prestigious and no doubt safer job teaching theology in the United States. He turned this offer down, saying, "I don't think I can leave my colleagues and the struggle for South Africa. It is a critical moment and that is where God has placed me." In several of his works, most notably his masterpiece *Transforming Mission* and the short but profound *Believing in the Future*, Bosch suggested that the modern missionary movement was coming to an end, and a new missionary movement was emerging.

Having reflected on Bosch's work, along with my own experience in the world of Christian missions (including nine meaningful years on the board of directors of International Teams, www.iteams.org), I would like to suggest eight emerging obligations of a generous orthodoxy—postcolonial, postmodern, whatever—in regard to other religions in God's world. Each builds on the previous obligation, and each enriches the others.

We must accept the coexistence of different faiths in our world willingly, not begrudgingly.

In the old modern-colonial world, Euro-American Christians could wish that everyone everywhere would just get with it and become proper Euro-American Christians like us. In fact, non-Christians could be seen as stubborn rebels who refused to capitulate to the dominating truth. They could be seen as "in the way," a problem to be removed through either conversion (forced or free) or ethnic cleansing (a euphemism the horrible reality of which has been too often perpetuated in the name of Christ). Now in the emerging postmodern, postcolonial world, it is largely only radical Islamists who speak this way—Islamists and some Christians of an ungenerous orthodoxy.

No, the fact is that different religions have been here for a long time and are here to stay for the foreseeable future. To be a Christian means that one follows Jesus' teaching of neighbor-love, *especially* to those whose religions are different—even those who might be considered enemies. To show love and acceptance toward people, again, is *not* to approve all they believe or do, as any parent knows. To show disapproval of divergent beliefs by withholding love and acceptance may be orthodox Phariseeism, and it may even be orthodox modern, Western, colonial Christianity, but it is not the generous orthodoxy of Jesus Christ. It is, rather, a betrayal of our Lord and his way.

Having acknowledged and accepted the coexistence of other faiths, Christians should actually talk with people of other faiths, engaging in gentle and respectful dialogue.

This dialogue will benefit others, but we need it as well. According to Macquarrie (quoted in *Transforming Mission*, 483), there are seven formative factors in theology: experience, revelation, Scripture, tradition, culture, reason—*and dialogue with other religions*. This has always been the case, beginning with Judaism and Greco-Roman religions in the first centuries of the church. History makes this clear: Christianity has discovered what it is about in large part through this kind of dialogue. Without non-Christian dialogue partners, there would be no Christian theology as we know it. Bosch said it like this: "One-way, monological travel is out, as is militancy in any form" (*Transforming Mission*, 483).

Many modern Christians believe that to engage in dialogue means that we sacrifice our own position, that respectful dialogue is seen as compromise. This is absurd. Dialogue is only possible among people who come to the table with commitments— along with the mutual respect required for conversation, respect that is also required of Christians in any dialogue. Again, Bosch: "Without my commitment to the gospel, dialogue becomes a mere chatter; without the authentic practice of the neighbor it becomes arrogant and worthless" (*Transforming Mission*, 484).

We must assume that God is an unseen partner in our dialogues who has something to teach all participants, including us.

Just as Peter and the early church experienced ongoing conversion through the conversion of Cornelius (Acts 10-11), God has much to teach us in and through our dialogue with others. As Bosch affirms: "We are not the 'haves,' the *beati possidentes*, standing over against spiritual 'have-nots,' the *massa damnata*. We are all recipients of the same mercy, sharing in the same mystery" (*Transforming Mission*, 484).

We must learn humility in order to engage in respectful dialogue.

Too often the dominant-but-receding modern, Western, colonial Christianity saw boldness and humility as opposites, not as partners. We showed boldness and confidence in the gospel through what appeared to outsiders (though not to ourselves) as bombast, arrogance, disrespect, and insensitivity. As a result we attacked and argued too often, and we apologized too seldom. In the emerging context, *apologetics* (the art of giving reasons for our faith, hope, and love) will often, perhaps always, require a prelude of *apology*. We will have to realize, and admit, that the line of error and injustice runs through, not between, all religions, including Christianity.[130]

This apology can become excessive, though. We can apologize for the sins of our fathers in such a way that we render ourselves arrogantly superior to them, insensitive both to the challenges of their milieu and to our present and anticipated failures in our own. So humility also means showing respect for our ancestors in the faith, for what they have handed down to us, Bosch says, even if we have reason to be painfully embarrassed by their racist, sexist, and imperialist bias. We have no guarantees, he reminds us, that we will do any better in our context than they did in theirs.

In addition, we can become so preoccupied with our Christian failures that we minimize two realities: that every religion has its dark side, and that Christian faith has, along with disasters, produced much beauty, much goodness, and many valuable articulations of truth. Again, Bosch says it well: "We delude ourselves if we believe that we can be respectful to other faiths only if we disparage our own" (*Transforming Mission*, 485).

If "love your neighbor as yourself" applies in interreligious dialogue, then self-hatred is not a good path to neighbor-love. Honest, humble self-appraisal is. Christianity-bashing is a popular sport and is perhaps a needed antidote to a version of Christianity that too often bashed, but wouldn't it be a positive step to get beyond bashing altogether?

---

[130] See Chapter 18.

We must realize that each religion is its own world, requiring very different responses from Christians.

In this way, there is no such thing as interreligious dialogue in general, rather there is dialogue between this Christian individual or community and that Jewish or Buddhist or Hindu individual or community. Practice in one kind of dialogue prepares one for the next, but each requires new learnings and new openness. Each brings new challenges and new blessings, too.

Only at this point are we ready to reassert that conversation does not exclude evangelism but makes it possible.

We share the good news of Jesus, seeking to make disciples of all peoples—always inviting, never coercing. In Bosch's words: "We affirm that witness does not preclude dialogue but invites it, and that dialogue does not preclude witness but extends and deepens it."

I must add, though, that I don't believe making disciples must equal making adherents to the Christian religion. It may be advisable in many (not all!) circumstances to help people become followers of Jesus *and* remain within their Buddhist, Hindu, or Jewish contexts. This will be hard, you say, and I agree. But frankly, it's not at all easy to be a follower of Jesus in many "Christian" religious contexts, either.

Vincent Donovan captured exactly what I mean in *Christianity Rediscovered*: "'...do not try to call them back to where they were, and do not try to call them to where you are, as beautiful as that place might seem to you. You must have the courage to go with them to a place that neither you nor they have ever been before.' Good missionary advice, and a beautiful description of the unpredictable process of evangelization, a process leading to that new place where none of us has ever been before."

At heart I think my main gift and calling is to evangelism. I want to help every person I can to become a follower of Jesus, beginning with myself. As much as I love to speak to pastors and church leaders about church health and missional vitality, I feel most alive when equipping them to speak to their undiscipled friends and neighbors about the Good News. The other statements in this list do not in any way undermine the evangelistic calling; rather, they make it possible in our emerging context.

We must continually be aware that the "old, old story" may not be the "true, true story."

In other words, we must be open to the perpetual possibility that our received understandings of the gospel may be faulty, imbalanced, poorly nuanced, or downright warped and twisted. Here we must retain the good Protestant, evangelical, and biblical instinct to allow Scripture to critique tradition—including our dominant and most recent tradition, and including our tradition's understanding of the gospel. In this sense Christians in missional dialogue must continually expect to rediscover the gospel.[131]

In fact, this is one of the great benefits of missional interreligious dialogue for the Christian community: it puts us in situations where we may discover misconceptions and distortions we never would have seen if we were only talking to ourselves in self-affirming, self-congratulating conversation.

This good Protestant instinct to allow Scripture to critique tradition, this desire to keep learning, is nowhere better exemplified than in the Roman Catholic missiologist Vincent Donovan:

Never accept and be content with unanalyzed assumptions,

---

[131] This openness to having been wrong is largely the point of my chapter in *The Church in Emerging Culture: Five Perspectives* (EmergentYS/Zondervan, 2003).

assumptions about the work, about the people, about the church or Christianity. Never be afraid to ask questions about the work we have inherited or the work we are doing. There is no question that should not be asked or that is outlawed. The day we are completely satisfied with what we have been doing; the day we have found the perfect, unchangeable system of work, the perfect answer, never in need of being corrected again, on that day we will know that we are wrong, that we have made the greatest mistake of all (*Christianity Rediscovered*, 146).

We must live with a paradox.

But what happens in our missional dialogue when we meet others whose piety and goodness and spirituality dwarfs our own? What happens when we share the gospel and others are informed and enriched, maybe even gratefully so, but not convinced?

According to Bosch: "We cannot point to any other way of salvation than Jesus Christ; at the same time, we cannot set limits to the saving power of God...We appreciate this tension, and do not attempt to resolve it." This means that anathemas and damnation can be invoked rarely if at all, which will disappoint all who have grown accustomed to resolving the above paradox by means of their invocation. (This ingrained fire-and-brimstone rhetoric so characteristic of Euro-American revivalism persists stubbornly wherever it has been exported, and will probably come back to haunt us.)

For the rest of us, rather than resolving the paradox via pronouncements on the eternal destiny of people more convinced by or loyal to other religions than ours, we simply move on (as Jesus told his disciples to do), giving all the respect and honor due those who are not convinced by our message (with the meekness Jesus taught), rather than calling down fire from heaven on them (as Jesus told his disciples not to do).

If members of other religions are under threat, we must seek to protect them.

If through Christ, God risks all for us, then we must do the same for people of other religions. They are our neighbors, and everything Jesus said about neighbors applies to them. Even if they approach us as enemies, to be faithful to Jesus we must love them and never let their status as non-Christians reduce them to non-neighbors. When Paul says, "Let us do good to all people" and then adds, "especially to those who belong to the family of believers" (Galatians 6:10), the second clause in no way nullifies the first!

With these thoughts in mind, then, I wish I could have given this chapter its more disturbing title. As a generously orthodox Christian, I consider myself not *above* Buddhists and Muslims and others, but *below* them as a servant. Better, I consider myself *with* them as a neighbor and brother.

I am here to love them, to seek to understand them, and to share with them everything of value that I have found or received that they would like to receive as well. I am here to receive their gifts to me with equal joy—to enjoy life in God's world with them, to laugh and eat and work with them, so we play with one another's children and hold one another's babies and dance at one another's weddings and savor one another's hospitality.

I am here to be their neighbor *according to the teaching of my Lord*, and if I am not a good one, *my Lord says* they have no reason to believe or even respect my message. In the process of our ongoing conversation, I hope that both they and I will become better people, transformed by God's Spirit, more pleasing to God, more of a blessing to the world, so that God's kingdom (which I seek, but cannot manipulate) comes on earth as in heaven.

Ultimately, I believe "they" and "we" can all experience this transformation best by becoming humble followers of Jesus, whom I believe (as I said in the earliest chapters of this book) to be the Son of God, the Lord of all, and the Savior of the world.

In this light, although I don't hope all Buddhists will become (cultural) Christians, I do hope all who feel so called will become Buddhist followers of Jesus; I believe they should be given that opportunity and invitation. I don't hope all Jews or Hindus will become members of the Christian religion. But I do hope all who feel so called will become Jewish or Hindu followers of Jesus.

Ultimately, I hope that Jesus will save Buddhism, Islam, and every other religion, including the Christian religion, which often seems to need saving about as much as any other religion does. (In this context, I do wish all Christians would become followers of Jesus, but perhaps this is too much to ask. After all, I'm not doing such a hot job of it myself.)[132]

To help Buddhists, Muslims, Christians, and everyone else experience life to the full in the way of Jesus (while learning it better myself), I would gladly become one of them (whoever they are) to whatever degree I can, to embrace them, to join them, to enter into their world without judgment but with saving love, as mine has been entered by the Lord. I do this *because of my deep identity as a fervent Christian*, not in spite of it.

This coming close to my non-Christian neighbor in understanding and love does not compromise my Christian commitment, but rather *expresses it*. If that point is missed, this

---

[132] If you have never heard about the quiet contextual revolution going on in missions around the term "C1-C6 Spectrum," you'll find a good introduction in Joshua Massey's article "His Ways Are Not Our Ways," found on the Web at http://bgc.gospelcom.net/emis/special%20articles/hisways.html. You will find a cautionary alternate view by Phil Parshall at http://bgc.gospelcom.net/emis/1998/danger.html. This conversation represents, in my opinion, first steps toward a postmodern and post-colonial understanding of evangelistic mission from within the evangelical missionary community.

chapter's original title will have confused and misled rather than stimulated thought. This is my best guess as to what the ethos of the next missionary movement will be. This is also the ethos of a generous orthodoxy.

My friend Diana Butler Bass embodies this ethos in a story from *Broken We Kneel* (Jossey-Bass, 2004). Diana lives near me in the Washington, D.C., area—rich in cultural diversity, tense after the 9/11 attacks, and the context for this story: [133]

> One day [my daughter] Emma saw a woman walking toward us covered in a veil and asked the inevitable, "What's that, mommy?"
>
> "Emma," I answered, "that lady is a Muslim from a faraway place. And she dresses like that—and covers her head with a veil—because she loves God. That is how her people show they love God."
>
> My daughter considered these words. She stared at the woman who passed us. She pointed at the woman, then pointed at my hair, and further quizzed, "Mommy, do you love God?"
>
> "Yes, honey." I laughed. "I do. You and I are Christians. Christian ladies show love for God by going to church, eating the bread and wine, serving the poor, and giving to those in need. We don't wear veils, but we do love God."
> After this, Emma took every opportunity to point to Muslim women during our shopping trips and tell me,

---

[133] Before some readers wish to embroil me in debates about whether Allah of Islam is the same God as Yahweh of the Bible, please allow me to show at least a few Muslims the same grace Jesus showed: (a) a Roman centurion when Jesus said he had not seen such faith in all of Israel and (b) a Syrophoenician woman when he told her she had great faith. And please allow me to believe that if God would use stars to lead wise men (astrologers) from the East to Jesus, God might also speak to Muslims in terms of their own worldview and vocabulary.

"Mommy, look, she loves God." One day, we were getting
out of our car at our driveway at the same time as our
Pakistani neighbors. Emma saw the mother, beautifully
veiled, and, pointing at her, shouted, "Look, mommy, she
loves God!"

My neighbor was surprised. I told her what I had taught
Emma about Muslim ladies loving God. While she held
back tears, this near stranger hugged me, saying, "I wish
that all Americans would teach their children so. The
world would be better. The world would be better."

I am more and more convinced that Jesus didn't come merely to
start another religion to compete in the marketplace of other
religions. If anything, I believe he came to end standard competitive
religion (which Paul called "the law") by fulfilling it; I believe he
came to open up something beyond religion—a new possibility, a
realm, a domain, a territory of the spirit that welcomes everyone
but requires everyone (now including members of the Christian
religion) to think again and become like little children.[134] It is
not, like too many religions, a place of fear and exclusion but a
place *beyond* fear and exclusion. It is a place where everyone can
find a home in the embrace of God.

If I have failed to help you see that place of generous
orthodoxy in these pages, I hope I have at least made you curious
to seek it. Even if it takes you 10 years, believe me, the struggle will
be worth it.

---

[134] The words *realm, domain,* and *territory* above should evoke the word *kingdom*—something bigger
than exclusive territorial or tribal religion and at the core of Jesus' message.

CHAPTER 18

WHY I AM DEPRESSED-YET-HOPEFUL

In the previous chapter, I suggested that Jesus didn't come to start another religion, which would include the Christian religion. I wasn't kidding. I do, in fact, believe that. That the Christian religion formed as it has is not surprising. It was no doubt necessary and in many ways good, and I know God is in it, and I am in it, too. But "the Christian religion" is neither the ultimate goal of Jesus nor the ultimate goal of God, in my view. Rather, the goal of Jesus is the kingdom of God, which is the dream of God, the wish and hope and desire of God for creation—like a parent's hopes and dreams for a beloved child.

Sometimes the Christian religion cooperates with that desire and serves as a catalyst for it. Sometimes it doesn't, obstructing or even contradicting the coming of God's kingdom. (This depresses me.) But even when it doesn't, that doesn't mean it can't cooperate again in the future—if it repents. The same can be said of every religion in the world. (Thus I am hopeful.)

Christians (rightly) tell non-Christian individuals that they must repent to be "born again": *You must repent to enter the kingdom of God. You must repent, or you will perish.* Now it is time for us Christians to practice our own preaching. We need to look back over our corporate history so far, and facing our failures and atrocities both ancient and recent, we need to repent. In terms of Gerald May's definition of denial (from *Addiction and Grace*, Harper, 1991), we Christians cannot continue *to avoid knowing what we already know*: that something is rotten in the state of our religion.

We must not separate ourselves from past and present Christian failures and atrocities in a holier-than-thou-schism, suggesting that "they" did it—Catholics, medievals, fundamentalists, liberals, whoever—not us. We must not indulge in a naïve-and-arrogant protest, denouncing the failures of our forebears or cousins in the faith with sufficient vehemence to somehow exonerate ourselves. No, rather, we need to say that those bad guys back there or over there are "us," here, now. We need to say, as the people did in Nehemiah's day, that we are no better than our fathers (Nehemiah 9). Only that kind of repentance will enable Christians to be truly born again in any way that matters.

Mormon novelist Orson Scott Card tells the story of a town that perpetrated a horrible atrocity.[135] The curse imposed on that town required that forever its inhabitants had to recount to all visitors and newcomers the sad story of what had happened there. But the curse, I think you'll agree, was also a blessing because by repeating the story, the townspeople were able again and again to repent of it, to affirm that the "we" who now tell the story do not want to be the same "we" who committed the atrocity.

It is ironic, in this regard, how it is primarily the Jews who say, "Never forget," regarding the Holocaust. Shouldn't the Germans also be saying it, even more? And shouldn't white Americans be saying it about their atrocities against slaves

---

[135] See Card's Alvin Maker series, beginning with *Seventh Son* (Tor, 1991). His Ender series has a parallel incident in *Ender's Game* (Tor, 1992).

and Native Americans and the Tutsis and Hutus about their mutual brutality in Rwanda? And all of us, in our own myriad, heartbreaking ways—because we are all Germans and Americans and Tutsis and Hutus?

A generous orthodoxy must, to be either generous or orthodox, look back on our first 2,000 years of Christian history and face our failures, our atrocities, our abdications, our cowardice, our complicity, our betrayal of Jesus, and say to ourselves, "Never forget."[136]

If the world, contrary to fundamentalist expectations, does not soon blow up in a *Left Behind*-style conflagration, but instead goes on for hundreds of thousands of years, we should realize that, from the perspective of our descendants, say in 224,000 A.D., we are still in the days of the early church. Years 1 to 2100 will be but a few brief pages in their church history textbooks. Wouldn't one of the greatest gifts to our descendants be to soberly face our early and continuing failures and sincerely repent of them, never forgetting them, but letting them educate us about the dangers of the human heart; of principalities and powers; of unholy alliances between spirit and money or God-talk and guns or fund-raising and fear; of fat and missionless religious bureaucracies; of both repressed and unrestrained sexuality; of subtle idolatries, including the worship of our concepts or feelings about God rather than God; of wealth and comfort; and of so much more?

For those of you who have never heard even one story of Christian atrocity I offer this one, which I share with shame, like

---

[136] "Remember the church's atrocities!" was the cry of the great French skeptic Voltaire, and it played no small part in the anti-religious tone of the Enlightenment. I am not recommending we go that reactionary, anti-religious route, of course. It has already been tried and produced no less terrible atrocities. Neither do I recommend we try to pause history and stop short of the Enlightenment in intentional premodern naïveté. Rather, what I am proposing here seeks to be enlightened about the Enlightenment, and pass through it and beyond it. If Christians themselves had listened to Voltaire and had humbly acknowledged our atrocities to date 300 years ago, could the Enlightenment have been brighter, less anti-religious, and less spiritually dismissive?

the people of Orson Scott Card's fictional village. (In a time of terrorism like ours, the word *terror* in this story should jump out at you whenever it appears.)[137]

It was November 16, 1532. The Spanish explorer Pizarro was crossing the Peruvian highland and came to Cajamarca. He was accompanied by 168 soldiers, 62 mounted and 106 on foot. He learned that the great Incan king Atahualpa wanted to meet him, having sent this message to Pizarro's envoy: "Tell your lord to come when and how he pleases, and that, in what way so ever he may come I will receive him as a friend and brother. I pray that he may come quickly, for I desire to see him. No harm or insult will befall him."

Pizarro had reason to be nervous, as he was slightly outnumbered: Atahualpa, head of the largest empire in the Americas, was accompanied by 80,000 soldiers (according to the reports of Pizarro's brothers, Hernando and Pedro, who were part of the Spanish contingent). As Atahualpa approached, 2,000 Incas swept the road ahead of him. The king himself was carried on an elaborate litter, covered with gold.

The brothers of Pizarro describe what happened next:

Governor Pizarro now sent Friar Vicente de Valverde to go speak to Atahualpa, and to require Atahualpa in the name of God and of the King of Spain that Atahualpa subject himself to the law of our Lord Jesus Christ and to the service of His Majesty the King of Spain. Advancing with a cross in one hand and a Bible in the other hand, and going among the Indian troops up to the place where Atahualpa was, the Friar thus addressed him: "I am a Priest of God, and I teach Christians the things of God, and in

---

[137] This account comes from Jared Diamond, *Guns, Germs and Steel* (Norton, 1997), 70-74.

like manner I come to teach you. What I teach is that which God says to us in this Book. Therefore, on the part of God and of the Christians, I beseech you to be their friend, for such is God's will, and it will be for your good."

Atahualpa asked for the Book, that he might look at it, and the Friar gave it to him closed. Atahualpa did not know how to open the Book, and the Friar was extending his arm to do so, when Atahualpa, in great anger, gave him a blow on the arm, not wishing that it should be opened. Then he opened it himself, and, without any astonishment at the letters and paper he threw it away from him five or six paces, his face in a deep crimson.

Then Friar Valveerde shouted to Pizarro and his men, "Come out! Come out Christians! Come at these enemy dogs who reject the things of God. That tyrant has thrown my book of holy law to the ground! Did you not see what happened? Why remain polite and servile toward this over-proud dog when the plains are full of Indians? March out against him, for I absolve you!"

Pizarro's men fired their guns, and the Incas were terrified: "The Indians were so filled with fear that they climbed on top of one another, formed mounds, and suffocated each other. Since they were unarmed, they were attacked without danger to any Christian. The cavalry rode them down, killing and wounding, and following in pursuit. The infantry made so good an assault on those that remained that in a short time most of them were put to the sword." The death toll was about 7,000, with many more suffering gunshot wounds and severed arms.

Pizarro grabbed Atahualpa to hold as a hostage for ransom. He lectured the Incan king:

"I have conquered greater kingdoms than yours, and have

defeated other more powerful lords than you, imposing upon them the dominion of the Emperor, whose vassal I am, and who is King of Spain and of the universal world. We come to conquer this land by his command, that all may come to a knowledge of God and of His Holy Catholic Faith, and by reason of our good mission, God, the Creator of heaven and earth and of all things in them, permits this, in order that you may know Him and come out from the bestial and diabolical life that you lead... When you have seen the errors in which you live, you will understand the good that we have done you by coming to your land...Our Lord permitted that your pride should be brought low and that no Indian should be able to offend a Christian."

King Atahualpa was held for eight months until his subjects could bring the required ransom: enough gold to fill a room 22 feet by 17 feet to a height of more than eight feet. When the room was this full of gold, the "Christian" Pizarro reneged on his promise and killed the "pagan" king who had said, "I will receive him as a friend and brother. No harm or insult will befall him."

The brothers of Pizarro assessed the whole story as follows: "The...battles of the Spaniards...will cause joy to the faithful and terror to the infidels...Such terror has been spread among the infidels, such admiration excited in all mankind."

Lest we American Protestants take comfort that European Catholics committed these atrocities, we should read an American history told from the vantage point of the First Nations of North America, like Dee Brown's *Bury My Heart at Wounded Knee*. In addition to horrible, heartbreaking stories about smallpox (biological warfare hidden in our own closet), broken treaties, massacres, and the like, we Americans will learn of less dramatic yet poignant events like this conversation in 1873, when President Grant sent a commissioner to convince the Nez Perces in what was then the Washington Territory to accept government schools.

This snippet of dialogue was written down to recount the commissioner's interchange with Chief Joseph:

> "Why do you not want schools?" the commissioner asked.
>
> "They will teach us to have churches," Joseph answered.
>
> "Do you not want churches?"
>
> "No, we do not want churches."
>
> "Why do you not want churches?"
>
> "They will teach us to quarrel about God," Joseph said. "We do not want to learn that. We may quarrel with men sometimes about things on this earth, but we never quarrel about God. We do not want to learn that."[138]

Stories like these bring us to repentance and regret.[139] There are many clever and pleasant ways of wriggling out of this repentance and regret. But to squirm out is to betray both orthodoxy and generosity of spirit. There is a high cost to repentance, to be sure: our pride, our superiority, our complacency, our smugness, our self-confidence, our judgmentalism all will feel the sharp sting of the shot of repentance. But there is a high cost to non-repentance, too, and I hope you will ponder that cost for a while before you read the next sentence.

Did you rush on to begin this sentence without pondering the cost of non-repentance, as requested in the previous sentence? Please do not read another page before doing so if you truly care about generous orthodoxy. Please. Put the book down. Just take a walk, or sit quietly. Breathe a prayer. Don't read any more, not yet.

---

[138] *Bury My Heart at Wounded Knee* (New York: Bantam, 1970), p. 302.

[139] On the value of regret, watch Danny DeVito's speech at the end of *The Big Kahuna*, available on DVD.

If enough of us can bear the truth of our failures as Christians, if we can let that truth humble us and bring us from denial to sincere and profound repentance, if our hearts are made soft and responsive to the Holy Spirit through this painful but needed process, then there truly is hope in the midst of depression.

CHAPTER 19

WHY I AM EMERGENT

In the late 1990s, I was invited to become part of Leadership Network's Young Leader Networks (YLN), also briefly known as the Terranova Project. I was grandfathered in as the network's "old guy," having moved beyond 39 in 1996. In 2001, I met with Doug Pagitt to discuss our future plans, YLN having just been launched by Leadership Network to continue on its own as an independent entity. Doug is a tall, Nordic-looking fellow with a mischievous smile. He's the pastor of Solomon's Porch (www.solomonsporch. com) in Minneapolis, former leader of YLN, and (then was) still well shy of 40. One of us—I can't remember which (a sign of good collaboration or an aging memory, or both)—came up with a new name for the group: *emergent* (www.emergentvillage.com). We had no idea how fitting the name was and how helpful it would be in our ongoing work.

Some time later my friend Stephen Freed called with added meaning for the name. Stephen, president of International Teams (www.iteams.org), spends a lot of time on airplanes, and on a recent flight met an expert in forestry. His specialty was rainforest ecology, specifically *emergents*—small saplings that grow up in the shadow of the mature forest canopy. In a sense, they may seem dwarfed, stunted, restrained by the shade of the mature trees, but in truth they are waiting. Whenever one of the mature trees dies, the emergents are there, ready to soar up and fill the gap and thrive in the light now available to them.

Meanwhile, as I mentioned in Chapter 16, I was volunteering with my state's Department of Natural Resources doing habitat surveys, especially in *emergent wetlands*—wetlands in which semiaquatic plants grow, plants whose roots are in the soil underwater but whose shoots grow up through the surface of the water to take in the full, unfiltered sun. In this sense, emergents are plants that live in different worlds simultaneously.

Also about this time Steven Johnson's best-selling *Emergence: The Connected Lives of Ants, Brains, Cities, and Software* was published.[140] The book explored how a community (of ants, of slime mold spores, of city dwellers) can be smarter than its constituents, how new levels of intelligence emerge from the interaction of lesser intelligences:

> Emergence is what happens when the whole is smarter than the sum of its parts. It's what happens when you have a system of relatively simple-minded component parts— often there are thousands or millions of them—and they interact in relatively simple ways. And yet somehow out of all this interaction some higher-level structure or intelligence appears, usually without any master planner calling the shots. These kinds of systems tend to evolve from the ground up.

The meaning of *emergent* as used in these and other settings is an essential part of the ecosystem of generous orthodoxy. A simple diagram can illustrate what we mean by *emergent thinking*. Think of a

---

[140] (Scribner, 2001)

cross section of a tree. Each ring represents not a replacement of the previous rings, not a rejection of them, but an embracing of them, a comprising of them and inclusion of them in something bigger. The tree's previous growth is integrated into, and in fact is essential to, the tree's continuing growth and strength.

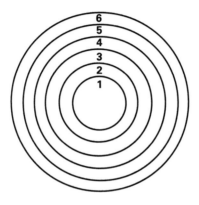

Each year nutrients from below (via roots and soil and rainfall) and energy from above (via branches and leaves, sunshine, and air) are combined to produce the durable, lasting residue of another ring. The production of that which is most durable and visible (the trunk) depends on that which is most ephemeral (the leaves) and that which is most invisible (the roots). The growth itself is hidden by the bark, as a new ring emerges secretly and gradually from the whole complex of soil, rain, sunlight, structures (xylem, phloem), and processes (photosynthesis). The soil in which the tree grows, of course, consists of the decayed remnants of its ancestors—their leaves and wood recycled through decomposition. It's an amazing process we too seldom contemplate.

There are many kinds of thinking. Some thought is discursive, tracing the development of an idea in a linear way. Some is polemical, staging a winner-takes-all fight between ideas. Some is analytical, breaking down complex wholes into simple parts or tracing complex effects back to simpler causes. But some thought seeks to embrace what has come before—like a new ring on a tree—in something bigger. This is *emergent* (or integral, or integrative) thinking.

Emergent thinking has been an unspoken assumption behind all my previous books. For example, in *A New Kind of Christian* I presented an admittedly simplified schema for talking about human history in five epochs or stages: prehistoric, ancient, medieval, modern, and postmodern. Some of my critics seemed to read this schema in an even more simplistic way than I intended it, as if each epoch represented a clean break from its predecessors. However, in my understanding, each epoch embraces, enfolds, integrates, and consolidates the gains of the previous ones and then extends those gains into new territories, like a ring on a tree.

In *The Story We Find Ourselves In* I similarly told the biblical story in seven episodes (creation, crisis, calling, conversation, Christ, community, consummation), each new episode adding new dimensions to the previous ones, embracing them while extending them into terra nova, integrating and transcending its predecessors without ending or obliterating them. So crisis throws a new twist and challenge into creation without obliterating it; calling reconnects with ongoing creation while engaging the crisis; and conversation continues creation and calling in the struggle with crisis; and so on.

In *Finding Faith* I presented (briefly) four stages of faith development—simplicity, complexity, perplexity, and humility. Again I was not seeing the stages as discrete and linear or as one replacing another in succession, but as helical—an ascending and widening spiral in which each new stage covers the same 360 degrees of territory as its predecessors but in a larger way. Each stage enfolds, embraces, integrates, and revalues the gains of previous stages, and, in so doing, rises to a higher level.

If this is unclear, think of what you are doing at this moment: reading. A child starts by reading letters, then syllables, then words, then sentences, then paragraphs, then chapters and books, then authors or genres or whatever. When a reader decides to read all the works of an author, say, Wendell Berry (a worthwhile endeavor!), one uses the skills of kindergartners by recognizing letters, plus the skills of first graders by recognizing syllables and words and sentences, and so on. New levels embrace and build upon previous levels; they don't exclude them. One doesn't stop reading sentences to read paragraphs.

A generous orthodoxy does the same thing. In whatever ways Protestants feel they emerged from Catholicism—or in whatever ways post-Vatican II Catholics feel they emerged from pre-Vatican II Catholicism—they can't despise their roots or reject their past. Rather they have to see that without learning letters and syllables and simple sentences at those earlier stages, they couldn't understand poetry now. Pacifists, in this sense, realize they wouldn't exist if it weren't for their ancestors who were good fighters.

The "Great Chain of Being" (better called, says integral philosopher Ken Wilber, the "Great Nest of Being") seeks to capture this emergence. Imagine the numbers on the previous diagram representing these realities:

1. Space and Time: the primal creation in which everything emerges.
2. Inanimate Matter: the domain of physics and chemistry in space and time.
3. Microbiotic and Plant Life: the domain of microbiology and botany, which embraces domains 1 and 2 and adds life.
4. Animal Life: the domain of zoology, which comprises domains 1 through 3 and adds increasing levels of sentience and intelligence.

5. Human Life: the domain of anthropology and psychology and art and ethics, which comprises domains 1 through 4 and adds increasing levels of consciousness and culture.

6. Spiritual Life: the domain of awareness of God, accessed through theology and spirituality and mysticism, which encompasses domains 1 through 5, and adds the experience of the sacred and conscious relationship with God.

One of the frustrations, but also stimulations, of this way of thinking is that we usually think of space and time as "big," matter as "small," plant life as "smaller," and animal and human life as "smaller still." This diagram doesn't picture size but emergence. The outer ring embraces everything within it, and it *needs* everything within it. Without the smaller rings, it wouldn't exist.

A similar kind of diagram could picture human life:

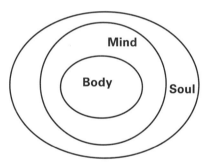

From the integration of the faculties of the human body—which includes the brain—(senses, hunger, digestion, respiration, attention, etc.), the mind emerges with its own faculties (will, memory, anticipation, analysis, classification, contrast, cause and effect, imagination, etc.). It can be differentiated from the body (think of someone in a persistent vegetative state), but it is not disassociated from the body (think of mental illness, learning disabilities, the effects of narcotics or alcohol or caffeine). From the integration of the faculties of the body and mind, the soul emerges with an ethical and aesthetic and relational dimension— the person whose story includes a body and mind, but is not limited to a body and mind.

Again, this kind of diagram frustrates us because we're more used to thinking of ourselves in the neoplatonic and Cartesian ghost-in-a-machine model, where the body is the bigger machine and the soul is a little disassociated tenant, fluttering around in the machine like a tiny moth in a tin can. This model says something very different: the soul is the "bigger" reality, the higher emergent reality, differentiated from the body and mind but never disassociated from them.

Similar diagrams could picture individuals in families, in communities, in cultures, in a world, in God's kingdom. Individuals are wonderful, but they aren't the highest expression of humanity. Neither are families, though families are wonderful, and without families, individuals can never reach their full fruition. Neither are communities, or cultures, or even the whole planet. All things are nested in a larger reality, and the largest reality, the one that comprises them, the ultimate domain is, I believe, what Jesus meant when he announced "The kingdom (or domain) of God."

Sin, in this model, can be understood as lower levels or rings resisting the emergence of higher levels or rings, body-lusts refusing to be integrated with mental ideals in an ethical soul; individual wills (a mental faculty) refusing to develop the virtues of soul necessary so that healthy families and communities and cultures can emerge; individual kingdoms (which we could call me-isms) or national or religious or ethnic kingdoms (which we could call we-isms) refusing to yield territory to the emergence of the larger (and largest) reality—God's kingdom (which we could

call good theism).[141] Like physical illness, which involves the parts
not integrating with ease (hence *dis-ease*) to yield the emergent
reality of health, sin mucks up God's original intent for the story
of creation, sabotaging emergence by replacing it with stagnation
and decay.

Because of this counter-emergent virus we call sin, the
stages, episodes, and levels don't always unfold as they should.
There are setbacks, stagnations, false starts, premature births,
retardations, impatient rebellions, emergence defects, and failed
attempts at emergence. For example, if parents do a good job of
raising an infant, she becomes a child. If parents do a good job
of raising the child, she becomes an adolescent. But if parents
become afraid of releasing the adolescent into adulthood and
instead try to freeze the adolescent in the adolescent phase, she will
not comply. She cannot comply even if she wants to. She may rebel.
She may become depressed. She may shrivel up in disheartened
outward compliance but inward despair. She may run away. She
may become a twisted semi-adolescent or even a suicide statistic.
But she cannot simply stay the same. Similarly, a child may want to
act like a teenager too soon, before she is ready, and if she succeeds
in acting out her wish, she will suffer consequences that bring pain
to her, her family, and others as well.[142]

Emergent Christians look at the world as "our Father's
world." We stand wide-eyed, trying to take in what's going on here,
understanding it as an unfolding story, an emergent family drama,
with birth, growth, struggle, maturity, death, and resurrection.

---

[141] Having read this sentence, you may perhaps better understand why I believe a person
can affiliate with Jesus in the kingdom-of-God dimension without affiliating with him in
the religious kingdom of Christianity. In other words, I believe that Christianity is not the
kingdom of God. The ultimate reality is the kingdom of God, and Christianity at its best is
here to proclaim and lead people into that kingdom, calling them out of smaller rings, smaller
kingdoms. Christianity at its worst, using the definition in this paragraph, can become a
sin when it holds people within its ring and won't let them enter the kingdom of God. Jesus
diagnosed the religious leaders of his day as doing this very thing.

[142] Using this analogy, consider how a religion can malfunction, either in the role of parent in
relation to children, or in the role of child in relation to God.

We see God not as a potentate trying to keep serfs under control in the stasis of perpetual childhood, but rather as a parent inviting us to grow and mature, to become as good and beautiful and true as we can become—to emerge.

It's risky business. God is a brokenhearted Parent when we squander our birthright and leave our proper spiritual home. God is full of joy when prodigal daughters and sons come home and rejoin the family and reenter the family story. Always God is wise and kind, neither seeking to freeze us at a manageable age nor to push us beyond our abilities. Rather, God's wish and hope is for us to grow toward the measure of the stature of the fullness of Christ—at the pace we can, remembering that "we are but dust," yet we are children of God.

To return to our tree analogy, God is the air that surrounds the tree, the soil in which it is rooted, the sunlight and rainfall that beckon it to grow and become, season by season, ring by ring. In God we live and grow and have our being. In God's wind we sway and our leaves dance.

In this way of seeing, God stands ahead of us in time, at the end of the journey, sending to us in waves, as it were, the gift of the present, an inrush of the future that pushes the past behind us and washes over us with a ceaseless flow of new possibilities, new options, new chances to rethink and receive new direction, new empowerment. This newness, these possibilities are always "at hand," "among us," and "coming" so we can "enter" the larger reality and transcend the space we currently fill—language you will recognize as being, again, the language of the kingdom of God, which is the language of the gospel.

What we will be is not yet clear to us. What we are becoming is presently only visible as through a glass darkly. As we see the glorious image of God in the face of Christ, as we lean toward that image that beckons us forward, as we identify it as our true destiny and the pearl of great price that we seek, we are purified and transformed inwardly, from glory to glory. We constantly emerge from what we were and are into what we can become—not just as individuals, but as participants in the emerging realities of families, communities, cultures, and worlds.

For too many, the process of emergence is fitful, stalled, aborted, like a butterfly halfway in and halfway out of its cocoon. It is to these trapped people that Jesus calls, "Follow me." We follow him into full emergence as children of God. It is for this full emergence that we thirst with aspiration, longing, and hope.

This God-given thirst for emergence brings us beyond where we have been. It caused ancient Christians to emerge from first-century Judaism. It caused their descendants to emerge from apostolic Christianity to the era of the martyrs and apologists, showing both courage and intelligence in dealing with their evolving situation. It caused the Celtic Christians to emerge from the parochial, Constantinian Roman Christianity that threatened to stifle and stagnate ongoing Christian emergence.[143] It caused late-medieval Christianity to emerge from the chaos and struggle of the early Middle Ages. It caused modern Christianity (in its Protestant and Catholic forms) to emerge from its late-medieval stage. And it is causing new forms of Christian spirituality, community, and mission to emerge from modern Western Christianity.

No emergence is perfect. Old things, previous gains that should be retained and integrated, are forgotten or rejected. Scars that should be embraced and thus healed are rejected,

---

[143] "Constantinian" refers to the Roman Emperor Constantine, whose edicts in the fourth century led to Christianity becoming, first, a legal religion, then the preferred religion, then the official religion of the Empire. This mingling of church and empire created what is known as "Christendom," a necessary stage, perhaps, but something from which many of us are glad to have emerged. (Others have what Diana Butler Bass calls a Constantinian hangover, a nostalgia for the "good old days" when church and state were entwined.)

and infection results (think of a lightning scar on a tree and of forgiveness and repentance as ways of embracing and healing such a scar). New things that should be added are similarly feared and shunned. True prophets (those who bring a new word from God to assist in the current process of emergence) are crucified; false prophets (those who promise shortcuts that will cause regression or stagnation) are made rich and famous. The process is messy.

So will our current emergence yield a superior and ultimate form of Christianity? Will this emerging form finally get it right? *Of course not.* No more than a teenager is superior to a child or than a senior citizen finally gets it right in comparison to a middle-aged mother. No more than a dying person is the ultimate and final form of a human being. Thus a generous orthodoxy is an emerging orthodoxy, never complete until we arrive at our final home in God.

Perhaps this sounds to you like heresy, not orthodoxy. Perhaps (as one of my dialogue partners once said) this seems to present you with only two options: a non-emergent gospel that is definitive, clear, sure, and certain, or a "radically indeterminate," anything-goes gospel that means anything, and thus is worth nothing.[144]

Perhaps this sounds to you like a heterodox compromise with pluralistic relativism, which philosopher Ken Wilber has aptly described like this:

> It claimed that all truth is culturally situated (except its own truth, which is true for all cultures); it claimed there are no transcendental truths (except its own pronouncements, which transcend specific contexts); it claimed that all hierarchies or value rankings are

---

[144] Michael Horton in *The Church in Emerging Culture: Five Perspectives* (emergentYS, 2003).

oppressive and marginalizing (except its own value ranking, which is superior to the alternatives); it claimed there are no universal truths (except its own pluralism, which is universally true for all peoples).[145]

Wilber rightly notes how this kind of pluralism (which, if it is universally true when it says there are no universal truths, self-refutes and therefore can't be universally true) becomes the unwitting ally of narcissism (a preoccupation with the self): "Narcissism will therefore not acknowledge anything universal, because that places various demands and duties on narcissism that it will try to deconstruct, because 'nobody tells me what to do.' This egotistic stance can easily be propped up and supported with the tenets of pluralistic relativism." This syndrome—a synergy between narcissism and pluralistic relativism—Wilber calls "boomeritis," and if you're against it, I can see why. Me too.

But please understand: *that's not what I'm talking about, not at all!* I know it might appear to be so, because I and others, while we aren't "for" pluralistic relativism, do see it as a kind of needed chemotherapy. We see modernity with its absolutisms and colonialisms and totalitarianisms as a kind of static dream, a desire to abide in timeless abstractions and extract humanity from the ongoing flow of history and emergence, a naïve hope to make *now* the end of history (which actually sounds either like a kind of death wish or millennialism).

In Christian theology, this anti-emergent thinking is expressed in systematic theologies that claim (overtly, covertly, or unconsciously) to have final orthodoxy nailed down, freeze-dried, and shrink-wrapped forever. Emergent Christians (post-liberal, post-conservative) see pluralistic relativism as a dangerous treatment for Stage 4 absolutist/colonial/totalitarian modernity

---

[145] *A Theory of Everything* (Boston: Shambala, 2001), p. 37.

(to use language from cancer diagnosis), something that saves a life by nearly killing it. It's dangerous medicine—but stagnancy, getting stuck too long in the cocoon, is dangerous too. (As in any good story, all of our choices run between Scylla and Charybdis, between dangers to the left and right.)

Again, I understand why people often accuse me (and others on this emergent path) of pluralistic relativism. If you hold to a modern, exclusivist, absolutist, colonial version of Christianity, anything not "us" seems to be "them."

But please, ask yourself: is it possible that there is a way of seeing and being that is beyond modern exclusivism/absolutism *and* beyond pluralistic relativism? Could there be an approach that avoids both stagnant, modern fundamentalism and narcissistic boomeritis? Is it possible that modern, exclusivist, absolutist Christians are right—pluralistic relativism is dangerous? But is it possible that the way ahead is not to *stop short* of a pluralistic phase, but rather to *go through it* and *pass beyond it*, emerging into something beyond and better? Do you see why words like *postmodern, post-liberal*, and *post-conservative* keep coming up—why the word *beyond* is so prevalent these days?

In this chapter I am trying (with Ken Wilber's help) to make clear that I believe there is something above and beyond the current alternatives of modern fundamentalism/absolutism *and* pluralistic relativism. I know this is so hard to envision because I struggled to envision this myself for about 10 years and have only begun in the last few years to see it, and even now, only faintly. This "above and beyond" is, I believe, the way of Jesus, which is the way of love and the way of embrace.[146] It integrates what has gone before so that something new can emerge. It is, again, what I

---

[146] With the word *embrace*, I'm also enlisting the help of Miroslav Volf, *Exclusion and Embrace* (Abingdon, 1996).

believe Jesus means by "the kingdom of God," a reality into which we have been emerging through the centuries, which is bigger than whatever we generally mean by "Christianity" but at the same time is what generously orthodox Christianity is truly about. May it come to us; may we come into it.

CHAPTER 20

WHY I AM UNFINISHED

The preceding chapters are as close as anything I have written to a kind of personal confession or testimony of faith. They are still a far cry from anything like a systematic theology, which I am neither qualified nor disposed to write. It would be more likely that I would turn to music, scriptwriting for film or theatre, poetry, fiction, or pottery making in the years ahead. I understand why German theologian Karl Barth celebrated Mozart so enthusiastically: music could do something "dogmatics" couldn't.

As I've said already, I believe that the kind of generous orthodoxy I am exploring here will pursue a more narrative approach to theology, in the tradition of the great James William McClendon and others. Rather than trying to capture timeless truth in objective statements systematized in analytical outlines and recorded in books and institutionalized in schools and denominations, narrative theology embraces, preserves, and reflects on the stories of people and communities involved in the romance of God—always beginning with and always returning to the treasury of stories in Scripture: the good, bad, ugly, and undetermined lives of those who have sought God and found God and lost God and served God and heard and ignored God and opposed God and betrayed God and returned to God and loved God all the more for having been forgiven much. In the process, it seeks to understand the direction and purpose and meaning of the larger narrative (the story of emergence) that these individual stories constitute.[147]

Interestingly and ironically, narrative theologian James William McClendon did write a three-volume work entitled *Systematic Theology*. But the titles of the three volumes betray a subversive dimension to the title. If you wrote a systematic theology with three titles, Doctrine, Mission (or Witness), and Ethics, in what order would you place them? Wouldn't you begin with Doctrine—laying the conceptual foundations for the systematic theology, followed by Ethics—how the community shaped by doctrine should live, and concluding with Mission—what the doctrinal, ethical community does in the world?

But McClendon's approach is profoundly different. He begins with *Ethics* because a community of faith, in order to exist as a community at all, must have virtue sufficient to forgive, reconcile, and otherwise get along. Without roots in virtue, without practices that strengthen virtue, and without a participatory experience of community made possible by virtue, no one is spiritually prepared to explore doctrine or pursue mission, McClendon implies. From this narrative perspective, the practices of humility, compassion, spirituality, and love—which develop only in community—are more essential to a good and healthy theology, more primal and important than scholarship, logic, intellect. Without love the latter are nothing.

Then McClendon engages *Doctrine*, but he doesn't present doctrine as a list or outline of information to be conveyed.

---

[147] I intentionally avoid using the term *metanarrative* for a number of reasons. See *A Is for Abductive* (Zondervan, 2003) and "An Open Letter to Chuck Colson" on my Web site, www.anewkindofchristian.com.

Rather he presents doctrine as a *practice* of the church—a practice of reflecting, discussing, articulating, critiquing, rethinking, rearticulating, and so on. Finally, a community practicing love and the pursuit of understanding is ready to engage in mission (*witness* for McClendon), in a dynamic cycle that spirals upward in ethics, doctrine, and mission.

In this narrative conception, then, orthodoxy isn't a destination. It is a way—a way on which one journeys, and on which one progresses, even if one never (in this life) arrives. Paul put it this way: "Not that I have already obtained all this...I do not consider myself yet to have taken hold of it" (Philippians 3:12-13).

My favorite musician for many years has been Bruce Cockburn, and as I said in an early footnote, I think my favorite line from all his songs is found in "Understanding Nothing": *All these years of thinking*, he sings, *ended up like this—in front of all this beauty, understanding nothing.*

I love that line for more reasons than I can articulate. There is humility in it. There's a certain sadness, too, expressing a sense of frustrated effort. But there is also insight, betraying the words *understanding nothing*, because if one understands that beauty surrounds us, one understands something unspeakably grand. One can solve a math problem. One can contain a chemical reaction in an equation. But one never "gets" beauty—one stands (or falls) in front of it astonished, amazed, open-mouthed, speechless, and humbled.

At this moment I'm sitting in a humble little restaurant in New Mexico, writing while I wait to pick up a friend at the airport. Around me are several people, unknown to me, but currently my neighbors—that guy over there, reading about the first game of the World Series in a local paper; that young employee sweeping the floor, pretty in her apron and humming a Latin tune; that tall man in a cowboy hat; his little boy in a bright red sweatshirt, looking mischievous and overfull of energy. In front of me, through the picture window, is a shabby, littered, half-empty parking lot typical of strip malls everywhere, and beyond that a road, and beyond that some shops and brightly painted houses. Scattered among the houses are tall aspen trees—three, four, five, seven of them—resplendent in peak fall yellow. And off in the distance, the brown, dusty mountains with fringes of dark forest rise up with a serenity that reaches back to touch me across the miles of clear October air.

Everything is bathed, directly or indirectly, in this distinct, pure, desert sunlight that somehow illuminates differently here. Now the wind blows, and the yellow aspen leaves undulate, shimmer, like hands clapping, applauding the cool glory that flows through them, stark against that stunning, pure blue desert sky.

A thousand artists could spend the rest of the millennium describing the diverse beauties before me at this one moment—now including the college student who just rolled by on his skateboard, a wry look on his face, earphones in his ears, backpack slung over his shoulder, leaning, swerving around litter, swinging across the sloping parking lot, dancing to an unknown rhythm. A thousand artists given a thousand years could never capture the world of wonders that surround me just now.

I am sure that what I see through this restaurant window here—the movement, the stability, the light, the color, the life— is radiant with the glory of God. So I just try to take it all in ("beholding as in a mirror the glory of the Lord"), to receive it as a gracious gift, to let it do to me whatever it will do to me. I know that in so doing, God is blessing me, transforming me from the *I* who I have been, creating the *I* who I am becoming. To be in this *creatio continua*, this ongoing and emerging creation, in front of all this beauty and glory, means that there can be no last word. Like a child breathlessly telling a story, just when you think you're finished, another conjunction comes: and then...and also...and then...and you know what?...and...

How ironic that I sit writing about orthodoxy, which implies to many a final capturing of the truth about God, which is the glory of God.[148] Sit down here next to me in this little restaurant and ask me if Christianity (my version of it, yours, the Pope's, whoever's) is *orthodox*, meaning *true*, and here's my honest answer: *a little, but not yet*. Assuming by *Christianity* you mean the Christian understanding of the world and God, Christian opinions on soul, text, and culture...I'd have to say that we probably have a couple of things right, but a lot of things wrong, and even more spreads before us unseen and unimagined. But at least our eyes are open!

To be a Christian in a generously orthodox way is not to claim to have the truth captured, stuffed, and mounted on the wall. It is rather to be in a loving (ethical) community of people who are seeking the truth (doctrine) on the road of mission (witness, as McClendon said) and who have been launched on the quest by Jesus, who, with us, guides us still. Do we have it? Have we taken hold of it? Not fully, not yet, of course not. But we keep seeking. We're finding enough to keep us going. But we're not finished. That, to me, is orthodoxy—a way of seeing and seeking, a way of living, a way of thinking and loving and learning that helps what we believe become more true over time, more resonant with the infinite glory that is God.

If, for you, *orthodox* means finally "getting it right" or "getting it straight," mine is a pretty disappointing, curvy orthodoxy. But if, for you, orthodoxy isn't a list of correct doctrines,

---

[148] Speaking of orthodoxy, you may wonder why I haven't written more on Eastern Orthodoxy. It's because others are far more qualified for that task. See Kallistos Ware, *The Orthodox Way* (St. Vladimir's University Press: 1995).

but rather the *doxa* in orthodoxy means "thinking" or "opinion," then the lifelong pursuit of expanding thinking and deepening, broadening opinions about God sounds like a delight, a joy.

Consider for a minute what it would mean to get the glory of God finally and fully right in your thinking or to get a fully formed opinion of God's goodness or holiness. Then I think you'll feel the irony: *all these years of pursuing orthodoxy ended up like this—in front of all this glory understanding nothing.* It's like claiming to love your spouse "right," with technical perfection or by following appropriate directions and rules, which sounds like grounds for marriage counseling.

In the Middle Ages, "straight thinking" was a kind of government function—like right business practices, similarly enforceable by censorship, imprisonment, torture, inquisition, and massacre. In the Modern Era, protest and conquest were the spirit of the age, so "right opinions" were one's ticket to power and dominance. But in the world that is emerging out of roots in the modern and medieval worlds, perhaps we will believe again that the meek will inherit the earth and that truth is a treasure not best found or held through coercion and threat or competition and dominance, but by humble seeking, sincere faith, resilient hope, patient love.

So perhaps orthodoxy will mean not merely correct conclusions but right processes to keep on reaching new and better conclusions, not just correct ends but right means and attitudes to keep on discovering them, not just straight answers but a straight path to the next question that will keep on leading to better answers. This kind of orthodoxy will welcome others into the passionate pursuit of truth, not exclude them for failing to possess it already.

Yes, there's a time and place to debate and dispute, to make noise, to overturn the tables in the temple if need be. When our Lord did so, it was not to finally get opinions right so all the wrong could be excluded. No, Jesus turned the tables and scattered the doves and coins so that the temple could once again become a house of prayer *for all the nations*—an inclusive place that welcomes *all* into the transforming mystery of prayer and worship, not only the "already right" or the "rich in spirit."

Jesus debated the Pharisees not so that his super-orthodoxy of *the exclusively right* could finally prevail over theirs, but so that his generous orthodoxy of *God's saving love for all* could open wide the doors to God's house, with a special welcome for the poor, the brokenhearted, the prisoners, the sick, and yes, even the mistaken.

If truth about the Divine is glorious beyond full comprehension; if glory itself is a wonder and surprise; if glorification is the doxology to which orthodoxy leads; if orthodoxy always culminates in an unending, joyous astonishment that erupts in gratitude and honor and humility and delight in response to the perception and contemplation of the truth about God, then these things are never done "finally right" or achieved or completed with mere technical correctness (that's not the point). They are never finished, never captured, never done justice, any more than the aspen leaves shimmering yellow against a pure blue sky outside this little Mexican restaurant can be done justice or sufficiently honored by a single poem or song, or that two lovers can be satisfied for having made love "correctly."

"Bach (or the Beatles) finally got it right. They finally captured beauty once and for all." Only a fool would say that. "Mozart (or Bob Dylan) finally got it right; there's no need for more musical composition after him." Ridiculous. The more Bach and Mozart (or Radiohead; Keillor and Monet; or Augustine, Aquinas, Luther, Kierkegaard, and Dr. King) honor the glory for us, the more our eyes and hearts are opened up to see more and deeper glory than we previously imagined.

Remember what Vincent Donovan said:

> The day we are completely satisfied with what we have been
> doing; the day we have found the perfect, unchangeable
> system of work, the perfect answer, never in need of
> being corrected again, on that day we will know that we
> are wrong, that we have made the greatest mistake of all
> (*Christianity Rediscovered*, 146).

The achievement of "right thinking" therefore recedes, happily,
farther beyond our grasp the more we pursue it. As it eludes us, we
are strangely rewarded: we feel gratitude and love, humility and
wonder, reverence and awe, adventure and homecoming. We shout
hallelujah, and we weep tears of joy. So we pursue it all the more
until the end when we find it has been pursuing us and we are
caught up into the Pursuer we have so long pursued.

"People have fallen into a foolish habit of speaking of
orthodoxy as something heavy, humdrum, and safe," Chesterton
said. But the generous orthodoxy we're exploring here is far from
that. It's a wild, inspiring, high-risk pursuit that Chesterton called
"one whirling adventure":

> There was never anything so perilous or so exciting as
> orthodoxy. It was sanity: and to be sane is more dramatic
> than to be mad. It was the equilibrium of a man behind
> madly rushing horses, seeming to stoop this way and to
> sway that, yet in every attitude having the grace of a statuary
> and the accuracy of arithmetic...

> It is always simple to fall; there are an infinity of angles
> at which one falls, only one at which one stands. To
> have fallen into any one of the fads from Gnosticism to
> Christian Science would indeed have been obvious and
> tame. But to have avoided them all has been one whirling
> adventure; and in my vision the heavenly chariot

flies thundering through the ages, the dull heresies sprawling and prostrate, the wild truth reeling but erect (*Orthodoxy*, 106-107).

True, orthodoxy has a conservative dimension, seeking "the grace of a statuary" and "the accuracy of arithmetic," but it also has a radical dimension, the paradox captured by Chesterton in this painting analogy:

> How can we keep the artist discontented with his pictures while preventing him from being vitally discontented with his art? How can we make a man always dissatisfied with his work, yet always satisfied with working? How can we make sure that the portrait painter will throw the portrait out of the window instead of taking the natural and more human course of throwing the sitter out of [the] window? (*Orthodoxy*, 116)

So here's the tension: we must always be discontented with our portraits of orthodoxy, but we must never, in frustration, throw the Subject of our portrait out the window. Otherwise, the revolution fails and falls, sprawling facedown in the dirt, and the whole whirling adventure is over. Until God's kingdom comes in fullness, the revolution of generous orthodoxy must continue: "In the upper world, hell once rebelled against heaven. But in this world heaven is rebelling against hell. For the orthodox there can always be a revolution; for a revolution is a restoration" (*Orthodoxy*, 117).

And so for this reason also, the adventure of generous orthodoxy is always unfinished and

Brian D. McLaren
www.anewkindofchristian.com
www.emergentvillage.com
www.crcc.org